I DIDN'T BELIEVE HIM

ALSO BY IRENE DARIA

The Fashion Cycle: A behind-the-scenes look at a year with Bill Blass, Liz Claiborne, Donna Karen, Arnold Scaasi and Adrienne Vittadini

Lutece: A Day in the Life of America's Greatest Restaurant

A Woman Doctor's Guide to Miscarriage

Steps to Reading Book 1: Short vowels

Steps to Reading Book 2: Blends

Steps to Reading Book 3: Digraphs

Steps to Reading Book 4: Silent e

I DIDN'T BELIEVE HIM

Irene Daria, Ph.D.

Copyright © 2024 by Steps Publishing, Inc

All rights reserved. No part of this publication may be reproduced, distributed, or transmitted in any form or by any means, including photocopying, recording, or other electronic or mechanical methods, without the prior written permission of the publisher, except for quotations used for critical reviews and other uses permitted by U.S. copyright law.

The events portrayed in this book are true and have been written about using journals and a blog the author wrote at the time. The name of the school has been changed, as have the names of all the children, parents, teachers, and administrators there. For the sake of narrative flow, a few teacher meetings that took place on separate days have been condensed into one.

For more information, see www.StepsPublishing.com.

1st edition

ISBN Print edition: 978-0-9864329-5-8

ISBN eBook: 978-0-9864329-6-5

"Statistically, more American children suffer long-term life-harm from the process of learning to read than from parental abuse, accidents, and all other childhood diseases and disorders combined. In purely economic terms, reading related difficulties cost our nation more than the war on terrorism, crime, and drugs combined."

– David Boulton, Children of the Code

"Many changes are needed to ensure that families can trust schools to teach their children to read and write well."

– Margaret Goldberg,
teacher and founder of the Right to Read Project

"Faced with a diagnosis of dyslexia or, more generally, a learning disability, too many parents fail to ask the school an important question: 'Well, what, exactly, did you teach my child?'"

– Los Angeles Times

"It is our experience that children with reading problems who ultimately catch up to grade level often have at least one parent who played a major role in this success story."

– *Parenting a Struggling Reader*,
by Susan Hall and Louisa Moats, Ed.D.

Welcome to our story.

Introduction

No one knows what goes on behind closed doors certainly applies to kids' elementary schools. In no other area of life do parents so blindly turn their children over to unknown experts. We hand-pick our kids' pediatricians, dentists, and babysitters. But most parents send their kids off to school without asking any questions about curriculums, teaching methods, or the kind of training the teachers have received.

Every year, 3.6 million children in the United States begin kindergarten, and very few parents think there is any reason to worry about whether their kids will learn how to read. I mean, what could be simpler than teaching a child the ABCs and how to read words like "Sit, Spot, sit?" That is a total no-brainer. The Jackson 5 even sang a song inspired by it: "ABC. Easy as 1, 2, 3."

Of course, we hear the often reported, terrible literacy statistics on the radio or glance at them in the newspaper or online:

- Two-thirds of children in America grow up without learning how to read well.
- 67 percent of fourth graders are not proficient in reading.
- Students who don't read proficiently by the time they enter fourth grade are four times as likely to eventually drop out of school. Two-thirds of those who are not proficient will wind up in jail or on welfare.
- 85 percent of juvenile offenders are functionally illiterate.
- 3 out of 5 inmates in American prisons do not know how to read, and that is a huge contributing factor to why they landed in prison in the first place.

Sad, we think. A shame. Maybe we can donate money to the cause, a cause that feels as distant to us as a tsunami, or a war in a foreign land. We feel empathetic, but immune. We believe our children will never have a problem learning how to read. After all, most of us are educated. We read to our kids. We talk to them and answer all their questions, thereby developing their vocabularies and their awareness of the world. Our kids went to preschool.

But, trust me, all children are potentially at risk of not learning how to read in school. They are at risk, no matter what race you are. They are at risk if you are rich, or if you are poor. They are at risk if you are well educated, or if you do not have a high school diploma. Not learning how to read in school has happened to poor Black and Latino children, as well as to the children of celebrities, politicians, and wealthy families like the Rockefellers.

Of course, many schools do a great job teaching kids how to read. But many do an abysmal one. Not learning to read in school has happened to millions of children in the United States, Canada, the United Kingdom, and Australia. Each of those places has conducted massive investigations into the problem. Each of those investigations revealed that children were having trouble learning how to read, not because there was anything wrong with the kids, but because many teachers were using flawed methods to teach them how to do so.

Some families have taken legal action. Ten students were awarded a $53 million settlement by the state of California because their schools caused them to be struggling readers. Michigan also awarded millions in a lawsuit brought by seven students who were similarly harmed by their schools.

The most recent investigation into how reading is being taught occurred in Canada. The Human Rights Commission in Ontario launched a public inquiry into why so many children were not learning to read. Can you imagine? The **Human Rights Commission** had to get involved. On February 28, 2022, the commission announced its findings: kids were struggling with reading because Ontario schools were using disproven, ineffective methods to teach them.

Typically, we equate the withholding of basic human rights with great suffering. Of course, it is painful for adults when they don't know how to read. But most adults don't realize the level of emotional pain and trauma young children feel when they go through the experience of being taught incorrectly. Little children sit silently in the back of the classroom, or become behavior problems, to hide the fact that they don't know how to read. After floundering for months, they begin to feel they are "bad" at reading. For many, that feeling becomes the truth and sets them on a terrible negative trajectory (often referred to as the "school-to-prison pipeline") all because of something that could easily have been prevented.

It is important to remember that behind every one of those grim literacy statistics is a living, breathing child.

One of those statistics was my son, Eric.

He did not learn how to read in school.

That happened even though his school is top-rated—a school any parent would be proud to send their child to. It happened even though his background and environment checked all the boxes for a child destined to learn to read with no problem. He was healthy, middle class, and the son of two parents with advanced degrees. My undergraduate degree was in English and journalism. At the time he entered kindergarten, my career revolved around words—I had worked as a newspaper reporter (*Women's Wear Daily*), magazine editor (*Harper's Bazaar*), magazine writer *(W, Parents, Money, Family Circle, Glamour, Elle Decor, Mademoiselle* and many others), and was the author of three critically acclaimed books published by top publishing houses like Random House and Simon & Schuster.

Reading and writing were my passions. Through example, without ever consciously thinking about it, I had passed my love of books on to my son. Eric started kindergarten ready and eager to learn how to read.

So why did he—and millions of other children—not learn how to read in school?

Sit down for this answer. It is so unbelievable that it will knock the wind out of you: Millions of children have not learned how to read because, for over one hundred years, a majority of teachers have had no idea how to teach a child to read.

Don't believe me? Google it. You will find many quotes similar to this one from neuroscientist Mark Seidenberg, Ph.D., author of a definitive book on learning to read *Language at the Speed of Sight*:

"Parents who deliver their children to school on that momentous first day of kindergarten, proudly starting them on the venerable path to education, make a big mistake: they assume that their child's teacher has been taught how to teach reading. They haven't."

Or this one from former First Lady Laura Bush on her experience as a teacher: "People leave college with their teacher certificate in hand, and they go into a classroom and come to find out they've never really learned how to teach somebody to read."

Or this one from psychologist G. Reid Lyon, Ph.D., former Chief of the Child Development and Behavior Branch at the National Institutes of Child Health and Human Development. He began his career as a teacher and says, "I had no idea what I was doing when I got into my third-grade classroom other than calling the roll and recess. What struck me (in my first year of teaching) was about 30 percent of these nine-year-olds couldn't read well at all, some not at all... I think by the end of the year the 30 percent that I didn't help had actually extended to about 40 percent because I screwed another 10 percent up. I just didn't have any idea what I was doing."

Or this one from a teacher testifying in front of the Ontario Human Rights Commission: "I am a specialist in special education, yet I was still not equipped to teach the children in front of me to read ...(I and my colleagues) truly really want to help and care deeply about the students, but we are ... not trained effectively."

Since the time they were established in the U.S. in the late 1800s, many teacher training institutes have failed to teach the nuts and bolts of how to deliver effective reading instruction. In recent decades, most teacher training programs have been disconnected from the valuable research being done at other parts of their campuses by cognitive psychologists—the people who have done hundreds of thousands of studies on how kids learn how to read.

In 2023 Heather Penske, president of the National Council of Teacher Quality, urged colleges and teacher training programs to take steps to ensure "new teachers have the knowledge and skills to be effective on Day 1." Some colleges are beginning to do so. Others are not.

At the moment—in both national and local media—there are many reports on how thoroughly the U.S. has mucked up the teaching of reading.

Of course, the news has seemingly *always* been full of reports about how thoroughly the U.S. has mucked up the teaching of reading. But the recent reports are different. Spearheaded by an excellent series of podcasts by American Public Media's Emily Hanford, these reports go deeper and point out specific weaknesses in popular reading curriculums. Thanks to social media, Hanford's podcasts reached many teachers who then took to the internet and, for the very first time, did their own research into the science behind the teaching of reading, science that teachers before them had previously ignored—or had not been taught.

Teachers who delved into the issue were horrified by what they found. These informed teachers are now scrambling to learn how to teach reading. To support each other, they are forming Facebook groups with names like "Science of Reading—What I Should Have Learned in College," and are writing open letters to the deans of their colleges complaining about the incorrect methods they were taught. Parents are successfully suing school districts and actively advocating to get schools to change curriculums. Elementary schools are creating "safe places" for teachers to deal with the guilt they feel over the harm they have caused to children. At a meeting of the chiefs of education from 13 states, getting teachers to teach reading correctly was called "the civil rights issue of our time," and the NAACP is now lobbying all across the country for effective reading instruction. Because of these combined efforts, many states are passing legislation saying reading needs to be taught using scientifically validated methods. Those states must now try to figure out how to retrain millions of teachers so that they can begin teaching effectively.

Mass teacher re-training has not yet begun in most states (Mississippi is a notable exception) and real change has happened in only a minority of classrooms. Every day, parents, journalists, and politicians continue to feverishly campaign for effective reading instruction. Their actions are to be commended and their goals are reflected by a tweet posted by Parents for Reading Justice: "Imagine—96 % of our children learning to read vs our current abysmal approximately one-third."

As I mentioned before, the process of not being taught how to read is extraordinarily painful for a child. I know this because I witnessed my son live through it. I watched the terrible downward spiral a child goes through when he goes to school day after day after day wanting to learn how to read and not being taught how to do it.

This book does something no other book has done before. It gives you an intimate look at how not being taught how to read affects a child and his family. It takes you into our home and also behind closed doors at one of the best public schools in New York City. It shows you exactly how the kids at that excellent school—and at thousands of others across the country—were "taught" how to read so that you can fully understand why those methods do not work. It explains how those methods—which seem unbelievably crazy to an outside observer—came to be the norm in teaching and shows you how easy it is to teach a child to read if you use correct methods from the very beginning.

At the time my son was not taught how to read in school, I was pursuing a Ph.D. in developmental psychology but had absolutely no idea how kids learned to read. Witnessing how my son suffered because of the ineffective teaching he was getting caused me to eventually do my dissertation on how children learn to read and to devote much of my second career as a developmental psychologist to helping children whose schools were using incorrect methods to teach reading. I opened an office in Manhattan and word of how quickly kids learned to read when they worked with me spread like wildfire. (Their success was not due to any special magic I had—it was simply because I used correct methods based on what research had found to be most effective, a body of research now referred to as "the science of reading.")

Even though I had no website, no business cards, and not even a listed business phone number, my client list soon included the children of celebrities such as Kate Winslet, Cate Blanchett, Tom Brady and Bridget Moynahan, Philip Seymour Hoffman, and Bob Kerrey, the former governor and state senator of Nebraska. I also taught hundreds of other children and volunteered at an elementary school in Harlem where I taught reading in summer school to kids whose teachers had failed to teach them how to read, and trained teachers at the school how to teach reading using scientifically based methods.

My work with children was—and continues to be—very gratifying. But, although it is indeed better—or at least psychologically healthier—to light a candle than to curse the darkness, it makes me sad to realize how many children out there are not being taught effectively. I hope this book helps parents and teachers recognize when reading instruction is based on effective methods, and when it isn't, and that the book will inspire and empower them to know what steps to take to help all children learn to read.

As I've said, what happened to my child has happened – and is continuing to happen—to millions of children across the country. If it happened to your child, you will probably find pieces of your story in ours. I hope our story will help you find a way to let go of the self-blame we parents are haunted by.

If you are the parent of a beginning reader—or of a struggling, older one—this book will help ensure your child will learn to read well since an informed parent is his or her child's best advocate. If you and your child are already on the same frightening road my son and I traveled, simply by going on this journey with my son and me, you will wind up knowing how to teach a child to read and will be empowered to quickly get your child on the road to becoming a joyful, proficient reader.

Your journey, truly, can have a happy ending.

1

"If only" moments happen when we least expect them. You know the moments I mean—"if only" they had left five minutes later, they wouldn't have been in the intersection when the car hit them. "If only" she had taken action the first time he hit her, she wouldn't have ended up in an abusive marriage. "If only" moments are moments that, for the rest of our lives, we wish we could go back and change.

My "if only" moment happened towards the beginning of my younger son, Eric's, kindergarten year. I was preparing dinner when my 5-year-old walked into the kitchen and said, "I want to learn how to read, Mommy, but my school isn't teaching me how to. They tell us to look at the pictures and guess what the words are, but that's not reading, Mommy. How do you read?"

I should have realized what an important moment that was. All motion and sound should have stopped. Instead, pasta sauce simmered on the stove and the salad spinner clattered and whirled as I kept drying romaine lettuce. I didn't even look up.

Rather than saying I would help him, I uttered words I lived to regret: "I don't understand how your school teaches reading, but it's a really good school and we need to trust that they know what they are doing. They will teach you how to read."

My little boy nodded and went back to playing with his blocks in the living room. If Mommy said he should trust his school, then that was what he would do.

Blind faith

A few weeks before Eric made that pronouncement, his teacher and principal had given a presentation on how his school taught reading. *(Their approach, known as Balanced Literacy, is the prevalent way of teaching reading in schools across the country.)*

Standing before a room full of well-educated parents, his kindergarten teacher had held up a very slim paperback book and opened it to a page that looked like this:

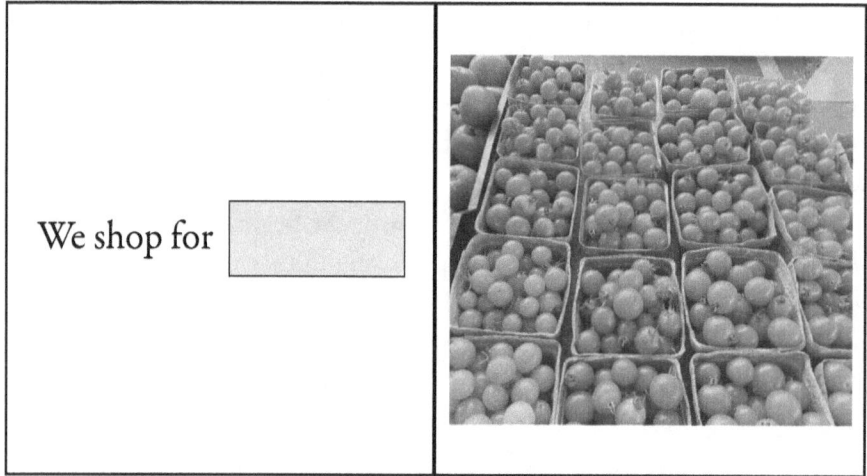

On the right-hand page was a color photograph of tomatoes. On the left-hand page was the sentence, "We shop for _____." The last word of the sentence was hidden by a small, yellow sticky note.

"We teach your kids to read by reading books like this out loud to them," the teacher said. "When we reach words that we've covered up with sticky notes, we tell the kids to guess what the words could be by looking at the pictures."

That made no sense. Why would the teacher hide words she wanted the kids to read? It was impossible to read words you couldn't see.

The teacher continued: "When you read with your children at home, and they reach a word they don't know, **don't** tell them to sound it out. If they start sounding it out, tell them, 'You could sound it out, but why would you want to when there are so many other strategies that are more effective?'"

She pointed to a hand-written poster hanging on the wall behind her. The poster had been made for this meeting and it listed the strategies the children were being taught to use when they encountered unknown words. The strategies included: look at the picture; skip the word and go back to it once you know what the sentence is about; ask yourself what word would make sense; and ask the person next to you if they know what the word is. "Sound out the word" was at the very bottom of the list.

"If they insist on sounding out the word when they read with you at home, tell them to skip the vowels," the teacher said. "Kindergarten is not the place for children to learn vowel sounds. Vowels are tricky because they make so many different sounds and the kids should ignore them."

I glanced at my fellow kindergarten parents—30 or so attorneys, financial executives, and other professionals. None of them looked confused. They all sat there, blindly accepting what the teacher was saying.

Or were they purposely remaining quiet like I was? I had been a journalist my entire working life and was studying to be a psychologist. Asking questions was part of my nature, part of who I was and what I did for a living.

Yet, I didn't ask a single question at that meeting.

Why not?

Because I was very much in awe of Hallowed School (*not its real name*) and thrilled that my son had earned a seat there. Hallowed was one of the most sought-after gifted and talented schools in Manhattan. Thousands of children applied for admission each year and only 56 were accepted. You could actually see acquaintances look impressed when you told them your child attended Hallowed. "Wow! That's a great school," they always said.

That's what I thought too. With such a great reputation, the school must know the most effective methods for teaching reading. Who was I to question them? *At the time, I had not yet earned a Ph.D. in cognitive developmental psychology and had not yet done my dissertation on how children learn to read. At the time, I saw myself as "just" a mom.*

At the end of the reading presentation, Eric's all-powerful principal held up a stack of slim books full of bright, bold pictures and words that no beginning reader could possibly read—words like "astronaut" and "dinosaur."

"These are the books that will teach your children how to read," she said. "Trust us."

I did.

And so, I never raised my hand and said what I was thinking: Books don't teach children to read, do they? Aren't teachers supposed to do that?

Witnessing my son's shame

Eric's kindergarten classroom was a happy place. The room was clean, and bright, and well-stocked with books, markers, and shiny plastic bins full of math manipulatives and other educational supplies. Sunshine poured in through the large windows and children's artwork—mostly smiling stick figures drawn in bold, primary colors—hung on the walls and dangled from ropes draped like clotheslines from the ceiling. The school's motto was "nothing without joy," and my son's classroom reflected that motto.

My son did not.

It was November, and I was in Eric's classroom for Open School Week, a time when parents were allowed to observe their children's classes.

Eric's 27 classmates were sitting cross-legged on the classroom rug, either chatting with each other or looking expectantly at the teacher, who was about to start the lesson. (*In Balanced Literacy classrooms, children do not sit at desks in rows facing the teacher. Instead, they sit on the floor for their lessons.*) In contrast to his eager classmates, Eric was sitting at the back of the room, staring at the rug in total silence.

Eric was not a silent kid. He was a boy who made friends instantly in the playground and, within minutes, had a gaggle of children following him around. As a baby, he had frequently waved at passing strangers from his stroller and his adorable, infectious smile had made even the toughest-looking, leather-clad bicycle messengers smile back.

As a toddler, we had taken him to a beach in the Hamptons. He toddled over to a man and woman who had set up their beach chairs near us, plopped down next to the two strangers, and offered them his red plastic beach shovel.

"He's running for mayor of New York," I jokingly said to the couple as I walked over to retrieve my son.

"So is he," said the woman about her companion. She meant it. Mayoral elections were coming up and the guy who had accepted Eric's sand shovel really was a mayoral candidate. Eric's extraversion and happiness had brought many people into our lives and had cheered up the lives of others. He had such great spunk and spirit, that his preschool directors had affectionately called him "the cheerleader of the school." If anything negative was going to happen in kindergarten, I expected it to be that Eric would get in trouble for talking too much to his neighbors.

Not today.

Today, Eric didn't say a word.

Not once, did he raise his hand.

Not once, did he smile.

I had no idea why my son was being so withdrawn. Soon, unbeknownst to me, the reason was displayed before my eyes. Eric's teacher put a huge, over-sized copy of the book *Mrs. Wishy-Washy* on an easel and began reading the story out loud, pointing at the words with a long wooden pointer as she read…

"In went the cow. Wishy-washy. Wishy-washy.
"In went the pig. Wishy-washy. Wishy-washy.
"In went the duck. Wishy-washy. Wishy-washy."

Most of the kids read the story out loud with her. While his classmates read, my son looked out the window.

I was surprised that Eric's classmates were able to read, but I didn't worry about it. Every child accepted to Hallowed had passed a rigorous screening process. Knowing how to read had not been a requirement for admission. After all, this was only kindergarten, and it was only November. Eric was smart. He learned quickly. I was sure Eric's kindergarten teacher would do her job and teach him how to read.

I waited for the reading lesson to start, for the teacher to actively teach the kids something about how to read.

She never did.

Eighteen years have passed since Eric entered kindergarten. When I write in italics like this, it means you are reading information I did not have 18 years ago, information that is important for you to know so that you understand what you are witnessing in a way I was not able to back then.

What I didn't know at the time was that most of the kids in Eric's class had NOT been reading. Because their teacher had read Mrs. Wishy-Washy to them so many times, they had memorized the words and were simply reciting them like parrots. And that was exactly what their teacher wanted them to do.

*This will sound very strange to you—because it **is** very strange—but the initial goal of Balanced Literacy is NOT to teach kindergartners how to read. The initial goal is to get them **excited** about learning how to do it and to help them "develop the identity of being one who reads." That last phrase is taken straight out of a book called The Art of Teaching Reading, written by a Columbia University professor named Lucy Calkins. She is widely regarded as the godmother of Balanced Literacy and her 580-page book has been studied by elementary school teachers the way the Bible is studied by devout Christians and Jews.*

How, according to Balanced Literacy, do children "develop the identity of being one who reads?"

By pretending.

You read that right.

Just as children pretend to be mommies, or daddies, or fire fighters, Balanced Literacy intentionally teaches kindergartners all across the land to pretend to read.

Don't believe me?

Here is how The Art of Teaching Reading instructs teachers to teach children to read: "At the start of the school year…" Calkins writes, "gather children together and … say, 'You are all readers. Today I'm going to read (a story) to you, like I did yesterday and then you can read it and other books with each other.' Soon after children have heard us reread the familiar tale… they disperse with their own copy of this book or other familiar story books in hand and reread those books to each other.

"But… they can't read, you may think and that's probably mostly true," Calkins continues. "At the start of kindergarten, most of our readers can only approximate reading… But children need opportunities to approximate reading… because children learn any language—the reading of it, the writing of it, and the speaking of it—by approximation. They learn by being immersed … in written language, by seeing us and their classmates demonstrate what seems doable and worth doing."

It is important for you to understand what Calkins wrote because it is the fundamental, underlying belief in Balanced Literacy classrooms—children learn to read by being surrounded by books, and having stories read to them. Teachers have been taught that, if they read to their students often and give them books that interest them, the kids will pick up reading on their own. Children are taught to memorize some frequently occurring words and to use pictures and context to help them guess what unknown words could be. Other than that, very little explicit instruction takes place.

According to Calkins, the crucial message kindergarten and first grade teachers are to convey to their students is "the expectation that they can do this."

But Eric knew that he could not.

And he thought the rest of his classmates could. What I had witnessed when I saw him sitting in the back of the room, in silence and with his head bowed, was my son feeling terribly ashamed. He had known the reading "lesson" was about to start and he was afraid of being exposed.

Children all across the country are having the same experience. "Reading is the most frequent and visible behavior visible to peers as kids enter school," says Dr. G. Reid Lyon, former Chief of the Child Development and Behavior Branch at the National Institute of Child Health and Human Development (NICHD). "Kids look at reading as a proxy for intelligence … Lousy reading produces a perception of stupidity and dumbness to peers and clearly to the youngster who is struggling. That is (why they feel) shame … They feel like they're failures."

Imagine what it feels like to be five years old and feel like a failure in the third month of kindergarten. Imagine how that would affect a child…

"I hate school!"

Something was haunting Eric. By December, that haunting began to permeate our existence as a family. Every morning, Eric said he didn't want to go to school. Every night ... many times every night ... he woke up anxious and would come into our room to be comforted and tucked back into bed.

He began having terrible nightmares. He dreamed he fell off a boat and into the ocean and drowned. One night, he woke up screaming so loudly that I thought he had fallen out of his bunk bed and broken a limb. Instead, he said, "I dreamed I got lost forever."

I did not know my son's dreams reflected how he was feeling about reading. Drowning. Lost forever.

Every school day, Eric woke up sad. If you have kids, you know how disturbing it is when your child is upset. I'm not talking about the annoying whining you hear when a spoiled child doesn't get his way. Or the heartfelt sadness a young child feels when, say, a scoop of ice cream falls off his ice cream cone and onto the ground. Those scenarios are fixable. I'm talking about when a young child feels the deep, all-encompassing sadness that all humans, no matter what age, feel when something is terribly wrong, and they are unable to do anything about it.

Eric had, quite clearly, told me what was upsetting him:

"I want to learn how to read, Mommy,
"but my school isn't teaching me how to.
"They tell us to look at the pictures and guess what the words are,
"but that's not reading, Mommy.
"How do you read?"

I had dismissed him. He had said those words very matter-of-factly and I had no idea how much upset his words had contained. I also had no idea that his words—*my school isn't teaching me how to read*—were the honest-to-God truth.

I tried to figure out what was making Eric so upset but was stumped. Whenever I volunteered at school lunch or recess, Eric was always happy. He had nice friends, was invited to an endless stream of classmates' birthday parties, and joyfully played in the schoolyard. All seemed to be well, except for the miserable heartfelt declaration he made every morning—"I hate school!—and for his continuing night-time awakenings.

When his unhappiness showed no sign of abating, I emailed his kindergarten teacher and asked her if she saw any signs of stress or unhappiness in school. In her typical supportive way, she responded almost immediately:

> From: KindergartenTeacher@schools.nyc.gov
>
> To: Me
>
> Subject: Eric
>
> No, not really. I read with him on Friday and he did a great job. At first he looked at the book and said, "I can't do that!"
>
> I said, "Yes you can. Use the pictures to help you and if you really get stuck I'm right here."
>
> He read very well, figured out the pattern in the book and went with it! Afterwards I said, "See I knew you could!" He looked at me with a big smile. I told him that you had told me he was sad before coming to school and he said, "Yeah, a little."
>
> I asked how come and he shrugged his shoulders. I told him that school was fun and challenging but that everyone was here to learn and soon he'll be reading and writing just like his brother, but that kindergarten was for learning and for playing and that he should just worry about doing his best. He got a little silly and seemed to be okay about it. Let me know if we should talk again.

At the time, I was focused only on whether my son was happy in school and zeroed in on the fact that he had smiled "a big smile." I completely missed the fact that Eric had said, "I can't do that!" about reading.

I had never heard Eric say, "I can't do that" about anything.

In fact, he regularly said the opposite. The very first sentence he ever uttered had been, "Eric do it." Those words became his unspoken motto. He always wanted to do everything on his own—from feeding and dressing himself, to getting a stepstool and climbing onto the kitchen counter to retrieve a box of graham crackers from the cabinet instead of asking an adult to get it for him.

If someone had asked me to use one word to describe my son, I would have said, "determined." He was also a problem solver. For example, my older son's best friend had recently told us about a "special ed girl" on his school bus who couldn't remember her name.

"What do you mean?" Eric had asked.

"She forgets who she is," the friend had replied.

"Well, why doesn't she wear a name tag?" my 5-year-old had asked.

His problem-solving ability had been part of what had gotten him accepted to Hallowed School in the first place. For his admissions interview, he was supposed to bring in an object he could talk about. He chose to bring in a house he had built in his preschool woodworking class.

As he was describing the house during his interview, the chimney (made out of a cardboard toilet paper tube) had fallen off. The teacher interviewing him later told us she had been impressed when he didn't miss a beat. He had simply asked for tape, used it to fix the broken chimney, and had gone on explaining various aspects of the house.

For this child to say, "I can't do that!" when asked to read a book was a sign that things were going terribly wrong.

It was a clear cry for help.

But I did not hear his cry.

And neither did his teacher.

Here is something else I missed: In her email, the teacher had written that Eric had "figured out the pattern in the book and went with it."

What is a "pattern in a book" and what did a pattern have to do with reading?

Eric would be in first grade before I thought to ask that question.

Eric's report card says all is well!

In January, Eric brought home his first report card.

It was excellent.

His school gave numerical grades (1 through 4) to signify whether a child was above, at, approaching, or below grade level. Eric was above, or at, grade level for every single item listed on his report card, including reading.

In the comment box, his teacher had written, "Eric is a bright, kind child who enjoys his time in school. He is interested in learning to read, and he is becoming comfortable and confident using the early reading strategies that are taught in class. Eric reads for meaning and is able to identify a growing number of sight words. He is working on paying close attention to matching the words on the page with the words that he reads."

*I ask you now, years later: How can anyone read **anything** without "matching the words on the page with the words that he reads?" I did not yet know that Balanced Literacy allowed children to narrate any story they wanted to, as long as what the kids said reflected what was happening in the pictures. The children were not expected to read the actual words on the page. This is part of the pretending-to-read that goes on in Balanced Literacy classrooms.*

The report card also said, "I am confident that Eric is following the class conversation, but I would like him to share his thoughts and ideas more often."

My extraverted chatterbox was still being unusually quiet in school.

"He gets along well with his peers and is always willing to help a friend in need. Eric is a very sweet boy and a pleasure to have in class!"

At the time, that report card had been a pleasure to read. Now, years later, it brings tears to my eyes. A sweet boy. A kind boy. A boy who was suffering—having nightmares, hating school, and crying, I can't do that!—because, as he had clearly told me, "I want to learn how to read but my school isn't teaching me how to."

That's not what the word says

In January, Eric began bringing home very short, little books to read for homework. The very first book he brought home was called *After School*. "After" and "school" were very hard words. Could he really read them?

Eric looked at the cover and, much to my surprise, read, "After School." He turned the page and continued, "What do you do after school?"

That was amazing reading for a kindergartner! The school's teaching methods were strange, but they certainly seemed to work. Look at what he was able to do!

He turned the page and saw:

After school,
I like to have a snack.

He read: "After school, I like to have a…"

He paused.

He looked at the word at the end of the sentence, and then he looked at the picture. It showed a girl bringing a glass of milk to her lips while holding a plate with a sandwich on it in her lap. *(The photo above is a reenactment. It is not the photo from the actual book.)*

Eric eyed the sandwich in the picture.

"Sandwich," Eric guessed.

He was doing exactly what his teacher had taught him to do; he was guessing what the word could be by looking at the picture.

"No. Try again," I said.

He squinted at the picture. "Drink?"

The girl in the picture was holding a glass to her lips, so drink was a good guess.

"No."

Eric stiffened and sat up straighter. "Glass of milk?" His voice rose in frustration.

"No."

Eric stared and stared at the picture, looking for another clue. He was clearly stumped. "It *has* to say sandwich!" he cried. "That's a sandwich in the picture!"

"Yes, that's a sandwich in the picture, but that's not the word on the page. The picture doesn't really show what the word is. See if you can sound it out."

He looked at me blankly. He had no idea what I was talking about.

"Make the sound of each letter and then put the sounds together."

He blinked hard, still not comprehending.

I didn't understand what the problem was. His kindergarten teacher had taught his class the sounds that all the letters make. In fact, the kids had spent a lot of time working on mastering those sounds. Why did Eric not know how to sound out the word snack?

"Look," I said, pointing at the letters. "S says sss. N says nnnn. A says aaaaa. C and k together make the kkkkk sound. S—n—a—ck. The word is snack."

"How am I supposed to know that?" he exclaimed in righteous indignation.

At the time, I didn't realize what an excellent question Eric had asked.

In fact, I thought just the opposite.

*I thought, how can he **not** know how to sound out snack?*

Even though his teacher had told parents they should not have the kids sound out words when they read with us at home, I assumed she was teaching them how to do so in school. Up until that point, kindergarten had been all about learning the sounds that letters make. In fact, the single issue Eric's teacher had ever raised with us about his performance in kindergarten had been about letter sounds.

At our first parent-teacher conference, his sweet, young teacher had told us what a pleasure Eric was. What a joy to work with. What a nice kid. How good he was in math. "That is his strength," she had said.

Then, forehead furrowed, she had delivered what she clearly thought was worrisome news: "This is hard for Eric," she said, placing two white 8 ½ x 11 pieces of paper on the table. At the top of each page was a big rectangle inside of which Eric had drawn a picture. Underneath the rectangle were wide lines where he should have written words describing his picture.

The subject that was "hard" for Eric was not reading. The subject that was hard for Eric was writing.

Writing?

Kids were expected to know how to write in November of their kindergarten year? That was news to me.

His teacher was showing us work Eric had done in Writing Workshop, a class period during which the children were supposed to draw a picture and then write about what they drew. The first picture Eric had made was an abstract design consisting of colorful squiggles and lines.

The lines underneath it were blank. Eric had not written a single word.

That was actually pretty clever: Eric had known he was supposed to write about the picture he drew. He knew he didn't know how to write, so he drew an abstract picture that was impossible to write about.

His teacher must have reprimanded him because his second picture was of a truck. Underneath the picture, the letters "KRT" were printed in large, childish handwriting.

The teacher waited for our reaction.

I didn't see what the problem was.

"I'm not surprised he can't write yet," I said. "When he started kindergarten, he didn't know the sounds of any of the letters. (His preschool, and I, had believed that playing and learning to socialize well with other children, was more important at that young age than academics.) Now he knows a lot of sounds, but I think the only word he can write is his name."

Kindergarten Teacher looked shocked. "So, he's learning 52 new letters all at once?" By 52 she meant the upper and lowercase versions of the 26 letters of the alphabet.

"Yes," I said. "He's come a really long way since September."

Kindergarten Teacher looked impressed. "Well, then, it's definitely not a problem. There's a problem when kids don't make progress and if Eric didn't know any of his letters when he started school then he's definitely made progress. But it would be a good idea if you got some magnetic letters and worked with him at home."

I did. I put magnetic letters up on the refrigerator and quizzed Eric on their sounds. We also played a game called "I Spy" in which I would say things like, "I spy with my little eye something that begins with a t," and he would look around and find the object I was referring to. Maybe a truck, or tape, or a toy tank.

A few weeks after we started playing I Spy, I was getting ready to take him for a walk. As I zipped him into his little ski jacket, my gaze fell on a lamp and I said, "I spy with my little eye something that begins with an L."

Eric sighed in annoyance, straightened his shoulders, and said, "Lamp. L…l…l…l…lamp."

Sounding quite annoyed, he said, "I get it."

To prove that he got it, he looked at the table and said, "Table, t…t…t…t." Then he said, "Floor, f…f…f…f." Then, "Door, d…d…d…d."

I never played the game with him again. There was no need to. He clearly knew his letter sounds. So why couldn't he sound out the word snack?

Never in my wildest dreams did I think it was because Eric's teacher had not taught his class how to sound out words. His teacher had said that sounding out was the **least desirable** reading strategy, but I did not realize Balanced Literacy viewed it as an **undesirable** strategy.

I did not realize that the teacher expected the kids to use their knowledge of letter sounds only when they wrote. I did not know that Balanced Literacy believed kids discovered phonics rules **on their own** as they wrote out the letters that stood for the sounds they heard in each word.

That sounds like it might be plausible until you consider the fact that the kids were allowed… Strike that… Kids were **encouraged** to spell words incorrectly, as long as the words were written the way they sounded. In Eric's classroom, it was perfectly fine for a kid to spell "of" as "uv" or "cat" as "kt." This was called "invented spelling."

There are a lot of things wrong with teaching kids to use "invented spelling" but, for our purposes, the most important issue with it is this: Spelling "of" as "uv" does not help you recognize the word "of" when you read it. And writing letter sounds that you hear is not a skill that helps you recognize words when you see them written on a page. That's because sounding out words that you **see** sitting quietly and statically on a page is very different from writing down sounds that you **hear**. *(The first is called decoding, the second is called encoding.)*

I can't tell you how many times in the future I would see Eric, and other kids, write something in school and then, a week later, have no idea what they had written. Kids were not even able to sound out words that they, themselves, had created. Sounding out words—or decoding—is a skill that needs to be explicitly taught to children, and I had no idea it was not being taught to mine.

Every day for the rest of his kindergarten year, Eric brought home little books full of very big words.

Every night, he read them for homework.

Sometimes, he came across a word he didn't know and couldn't figure out by looking at the picture. At those moments, I told him what the word was. I listened to what his teacher had said in her presentation and did not tell him to sound it out.

The school's method seemed to be working. We used it for six more months—from January to June. *SIX MONTHS! Six precious months wasted, unbeknownst to me.* For those six months, Eric seemed to be reading very well, but he was miserable doing it.

Every night, his little body was stiff as cement as he read.

Every night, he looked so unhappy.

One night, after he finished reading one of the books he had brought home from school, he slammed it shut and declared, "I hate reading!!!"

His declaration was very disturbing. Eric had always loved being read to and had started school excited about learning how to do so. Last summer, I had taught him to read the word "the." He had learned the word quickly and easily and, excitedly, had hunted for "the" in anything I read to him. One day, he had even yanked *The New York Times* out of my hand and, unprompted, circled every "the" in one of the articles on the front page.

At the beginning of kindergarten, he couldn't wait to learn how to read. Now he hated it.

Eric's final kindergarten report card was full of great news

On his final kindergarten report card, Eric received the highest possible grade in the following reading skills:

- Demonstrates an interest in reading, exploring books and being read to.
- Attends to print and illustrations.
- Demonstrates an understanding of letters and their corresponding sounds.
- Recognizes sight words studied in class.

He was at grade level in the following:

- Reads for understanding.
- Reads with expression.
- Demonstrates an ability to apply strategies taught during mini-lessons into independent reading.
- Uses a variety of reading strategies.
- Self-selects books at an appropriate level.

No parent could have asked for a better report card.

No parent could have realized her child had absolutely no idea how to read.

School's out for summer!

The school doors swung open, revealing a gaggle of joyous kindergarten children ready to burst into the joy of summer vacation. But, first, each child needed to say goodbye to the teacher.

When it was Eric's turn to shake his teacher's hand, I stepped into the school foyer to also say goodbye and asked her to recommend some books for Eric to read over the summer.

She thought for a moment and then said, "*Biscuit.*" That was a series of early readers about a golden retriever puppy named Biscuit.

"He can definitely read those books," his teacher said.

The next day, with the afternoon sun streaming in through our living room window, Eric and I sat down on the couch. I handed him a *Biscuit* book. "I can't read this!" Eric cried, as he leafed through it.

Again, those words: "I can't."

Again, uttered in reference to reading.

I examined the words on the opening pages: "Woof, woof! What's in the basket, Biscuit? Meow. It's Daisy. Meow. Meow. Daisy has two kittens." Those words were hard, but the books Eric had brought home to read for homework had been harder. Why was he unable to read, "What's in the basket?" when, in *After School*, he had been able to read, "After school, I like to watch cartoons on TV?"

But what Eric had said was true: He was, indeed, not able to read a single word in the *Biscuit* book. *Not... one... word...* He had known how to read "the" before he started kindergarten, but now he no longer recognized it.

His inability to read didn't make any sense. He had read every book he had brought home from school. He had gotten great grades in reading on his report card. His teacher had said he could *definitely* read *Biscuit*. Over the course of the next few days, I had Eric try reading more *Biscuit* books, as well as a few other early readers. With each passing day, it became clearer and clearer that Eric had no idea how to read.

And I had no idea how to teach him. My older son, Jamie, had attended a different elementary school. He had picked up reading easily and I hadn't paid much attention to how he had done so. His teacher had sent home lists of short little words that had the same endings. There was a list for words ending in "at" like cat, hat, and mat, as well as for words ending in "an" like can, man, and ran. His teacher had called them word families. I assumed that, in working with those lists, she had taught kids how to sound out words. Jamie's school had also offered an after-school class called Fun with Phonics that I had signed him up for and where he learned to sound out words. Although I had no idea HOW to do it, I knew WHAT I needed to do—I needed to teach Eric how to sound out words.

The next day, I searched the shelves in the children's room of the Jefferson Market Library in Greenwich Village looking for books meant for beginning readers who were just learning how to sound out words. I didn't find a single book like that although I did find a book called *Who's a Pest* that had a few short words in it like "it" and "did" and "pest" and "yes."

I had come to the library hoping to find a summer's worth of books for Eric to read. I left with just one little book.

I was clearly doing something wrong…

Night after night, Eric moaned when I announced, "It's reading time."

Night after night, he moved to the other side of the couch, trying to place as much distance as he could between himself and the book *Who's a Pest*.

Night, after night, was torture.

In hindsight—how clear everything is in hindsight—*Who's a Pest* was much too hard for him. The few words I thought I could teach Eric to sound out (it, and, at, did) were hidden among much more difficult ones that were very intimidating (Molly, brother, turned, pest).

In the end, Eric was able to read only two words in the whole book: "the" and "and." I was glad he had remembered how to read "the." But in one whole year of school, the only new word he had learned to read was "and"?

Eric was not able to sound out a single word. Not even "at."

I told him what to do: "Make the /a/ sound—aaaa—then /t/—tttttt. Put those sounds together and you get 'at.'"

He looked at me as if I was speaking Swahili.

Night after night, I demonstrated how to sound out various little words in *Who's a Pest*, but didn't know how to teach him to do it in a way that he would understand.

Every night, Eric stared at the book in sheer misery.

Every night, he begged me to read to him instead.

He still loved books. He just hated reading them himself.

I sensed I was doing more harm than good and stopped asking him to read.

Clearly, I was doing something wrong and needed to figure out how to do it right.

Your son is smarter than his teacher

When you think of *InStyle* magazine, you probably think of beautiful models and stylish editors heading out to photo shoots wearing the shortest of skirts and the highest of heels.

When you look at the gleaming Time-Life building in Rockefeller Center that housed *InStyle* magazine at the time, you certainly wouldn't think one of its editors was sitting in a beautifully furnished office on the 17th floor Googling, "How to teach your child to read." But there I was, doing just that on my lunch break from the full-time freelance editing job I had taken at *InStyle* that summer.

One of the articles I found online was called "The Most Fulfilling Thing I've Ever Done," by Phyllis Schlafly. Yes, that Phyllis Schlafly—the woman responsible for derailing the adoption of the Equal Rights Amendment to the Constitution. I never imagined I would find use in anything Schlafly had written, yet here was this article. It had been written in 1992—***eight years before Eric was born***. *And its contents is still 100 percent applicable today.* The article began like so:

> "When people ask me, what is the most fulfilling thing I've done in my whole life, I answer—teaching my six children to read **before** (*emphasis hers*) they entered school....I urge you, and your family and friends, to do likewise.... It is terribly important that your child be taught to read by the correct method **before** he is taught bad habits such as **pretending** to read by looking at pictures and guessing at the words.
>
> Your children and grandchildren can avoid all those bad habits, and the disappointments that result, if you teach your child to read at home."

I paused to digest what I had just read. Guessing from the picture was bad?

But that's what my son's school was telling all the kids to do.

Guessing was much better than sounding out, the kids and parents had been told.

I kept reading:

> "Most public schools simply do not teach children the skill of reading. They just teach the children to guess at the words."

I swallowed hard. An entire school year had passed since my five-year-old had said,

> *"I want to learn how to read, Mommy,*
> *"but my school isn't teaching me how to.*
> *"They tell us to look at the pictures and guess what the words are,*
> *"but that's not reading, Mommy.*
> *"How do you read?"*

Schlafly continued:

> "What typically happens in (public schools) is well described ...by the Oklahoma State Department of Education. Instead of teaching children to read by learning the sounds and syllables of the English language so the child can sound out and read new words, the teacher is instructed to use the following techniques: 'Develop a sight vocabulary of high frequency words [*i.e.*, memorize about 25 words] *(the brackets are Schlafly's)* .... [Use] stories with a repetitive content [*i.e.*, stories that use the same words over and over again].... Predict unknown words.... Use pictorial clues [*i.e.*, look at the pictures and guess what the words mean].... Substitute another word [that seems to fit]... Skip the word.... [Figure out] the meaning of what is read rather than focusing on figuring out words.'

> "Guessing, predicting, looking at pictures, skipping, and memorizing a few dozen words are **not** reading," Schlafly continued. "They are very bad habits. The child who is trained in such bad habits is guaranteed to be a poor and inaccurate reader. Yet, most public schools use this guessing process with all first-graders."

After another three-and-a-half pages, Schlafly concluded:

> "Unless we are willing to become a society where only the elite can use the written language, mothers and fathers will have to assume the responsibility of teaching their own children to read. It is obvious that the public schools either can't or won't do it."

Oh my God, I thought.

Oh ... my... God.

Schlafly had written a book that parents could use to teach their kids to read. I fished a credit card out of my wallet, picked up the phone, and dialed the phone number posted on her website.

I told the woman who answered the phone that I wanted to order the book. I also told her how grateful I was for the article because it had opened my eyes to the fact that there was a problem with the way reading was being taught in Eric's school. I told her what Eric had said:

> *"I want to learn how to read, Mommy,*
> *"but my school isn't teaching me how to.*
> *"They tell us to look at the pictures and guess what the words are,*
> *"but that's not reading, Mommy.*
> *"How do you read?"*

The woman's response?

"Your son is smarter than his teacher."

Dialing for help

My next phone call was to the mother of one of my son's classmates. She was a speech pathologist, and teaching kids how to read was part of what she did for a living. Not surprisingly, she had taught her own son how to read.

I told her that although Eric had seemed to be reading fine in school, and had gotten a great report card, he was now able to read only two words.

"Have you heard of *Explode the Code*?" she asked.

"No."

"Buy those workbooks. They will help you teach him phonics."

I found the books online, clicked on "sample pages and lessons" and knew that I had struck gold. The first book in the series had 24 pages dealing with the short /a/ sound. These were followed by eight pages teaching short /i/, then eight pages reviewing short /a/ and short /i/. Then another short vowel sound was introduced. This was exactly what Eric needed—lots of step-by-step practice and reinforcement, instead of me kitchen-sinking all the rules together the way I had done with *Who's a Pest*.

Immediately, I ordered the first three books in the series.

If I could do it all over again, I would have ordered expedited delivery of the phonics workbooks and would have treated Eric's inability to read as an emergency.

But I did not. It took a long time for the workbooks to arrive. By the time they came, I was focused on working full-time at *InStyle* and enjoying the summer with my family.

Now that school was out, Eric was happy. We went to the park. We went to the beach. We went on vacation. I read to Eric every night for the sheer joy of reading, not to teach him how to do it.

I did not realize that while I was enjoying the lazy, hazy days of summer and not having Eric do any academic work—except for some math problems, which he asked for, and loved to do—most of the other kids in Eric's grade were busy reading, writing, and completing workbooks their parents had purchased for them.

Eric's classmates were moving ahead academically over the summer.

Unbeknownst to me, my son was falling way, way behind.

2

Sparkling stores. Marble brownstones. Chauffeurs. High academic achievement. All of these are part and parcel of New York City's Upper East Side, a glittering neighborhood snugly ensconced between East 59th and East 96th Streets. Manhattan is home to more millionaires than any other city in the world and the Upper East Side is where most of them have chosen to live. It is the wealthiest neighborhood in Manhattan; 44 percent of its residents earn over $200,000 a year.

Children raised in this elite area tend to do well in school and are regularly accepted to the best colleges in the nation. No surprise there, since socioeconomic status is the largest predictor of academic success. Rich parents are usually well-educated and have time and resources to invest in their children's educations. Those parents read to their little ones, are able to help their kids with homework, hire tutors when their children struggle, and send them to the best schools.

In Manhattan, "best schools' tend to be private, and private schools cost more than $40,000 a year. Those schools are housed in gorgeous buildings, often looking like they could be on an Ivy League campus, as opposed to gracing a narrow Manhattan sidewalk.

The offspring of New York's very rich never set foot in a Manhattan public school. Those schools primarily serve the tired, poor huddled masses, and the homeless—the same people mentioned in the Emma Lazarus poem engraved on the Statue of Liberty. Like the Statue of Liberty, New York public schools are seen by non-wealthy families as a gateway to a brighter future for their children.

Manhattan public schools also serve a second, smaller group of families. I will call them the Almost Theres. The Almost Theres are wealthy enough to afford gym memberships, Starbucks soy lattes, and SUVs. They frequently order in, and take their kids on beach and ski vacations, but can't afford to plunk down a quarter of a million dollars on an elementary school education. The Almost Theres make up the bulk of the parent body at Hallowed School, which is known for high academic achievement but which, in physical appearance, could never be mistaken for a private school.

Hallowed School is tucked inside a low, wide building whose campus takes up almost the entire square block between 95th and 96th Streets and Lexington and Third Avenues. It has the retro, metal and glass boxy look of all New York City public school buildings constructed in the late 1950s. Back then, the school must have looked modern; now it looks like a big warehouse with lots of windows.

Hallowed shares this building with PS 198, a school for kids who live in East Harlem, Manhattan's poorest neighborhood. The median household income in East Harlem is "barely a quarter of that of its wealthiest ones," according to Crain's New York. That means most families in East Harlem make $50,000 a year. At the time Eric attended Hallowed, most of the kids at PS 198 were Black and Latino and many lived in the low-income housing projects located north of 96th Street, the official dividing line between the Upper East Side and East Harlem.

Unlike PS 198, which was open to all residents of its East Harlem neighborhood, Hallowed School was a screened gifted and talented institution, educating children who had been identified as exceptionally bright. It was a small school with only two classes in each grade. The vast majority of its students were white and tended to live in one of the high-rise Upper East Side apartment buildings south of 96th Street.

The young residents of the wealthy Upper East Side and of impoverished East Harlem walked the same school hallways and shared the gym and cafeteria but never came together in a classroom. The schools even had separate entrances. At the 95th Street entrance to PS 198, the working-class parents dropped off their children and left.

Morning drop-off at the Third Avenue entrance to Hallowed School was a very different experience. Every morning, the parents—especially the mothers—would linger near the school entrance and talk...and talk... and talk. But this was not aimless chitchat. Instead, these mothers were engaging in what University of Pennsylvania sociologist Anne Lareau called "concerted cultivation."

Lareau studied the differences in how parents of various socioeconomic status raise their children. She found that wealthier families carefully plan and orchestrate their children's experiences. Working class parents, on the other hand, let their children develop naturally and give them a lot more time for free play.

It was the difference between raising an orchid and a daisy. Neither approach was better. Just different.

The first step financially comfortable New York families take in cultivating their child's future is getting him or her into the best school possible. The Almost Theres had done that. As I've mentioned, Hallowed School's reputation was stellar, and its test scores were among the best in the city.

The second step was finding enriching activities and experiences that would fertilize the young orchid's mind. That takes a lot of work and effort. And research. Well-off parents don't just sign their kids up for any afterschool activity; they sign them up for the best ones. And the best ones are discovered through word of mouth.

Word of mouth was the name of the game at morning drop-off. From a distance, the parents appeared relaxed and nonchalant, but if you ever looked closely at the mothers clustered near the entrance to Hallowed School, you would see intensity on their faces, anxiety almost. Every so often, you would hear an, "Ah!" and see them jot down the name of a resource another parent had just told them about, maybe an afterschool sports program, or a chess club. Of course, their conversations weren't only about children's activities. The moms would also discuss great new restaurants, the best vacation spots with and without children, or the best yoga classes. No matter what category it fit into, if it was the best, these mothers wanted to know about it.

I did too. But I was not typically part of this information gathering network. We were outliers at Hallowed because we were not residents of the wealthy Upper East Side. We lived in a one-bedroom, rent stabilized apartment at the northern tip of the West Village. Our two boys slept in bunk beds in the living room, and our German shepherd slept in the bedroom with me and my husband. During the school year I worked from home, but my husband worked in an office. Since he needed to get out of the house anyway, he was the one who brought Eric to school every morning.

Their commute was no small feat.

Every morning, my husband and little boy would walk one long block to the Union Square subway station, down the stairs, through the turnstile, and along the lengthy pedestrian tunnel to the Lexington Avenue line platform. Crammed in among rush hour commuters, Cary and Eric would wait for the train and then take it 10 stops to 96th Street.

They would then walk east for one very long block, turn the corner onto Third Avenue and walk another half a block to the school entrance. Eric would scamper into school and Cary would head back to the #6 train and take it downtown—hopefully switching to an express somewhere along the way—to his law office near Wall Street. Getting Eric to school every morning added at least an hour to Cary's daily morning commute.

Like immigrants who travel to America seeking a better life, my husband and son left our low-key West Village neighborhood and traveled to one of the best schools in the richest zip code in New York City because we, too, were seeking something better. Cary did not schlep Eric uptown to a gifted and talented school because we thought Eric was a baby Einstein who needed to be taught physics at age five. He schlepped Eric to Hallowed School because we wanted him to go to a school that taught math.

Yes, math.

But, you say, doesn't every elementary school teach math?

Ah reader, you are as innocent as I was when my older son, Jamie, entered the public school system. Let me be the first to tell you that there is math as you and I know it, and then there is constructivist math.

What is that, you ask?

So did I—and every other parent at Jamie's Greenwich Village public school. That school held workshop after workshop trying to explain to parents how its constructivist math curriculum—called Investigations—worked. Turns out, constructivist math believes children learn math best when they are allowed to find their own ways to solve problems. (It is called "constructivist" because kids are expected to construct their own knowledge, as opposed to being taught how to do math.) As a result, the memorization of math facts went out the window, as did learning how to add, subtract and multiply the traditional algorithm way in which you line the numbers up in columns.

There seemed to be no wrong answer in math anymore and maintaining children's self-esteem was paramount. Once, I was in Jamie's third grade classroom and his teacher drew a triangle on the board. "What shape is this?" she asked the class.

"A square," said a boy.

Instead of saying no, the teacher replied, "Well, it would be a square if we drew an upside-down triangle directly adjacent to it, and the sides were all the same size. But what shape is this shape?"

On another occasion, she asked what 10 plus 4 was. A child said, "12."

"Well, it would be 12 if we did 10 plus 2. But what is 10 plus 4?"

The words "no" or "wrong answer," were never uttered in that classroom. And tests were not administered. The curriculum was a disaster and I, like all the other parents at that school whose kids did well on New York State's annual state math tests, taught Jamie traditional math at home.

Dealing with the huge holes in that math curriculum had not been fun, and it was not something I wanted to repeat with Eric. Because of the way Jamie's school taught math, I believed Jamie's school was "bad." I wanted Eric in a "good" school that would teach him math and allow me to be his mom, and not his math teacher.

Few schools had a better reputation that Hallowed. I was sure its teachers would teach Eric how to do math.

How'd that work out for us?

I'll tell you later.

For now, let's focus on reading and the fact that my son had no idea how to do it.

Today was the first day of school, and I knew many parents—even those who, like me, were usually not able to drop off their kids—would be there. That's why, today, I was part of the stream of affluent looking parents and sun-kissed, glowing children approaching the school entrance. I was there to bring my son to his first day of first grade, but I was also there to talk to as many parents as I could about how their kids were doing with reading.

When we reached the large, metal doors—propped wide open to receive their little charges—I gave Eric a big hug and said, "Have a great day in school."

All around us, calls of, "Bye Mommy! Bye Daddy," and "I love you!" filled the air. Little girls in pastel patterned summer dresses, and boys in brand new athletic shorts and t-shirts detoured around us as they scampered into school.

Eric hugged me back, and then let go.

There was no resistance about heading inside. Maybe whatever had bothered him about kindergarten was no longer an issue. He was his usual, happy self and was ready and eager to be reunited with his school friends.

Soon, the doors closed and the parents were left standing on the sidewalk. Without the kids' happy chattering, the sound of traffic passing by and buses braking on busy Third Avenue was more noticeable. The weather was glorious and only a few parents—like Cary, who needed to get to his office—left immediately.

I waved to my circle of school-mom friends but didn't join them. I could talk to them any time. Today, I wanted to seek out parents I didn't have easy access to and joined two mothers who were chatting nearby. One I knew casually. The other was a Hispanic woman I had never seen before, one of the very few minority parents at Hallowed. The two women were comparing their daughters' experiences at two different summer camps, and I contributed what I could to the conversation. Then, when the timing was right, I casually asked, "So, how are your girls doing in reading?"

Both mothers moved a little closer. They were clearly interested.

"Mine is struggling," said my casual acquaintance. "She is pretty resistant to reading."

"Mine is reading at a third-grade level and is at grade 2.4 in math," said the Hispanic mom.

"So, your daughter learned to read really well in kindergarten,'" I replied.

"No. She's been going to a tutoring center three times a week since she was in preschool. They taught her how to read."

Her daughter had been going *to a tutoring center?*

Three times a week?

To learn how to read?

That was crazy.

I stood there in silence, trying to process what I had just heard.

"How is Eric doing?" asked the first mom.

"Not good," I replied, still feeling off-kilter after learning a kindergartner had been tutored. "He seemed to be reading beautifully in kindergarten, but he couldn't read anything over the summer. Nothing. It was as if he'd forgotten everything he'd learned in school. I don't know what's going on. Do you know how the school teaches reading?"

"No," both mothers said in unison. They said that they, too, had not understood the reading presentation the school had held last year. "Why would you tell kids not to sound out words?" the mother of the resistant reader asked.

"I trust the school," I said, "but what they are doing with reading doesn't make any sense to me."

The mother whose daughter was reading at a third-grade level looked at me as if I had just said the craziest thing in the world. "Don't trust the school," she said. "You can never trust the school. And you can't change them either. They do what they do. We need to let them do it and then we need to add whatever else we think our child needs."

She said this in the same tone you would use when instructing someone who had just relocated to Manhattan from a foreign, tiny, remote village where everyone knew each other and bartered for their goods. You would matter-of-factly tell that newly transplanted person that you need to lock your door at night, stop walking when you reach a red light, and pay for the groceries you want in a supermarket.

Those were facts.

It was how things worked in our society and, if you wanted to survive here, it was what you needed to do.

I was ranting as I paced back and forth in our apartment. "It's crazy!

"Tutoring kindergartners?

"Who tutors kindergartners?"

I had called Cary at work as soon as I got home, and he was listening.

"Do we need to have Eric tutored?" I continued.

"He is in *first grade*!
"Who tutors *first graders*?
"Why is that necessary?
"Shouldn't kids be learning to read *in school*?
"Why are they *not* learning how to read in school?
"Do we need to sign Eric up for tutoring too?"

"We know in our hearts it's not right," Cary replied, "but if the other kids are being tutored, we can't *not* do something to help him catch up. It wouldn't be fair to him."

He was right.

But a significant obstacle was standing in our way—money. Or the lack thereof. Cary was a maritime lawyer and the marine industry in our country was a sinking ship. Pun intended.

Even though he was a partner in his law firm, Cary had never made a lot of money and his firm was on the verge of disbanding. I was a journalist and I, too, had never made big bucks. On top of that, I was working towards a Ph.D. and was paying full tuition for the privilege. More accurately: I had taken out student loans to pay for the privilege. My summer freelancing at *InStyle* had ended and, since I was in school, I would have limited time to write freelance articles during the upcoming school year. We definitely did not have the money to hire a tutor.

That meant, if someone outside of school was going to teach Eric how to read, it was going to be me.

> "Want to see how I read, Mommy?"

The above sentence proves that words can be deceiving.

Read in isolation, they look like happy words uttered by a child who is proud of his accomplishment.

But Eric had just said those words, and he had not looked, or sounded, happy.

He had sounded angry.

I put down the apple I was slicing for him, rinsed my hands, and joined him in the dining area of our apartment's living/dining room. "Sure," I said. "I would love to see how you read."

Eric was holding a slim book called *Homes for People*. His mouth was set in a grim line of determination. One strap of his denim overalls had slipped down onto the sleeve of his white t-shirt. Normally, he would have adjusted the strap, but he was so focused on the message he was about to deliver, that he didn't notice it. He turned to the first page of the book and then put the book behind his back.

Huh?

Why was he putting the book behind his back if he was going to read it?

With his gaze locked on mine, Eric said, "A house is a home."

What was he doing?

His shoulders wriggled and paper rustled as, w*ith the book still behind his back*, he turned the page. He glared at me and "read," "A cabin is a home."

His shoulders wriggled again as he turned another page behind his back. "A hut is a home."

Paper rustled as, again, he turned the page and said, "A teepee is a home."

I leaned on the dining room table for support when I realized what he was showing me.

His gaze fixed on mine, he continued turning the pages behind his back and "reading" the rest of the book.

When he got to the end, his mouth was narrow.

His face was tense.

His little body was motionless.

He was waiting to see if I had finally, *finally*, understood what he had told me a full year ago.

> *"I want to learn how to read, Mommy,*
> *"but my school isn't teaching me how to.*
> *"They tell us to look at the pictures and guess what the words are,*
> *"but that's not reading, Mommy.*
> *"How do you read?"*

"Wow," I said, still processing what I had just witnessed. My son had just "read" an entire book while holding it behind his back. *Imagine the thought this six-year-old (he had turned six in July) had put into figuring out how to finally make me see there was a problem with the way his school was teaching reading. He was too young to even articulate it, to come right out and say, "My school is having us memorize sentences instead of teaching us how to sound them out so that we can really read them." He did not know what the school was doing wrong. All he knew was that what his school was teaching him to do was **not** reading.*

"That's amazing," I said. "You recited that whole book from memory."

Clearly, that was not the response Eric had been hoping for. Tense and angry, he said, "Watch me read it like this."

He put the book on the dining room table and closed his eyes really, really tightly. Again, he recited the whole book from memory, turning each page at exactly the right moment. He finished "reading" and opened his eyes.

"I understand," I said. "You memorized every book your teacher gave you. That's why your teacher thought you were reading. You will never have to memorize another book again. I will teach you how to read for real. I promise."

He visibly relaxed and pulled another book out of his backpack. "Want to see me read this one too?" This time, his tone was mischievous.

I nodded.

Again, he held the book behind his back, turned the pages, and recited it from memory.

Now, however, he looked happy.

Mommy had finally understood.

Mommy was going to help.

Mommy was going to teach him to read.

Ever try teaching short /a/ words to a kid who had spent all of kindergarten being told not to sound out words? To a kid who had been taught to guess what words are by looking at the pictures, instead of by looking at the words?

It is not easy.

In fact, it is MUCH harder than teaching a child from scratch because you have to undo a whole year's worth of bad habits.

I had taught Eric the sound short /a/ makes and, now, was waiting for him to read the word "hat" on a page in *Explode the Code*. He was supposed to read the word, then identify which of three pictures illustrated that word. There was an illustration of a house, a hat, and a chicken. Instead of reading "hat," he said, "house" because the picture of a house was right next to the word.

"No, that's not the word," I said. "Stop looking at the picture. Look at the word."

I pointed to the word, and he read, "hat."

I put my finger under the next word. "What's this word?"

The word was "sat," but he said "sun" because an illustration of the sun was directly next to it.

"No, that's not the word," I said. "Stop looking at the picture. Look at the word."

He was literally unable to do so. Over and over again, Eric misread the words because he kept looking at the pictures, instead of at the words. Finally, I covered all the pictures with a blank piece of paper. Only then, did Eric begin actually looking at, and sounding out, the words.

It took two weeks for Eric to master short /a/ words. Two weeks of hard, daily work on his part that involved me covering the pictures every time he read a word and then uncovering the pictures so that he could match the word he had read with the appropriate picture. If I didn't cover the pictures, he guessed at the words.

The fact that it took this very smart boy two weeks to learn how to read short /a/ words worried me. So did the fact that he sometimes read words backwards: he read "tag" as "gat" and "Nat" (a boy's name) as "tan."

I had heard that dyslexic children tended to read words backwards. Was it possible Eric had dyslexia? If yes, I wanted to get him help as soon as possible. I needed to ask his teacher if something might be wrong.

Every Friday, I took the afternoon off from freelance writing, or studying for my grad school courses, so that I could take Eric to play with his friends in the school yard. At dismissal on Friday, I sent Eric to the yard with a friend's mom so that I could talk to his teacher privately. I didn't want Eric to hear that I thought something might be wrong with him.

When she was done dismissing the class, and no one else was in earshot, I asked his teacher, "How is Eric's reading?"

The young teacher's unlined face remained placid. "Fine," she said.

"Fine?" We couldn't possibly be talking about the same child.

"Yes."

Knowing that was not true, I probed further. "How is he in relationship to the rest of the class? Where does he fall on the class curve?"

She thought about it for a moment. "He's towards the bottom." She said this matter-of-factly, as if she was telling me the sky was blue. Does being towards the bottom of the class sound "fine" to you? Especially when being towards the bottom means having no idea how to read?

"I'm worried about him," I said. "This summer, I realized he has no idea how to read. The other day, he got me to finally understand that he'd memorized all the books his teacher had given him in kindergarten. He wasn't really reading them. He was reciting them. I'm working with him now in a phonics workbook, but he's learning very slowly and he's reading some of the words backwards. Is there something more I can do?"

The teacher shook her head no. "Don't worry," she said. "Reading is developmental. Eric will read when he's ready to read, and reading words backwards is normal at his age. The one thing you want to see is progress and I'll be looking for progress in January."

January!?!

It was the end of September.

Eric was struggling, and she wasn't going to take any action until January?

I must have looked stricken because she said, "I'll sit and read with him and let you know if I have any advice."

Bang.
Slam.
Wham.

Those were the sounds of a hockey puck slamming against the sides of an indoor hockey rink in East Hampton, New York, where we had a weekend house. We rented the house out during the summer to help pay the mortgage but, off season, we were here pretty much every weekend. So were some other families from Eric's school.

Dressed head to toe in protective hockey gear, Eric was in the middle of an intense hockey game. I was in the middle of an equally intense conversation with Hockey Mom, a banking professional who was the mother of twins in Eric's grade at Hallowed. Both of her boys could read, and one of them was reading way above grade level.

As we sat side by side on the cold, hard bleacher, I told her how worried I was about Eric's reading. Thinking something might be wrong, I had brought him to an eye doctor. His eyes were fine, the doctor had said. When I'd told the doctor Eric was unable to read, he'd said, "You have a tutor for him, right?" I had not told him that tutor was me and that I was desperately looking for materials to use to teach him. I hoped Hockey Mom could help. "I've looked for phonics-based stories Eric could use to practice reading short /a/ words, but I haven't been able to find any in the library," I told her.

Hockey Mom did not come right out and tell me she had taught her sons to read. She did not come right out and tell me that she had worked with her kids on phonics, and that she (as I saw months later when I visited her apartment) had also labeled every conceivable surface in their home with words for the boys to learn: counter, hamper, refrigerator, couch, coffee table. But she did say, "Oh! I have some books in the car that are perfect for you. I just cleaned out my garage and I was going to donate them."

After the game, she gave me a stack of very little (5" x 4") books from a series called *Bob Books*. Most of the stories had just one word, or very short sentence, on each page. The first few books in the series consisted almost entirely of short /a/ words.

I felt like I had just won the lottery.

Later that day, I handed Eric the first book in Set 1 of *Bob Books*. The book, called *Mat*, was more like a booklet. It was so short and simple that an adult could have read it in 15 seconds.

Eric eyed the cover suspiciously.

"I can't read that," he declared and slid to the opposite end of the couch.

Again those words: I can't.

Again, uttered only in reference to reading.

His anxiety was understandable; I was asking him to enter uncharted territory—to read a book no one had ever read to him before, a book he had not had the opportunity to memorize. He would need to actually read this book all by himself and that scared him.

"You can read this," I assured him. "I promise. This book is different than the ones you get in school. It doesn't have any hard words in it. Almost all of the words in here are short little words with /a/ in them. They're the words you've learned to sound out in *Explode the Code*. This book will give you a chance to practice reading short /a/ words in a story."

Looking as if he was about to walk over a bed of nails, Eric wiggled ever so slightly closer. He glared at the *Bob Book* with distaste. Then he read the lone word printed on the first page: "Mat."

"Yes!"

Eric eyes widened in surprise.

I turned the page.

"Mat sat," he continued.

"Yes!"

Eric sat up straighter. "Sam."

"Yes!"

He continued: "Sam sat."

He kept on reading:

"Mat sat. Sam sat.

"Mat sat on Sam.

"Sam sat on Mat.

"Mat sat. Sam sat.

"The..." He looked at me.

"End," I said. "That last word is 'end.' You did it! You read the whole book!"

I thought Eric would be as happy as I was, but he looked pensive, as if he didn't fully trust what had just happened.

It had been a completely unfamiliar experience.

He had just read a whole book by himself, and he had done it by looking at the words, instead of by initially memorizing the words and then reciting them.

The tension in his body ebbed a bit, and he moved a little closer to me.

"Let's try another one," I said. He didn't argue. Relieved, I showed him the cover of the second book in the series. He read the title: "Sam."

I opened the book to the first page, and he read, "Sam and Cat."

I turned the page and Eric read, "Mat and Cat."

Next page: "Sam, Mat and Cat."

I continued turning the pages and Eric continued reading. He read the whole book without making any mistakes.

I pulled out a third *Bob Book* and, this time, he smiled. He was eager to read it, and he did.

I was so happy. If there had been a mountain nearby, I would have run up it, raised my arms towards the sky, and shouted, "Hallelujah!" My son had just read—*really* read—three little books!

A few days later, I received the following email from Eric's teacher.

> To: Me
>
> From: FirstGradeTeacher@nyc.schools.gov
>
> Subject: Eric's reading
>
> After spending some more time with Eric the other day I determined that one of the things he is struggling with are his sight words. These are words that we see all the time (ex. the, it, me, etc.) Children need to be able to read their sight words instantly, without sounding them out.
>
> Below is a link to a website which has all of the words as well as some activities and flash cards. We will be working with Eric on these words in school. It would be very helpful if you could work with him at home.
>
> It is a good idea to work with 2-3 new words at a time. When he is secure with one you can add another. You can have him create flash

> cards that he can go over with you or independently. I am hoping that this will help Eric in all of his reading (and writing).
>
> Let me know how things are going. Hope you had a good weekend.

I was surprised that the website the teacher sent me to was not run by a school, or some sort of educational association. It was run by a home-schooling mom.

These are the words Eric's teacher wanted him to memorize:

Kindergarten List

all	did	must	ride	under
am	do	new	saw	want
are	eat	no	say	was
at	four	now	she	well
ate	get	on	so	went
be	good	our	soon	what
black	have	out	that	white
brown	he	please	there	who
but	into	pretty	they	will
came	like	ran	this	with
		too	yes	

Eric was in first grade. If you notice from the title of the chart, *above*, the list Eric's teacher had sent me to was a kindergarten list. That meant Eric should have learned these words in kindergarten. Why had Eric's kindergarten teacher not made sure he knew them? Why had she not given me this list? But that was water under the bridge. I had the list now and, immediately, began teaching the words to Eric.

The next day, Eric came home from school looking gloomy.

"What's wrong?" I asked.

"Joshua and I are the only green stick dots in the class." The books in Eric's classroom were sorted according to reading levels and different color round stickers were placed on the back cover of each book to identify its level.

"What level is green?" I asked.

"The lowest."

Eric's teacher had told me Eric was *towards* the bottom of the class. She had failed to mention that he was *at* the bottom.

Eric reached into his school backpack and pulled out a book called *The Birthday Cake*. "I'm supposed to read this for homework, but I don't want to."

It had been a long day. I was tired, and I was worried about Eric's reading. Impatiently, I snapped, "You're unhappy being a green stick dot and you're refusing to read?

"I'm not refusing to *read*. I don't want to read *that*. I want to read a *Bob Book*."

Ah.

At age six, my son knew which books were helping him learn to read and which ones were not. "We don't have any more *Bob Books* that you can read now," I said. "You have to learn the sound of short /i/ before you can read the next *Bob Book*. But let's read the book your teacher sent home. There has to be a reason she wants you to read it. Maybe it's full of the sight words she wants you to know."

The book went like so:

Words	Illustration
Page 1: "A **red** cake."	A **red** birthday cake.
Page 2: "A **yellow** cake."	A **yellow** cake layer is added.
Page 3: "A **blue** cake."	A **blue** layer is added.
Page 4: "A **pink** cake."	A **pink** layer is added.
Page 5: "A **brown** cake."	A **brown** layer is added.
Page 6: "A **green** cake."	A **green** layer is added.
The last page said, "Happy birthday to you!"	

Brown was the only word in the book that was also on the list of kindergarten sight words. I had not taught Eric the word "brown" because I didn't think it would show up often in the stories he was reading.

Except for "A," as in "A red cake," Eric could not read a single word in *The Birthday Cake*.

I was stumped as to how a book like this was supposed to help Eric learn to read. "Your teacher must want you to learn how to read the words for different colors," I said to him. "Are you learning words for colors in school?"

Eric shook his head no.

"Well, there has to be some reason she wants you to read this book. If you want to move up a reading level in school, you have to know how to read the books that are in your classroom."

I made flashcards for all the words in *The Birthday Cake* and Eric began memorizing them. Because there were so many new words, we skipped working in the phonics workbook that night, and Eric also did not work on any words from the kindergarten sight word list.

The following day, Eric brought home a different book to read.

Again, there was almost no overlap with the kindergarten sight word list.

And there was no overlap with the words in *The Birthday Cake*.

None.

We made flashcards for all the new words in the second book and Eric set about memorizing those too.

Again, there was no time to work in the phonics workbook, or with the kindergarten sight word list.

The next day, the same thing happened—different book, different words. No time for the phonics workbook or for the kindergarten sight word list.

Fourth day—same thing.

I realized that if we continued to be guided by the books his teacher was sending home, Eric would just be memorizing endless new words.

My common sense told me to stop the infinite memorization. "We're going back to the phonics workbook."

Eric smiled and, happily, turned to the short /i/ page where we had left off in the workbook. His progress with short /i/ was faster than it had been with short /a/. He now understood what it meant to sound out words and he made good and steady headway learning to sound out words like "hit," "him" and "sip."

Two weeks later, Eric had completed all the short /i/ pages in the workbook. Tonight, I was excited about having him read the next *Bob Book,* which focused on short /a/ and short /i/ words. Eagerly, Eric sat down on the couch next to me. I handed him the book, *Lad and the Fat Cat.*

Confidently, Eric read: "Lad had a fat, fat cat."

I turned the page.

I expected him to continue reading but, suddenly, Eric tensed up.

"I can't read that!" Looking panic-stricken, he slid to the opposite end of the couch.

"You can read most of these words," I assured him. "I'll help you with the words you don't know."

Eric shook his head no. He was staring at the *Bob Book* with genuine fear in his eyes, as anxious as if he was in imminent physical danger.

Why would Eric be afraid of a *Bob Book*?

The words were as simple as could be.

Nothing about this page was intimidating.

Unless...

One of the words was "box." Eric had not yet learned how to sound out words with short "o." Could that one word be freaking him out?

I pointed to the word. "This word is box. You haven't learned the /o/ sound yet. I will teach it to you in a few weeks. You know all the other words on this page."

He made no move to come closer.

Clearly, "box" was not the cause of the problem. What else could have scared him so much?

In grad school, I was learning how to do scientific research. I was learning to examine outliers. What was different about this page?

It had two lines of print. All the previous *Bob Books* had featured only one line per page. Maybe the two lines made the book look difficult to him.

I retrieved a piece of blank paper, folded it in half, and used it to cover up the second line of print. "There. Now there is just one line to read. Now it's just like the pages in the other *Bob Books*."

I held up the little book so that Eric could see it from where he was sitting on the other end of the couch. He read, "That cat is Kit."

I uncovered the second line. He moved closer and read: "Kit sat in a box."

He continued reading, and his anxiety began to ebb as he easily differentiated between short /a/ and short /i/ words. He reached the end of the book and smiled as he said, "I'm so proud of myself!"

I was proud of him too. He had faced his fear, and overcome it, and read well. But I was also worried about the damage his school had wrought.

Eric had felt genuine, visceral fear about reading this little book.

Reading is something children should never, ever, need to be afraid of.

3

"I can't wait to read my book from school to you. It's my favorite book. I love it." Eric said. He was excitedly fishing through his school backpack.

My son had a favorite book?

My son couldn't wait to read?

I was as excited as Eric!

He pulled out a book called *One Frog Too Many*. "Can you help me with this?" Eric asked. "It's really hard, but I can read a lot of it."

"Sure," I said, relieved that his can-do spirit had resurfaced. He had recently moved up a reading level in school and was now a blue stick dot. Maybe that had given him the boost of confidence he so desperately needed.

Eric read the title: "One Frog too Much."

Not "much," I said. "That word is 'many.'"

"Okay," Eric said, beaming with happiness. "This is a chapter book!"

His happiness was infectious. I was smiling too. It was wonderful to see him so excited about reading.

Eric opened the book and read the cover page: "One Frog Too Many."

"Good," I said.

Turning the pages, Eric narrated the story of a boy who had a frog, a turtle, a dog and then got another frog as a present. As he read, I stared at each page in disbelief.

There were no words on the pages.

Let me phrase that another way because I really want to get your attention here: *The book contained no words.*

It contained only pictures.

Eric was "reading" by looking only at pictures and describing the events the pictures illustrated.

I looked at Eric. Knowing I was on to him, he smiled mischievously and kept "reading." He described how the first frog was jealous and did things to get rid of the second frog. The second frog disappeared, the first frog missed having the other frog in his life and, finally, there was a happy ending.

I had no idea what to say.

I certainly couldn't say what I was thinking, which was: "Is your teacher crazy?"

Instead of being able to play with—and enjoy—my son, I have been spending every single evening teaching him short vowels and helping him memorize sight words.

Meanwhile, instead of teaching him how to read, his teacher was giving him books that had no words in them. That really was nuts, but I wasn't going to say that to Eric. I wanted Eric to respect his school and his teacher. I also didn't want him to feel bad about the trick he had played on me.

I came up with a response that, I hoped, sounded reasonable: "That kind of book is a good introduction to reading for very young children who are learning what a story is and learning to look at the pages from left to right."

That was a lie. No child should ever be asked to "read" a book that had no words in it.

"You don't need those kinds of books anymore now that you know how to read," I told him.

He looked crestfallen. "I won't bring it home again. Sorry, Mommy."

My tone and expression must have given away how I felt.

I was devastated.

Reading Workshop

"You stole my book!" Joshua cried.

Eric looked at his reading partner, uncomprehendingly. "What do you mean?"

"That book." Joshua pointed to a slim book called *Fantastic Fish*. "You stole it."

This alleged crime occurred on November 16, during Open School Week. That was the annual week when parents were allowed to sit in on their children's classes and observe them learning. Specifically, the crime had occurred during Reading Workshop, a period I had turned heaven and earth to attend so that I could witness exactly how Eric's class was being taught to read.

The lesson had begun with the teacher retelling the plot of *The Little Engine That Could*. She must have recently read that book to the class, since many of the kids chanted, "I think I can, I think I can," at appropriate points in her narrative.

When she was done retelling the story, the teacher said, "Get your book baggies and go to your tables. I want you to read a story and then retell that story to your reading partner."

Joshua was at the same low reading level as Eric. Neither one of them was able to read a story that had anything resembling a plot, so how could they possibly "retell" a story? The other week, Joshua's mother had told me that pairing Joshua and Eric as reading partners was "like the blind leading the blind." I was glad that, today, I was going to be able to witness how, exactly, they read with each other.

I watched as the two worst readers in the class retrieved their zippered plastic bags from a large plastic bin. The two bags were each stuffed with about 20 of the same sort of books Eric brought home to read for homework—skinny books with big words that no beginning reader could ever sound out. Eric and Joshua walked to the back of the classroom, sat down on their child-sized chairs, and dumped the contents of their book baggies onto their table.

I was surprised at how many books Eric was reading in school. I had assumed he would be working on mastering only the books he had brought home for homework. Those books were scattered on the table, but so were many books I had never seen before, such as *Fantastic Fish,* the book Joshua had just accused Eric of stealing.

Eric had previously told me about that book. He had said he and Joshua looked at the pictures in it and made up names for all the fish. They called one of them "scrambled eggs fish" because it looked like scrambled eggs. They spent their time looking at the vivid, beautiful pictures, and talking about them, but they never actually read the words.

"You stole it," Joshua said, again.

"I did not," Eric replied.

"Yes, you did. It's mine. You stole my book."

Eric and Joshua bickered and bickered until, finally, I couldn't stand seeing them waste valuable reading time any longer. The teacher was reading with two kids on the other side of the classroom and was oblivious to Eric and Joshua's arguing and lack of reading. I was the one who would need to get them on track. "Guys, cut it out," I said. "You're supposed to be reading. Stop arguing and pick a book to read."

Both kids listened. They both chose a green stick dot book (the lowest level). Joshua chose *One Frog too Many*. He held the book up, with the cover facing me. "This book doesn't have any words.," he said. "Eric brought it home and you got so mad at him. He told me."

Wow. This kid clearly liked to stir up trouble.

"I didn't get mad at him. But I did tell him he shouldn't bring home any more books that don't have words in them."

"Don't talk to him," Eric said. At age 6, Eric already knew that sometimes the best way to handle a difficult person was to not allow yourself to be baited.

Joshua began examining the pictures in *One Frog too Many*.

"How about reading a book with words in it?" I asked. Recently, Joshua's mother and I had commiserated about how we both didn't understand how the school was teaching reading. We had also compared notes on how we were teaching our boys to read and had agreed to help each other in any way we could. I was trying to help now.

"No," Joshua replied, without looking up.

He was very definite in his answer and, so, I did not press him.

Eric, in the meantime, was leafing through the pages of his book so quickly that, even though his book *did* have words in it, he couldn't possibly be reading them. He was just looking at the pictures too.

Both boys finished their books in no time.

Now, they were supposed to tell each other what they had just read. Obviously, this was not possible since neither one of them had read a word.

Joshua glared at Eric and, again, said, "You stole my book."

Eric stood up, marched to where his teacher was sitting, and said, "Can I have a new reading partner?"

Teacher followed Eric back to the boys' table. "What's wrong?" she asked both boys.

Joshua said, "Eric is being mean to me."

Teacher looked at me for confirmation, and I shook my head no.

Teacher then said to Joshua, "What really happened?"

"Eric stole my book." Joshua pointed at *Fantastic Fish*.

"That book was in the basket for book shopping and Eric took it this week," Teacher replied. "That's his book this week."

Book shopping?

My little boy had been picking his own books? That's like a patient being let loose in a hospital and told to pick his own medication.

Had there really been no thought given to the books he was bringing home?

Was there really no method to this madness? (*That is correct. In a Balanced Literacy classroom, kids are allowed to pick which books they read, as long as they select them from books the teacher has deemed to be on their level. We will talk about how these books are leveled a little later in this chapter.*)

The teacher then said to both boys, "Do your flashcards. Assistant Teacher isn't here today so you're going to have to do them on your own."

She walked away.

The two lowest readers in the class were supposed to read their sight words *to themselves*? How would they know if they were reading them correctly if no adult was listening for mistakes?

"Read your cards to me," I said. "I'll do them with you."

My son accepted my offer; Joshua declined. He flipped through his flashcards on his own.

After both boys were done with the flashcards, Joshua told Eric, "Tomorrow I have blocks and I'm going to knock down your block building."

During a period called "choice time," the kids could pick one of several activities to do just for fun. One of those activities was building with blocks. The teacher allowed the block structures to remain standing for a few days. Eric loved building and treasured the elaborate structures he created. Joshua, obviously, knew this and was going for the jugular.

Eric ignored him. He picked up a few of his books, walked away from the table, sat down on the floor, and opened a green stick dot book.

I sat down on the floor next to him. "The other day, you were so happy when you became a blue stick dot. Read me a blue stick dot book." If his teacher wasn't going to help him make progress, at least I could.

Eric agreed and went on to read four blue stick dot books.

Four books!

If I hadn't been in the classroom, he wouldn't have read anything at all.

I realized that what was happening in his classroom every day was not what any reasonable person would call "teaching reading." It was unstructured, unsupervised time during which two struggling readers were left to their own devices. It was completely unproductive.

At lunchtime, I slid Eric's book baggie into my large handbag. While the kids were eating lunch, I was going to closely examine the books Eric was reading.

On my way out of the classroom, I said to the teacher, "With so many different reading levels in the classroom, how do you teach each child to read?"

"They're taught on an individual basis."

There were 28 kids in that class. Eric and Joshua had been the only kids "reading" green stick dot books, along with blue stick dot ones. But I had seen plenty of other kids reading blue stick dot books. That meant lots of kids in that classroom still had a lot to learn.

Today, I had seen the teacher work one-on-one with only a handful of children. That meant the rest of them had learned absolutely nothing.

Examining the evidence

Eric's class headed to the school cafeteria, and I headed to a nearby café where I ordered a Diet Coke and sat down to sort Eric's books according to stick dot color: there were 12 green stick dot books and five blue.

I examined the easier, green stick dot books first. None of them contained words kids could easily sound out. *(Many years later I would learn from a blog post by teacher Margaret Goldberg, co-founder of The Right to Read Project, that words kids could easily sound out had been left out of these books ON PURPOSE, to encourage them to guess from the picture.)*

Therefore, none of the books in Eric's book baggie reinforced the short vowel words he was learning with me. They were also not very useful for reinforcing the sight words his teacher wanted him to learn. For example, the word "like" was on the kindergarten sight word list, and it had been on the stack of flashcards he had just read to me in his classroom.

Since "like" was a common sight word, and since his teacher wanted him to learn it, I assumed it would appear in many of the books in his book baggie. But only two of his 12 green stick dot books included "like." I leafed through his blue stick dot books, searching for "like." It did not appear in any of them.

Among his green stick books, I found *One Frog Too Many*, the book with no words. I also found *Homes for People*, the book Eric had "read" while holding it behind his back. I examined the book closely and saw why that book had been so easy for Eric to memorize. In it, the same sentence was repeated over and over again: A ___ is a home. A ___ is a home. A ___ is a home.

On every page, the repeated sentence also contained a new, usually difficult, word that was illustrated with a picture. Here is how the non-repeating words in *Homes for People* were paired with illustrations:

Words	Illustration
Page 1: A **house** is a home.	Photo of a **house**.
Page 2: A **cabin** is a home.	Photo of a **cabin**.
Page 3: A **hut** is a home.	Photo of a **hut**.
Page 4: A **teepee** is a home.	You guessed it—photo of a **teepee**.

Fantastic Fish, the book Joshua had accused Eric of stealing, was structured similarly.

> You can see fish with <u>spots</u>.
> You can see fish with <u>stripes</u>.
> You can see fish with <u>spikes</u>.

Those sentences were accompanied by photos of fish with spots, stripes, or spikes.

As I paged through book after book, I saw that most of them were structured in the same way: one sentence was repeated over and over again. That was what his kindergarten teacher had meant in the email she had sent me last year. She had said Eric had "figured out the pattern in the book and went with it!" Really, she should have said, "Eric had memorized the pattern and was reciting it."

I could actually see value in these books if they were being used in a systematic way to support the teaching of sight words, or of phonics rules. *Homes for People* would be great practice for a child learning the words "A" or "is" if those were the only words the child was expected to read, and an adult read the harder words to him. It could also be used to support the teaching of long /o/, since the word "home" was repeated so frequently.

But these books were not being used in any systematic way. Eric had chosen these books himself, based on how interesting the pictures looked. One of the books (*The Space Ark*) had the numbers from one to nine written out as words. The illustrations were of a spaceship. The numbers were meant to be the countdown to the spaceship's takeoff. The last sentence said, "Lift off!" That was the contents of the whole book.

The book that made the least sense of all was a blue stick dot book called *The Green Snake*. This was what a beginning reader was given to read:

> "The green snake slides through the grass.
> It looks this way.
> It looks that way.

> It flicks its tongue.
> The snake sees a ladybug.
> Too small.
> The snake sees a toad.
> Too big.
> The snake sees a butterfly.
> Too fat.
> The snake sees a katydid.
> Just right.
> Gulp."

Gulp was right.

How in the world could a book like that have been labeled a blue stick dot? *Because the books were leveled according to the size of the typeface, and the number of words that appeared on a page. They were not leveled according to what phonics rules, or sight words, a child had learned. The word "astrophysics" would have made it into a green stick dot book, as long as it was written in large type and there weren't many other words on the page. But please keep in mind that I did not know this yet. I did know, however, that...*

Based on what I had witnessed in the classroom, and on the contents of the slim little books spread out on the scratched wooden café table before me, one fact was now indisputably clear: My son had been 100 percent correct when, at age five, he had told me his school was not teaching him to read.

Other parents knew

"Hi."

I looked up. A fellow first grade mother was standing next to my table. She looked down at the books spread out before me. Then, she looked at me. "What are you doing?"

I told her what I had just witnessed in Eric's classroom. My voice flat with shock, I said, "That school is not teaching our kids how to read."

"I know," she said, shaking her head in disgust. "I went into their classroom last year and was appalled at what I saw. Reading Workshop was a free-for-all. Instead of reading, they were pulling each other's hair and talking about everything except books. Instead of having them break up into groups and talk, the teachers should be standing in front of the room and actually teaching them how to read. But they don't do that."

She continued: "Last year, I taught my daughter how to read and, this year, I'm going to have to teach my son. He's in kindergarten at (another well-regarded Upper East Side public school). It's the same sort of bullshit there—this 'workshopping' where kids are supposed to just sit down and read even if they don't know how to."

She knew about this? Who else knew about this? And why hadn't anyone told me?

I wasn't going to keep this a secret. I was going to tell every parent I knew.

Spreading the word

The first person I told was Smiley, the father of a boy in Eric's class. Cary and I referred him as "Smiley," because he always smiled when he talked, even if nothing was funny.

Smiley was not the least bit concerned about the lack of instruction.

Smiling, he said, "We did all the workbooks we could find with David. Just go on Amazon and order them. David really liked working in them."

I was puzzled. Smiley's son was one of the best readers in the class. A few weeks ago, I had asked Mrs. Smiley what she had done to help him learn how to read.

"Nothing," she'd responded. "He picked it up by himself. He gets things really quickly."

Today, her husband was telling a different tale. He'd said David had completed "all the workbooks" his parents could find.

Why hadn't Mrs. Smiley told me that?

Was teaching a child how to read similar to experiencing a miscarriage, or having trouble breastfeeding? You never know how many other women have had a miscarriage until you have one yourself. Then many acquaintances—and even friends and relatives—tell you they have had a miscarriage too. But others never share their silent sorrow.

Same with nursing: it seems like every other mom on the planet simply puts her infant to her breast; the kid latches on; and, presto, all those immunities and vitamins flow directly from mother to child. It is only when a woman mentions she is having trouble nursing, that she finds out how many other women had problems too.

But there are some eternal holdouts. The ones who say, "I breastfed my child," even though they supplemented most of the feedings.

Clearly, some mothers were equally secretive about the fact that they had taught their children to read.

Next, I told a mom whose son was in the other first-grade class. She also had a story to share: "Noah is having a hard time recognizing words with short 'u' in them, words like 'mug,'" she said. "I talked to his teacher about it and told her he might have seen 'mug' a hundred times but he still says 'mag?' 'meg?'"

"What did his teacher say?" I asked.

"She said not to teach him the sound that 'u' makes."

"She actually said that?"

The mother nodded. "She said, 'Have him stretch out the "m" and the "g" so he says mmmmmmmm gggggggggggggggggggg. Then he should figure out what the word is from its meaning in the sentence or by looking at the picture.'"

"Nooo!"

"Yes! So I said, 'But what if he sees the word 'mug' without a picture? Shouldn't he just be able to recognize the word mug?'"

"What did she say?"

"She didn't really answer. She said to just have him use the pictures for now."

Finally, as we watched our kids play in the schoolyard after dismissal, I told three other first-grade moms what I had witnessed during Reading Workshop.

One of the moms looked very concerned. Her younger son, Luke, was in Eric's class and her older boy was in fourth grade at the school. "My older son, Robbie, is learning disabled," she said. "He's been working with the school's reading specialist since he was in first grade. Reading Specialist said Robbie needed help learning phonics. Now Luke is struggling with reading and is learning phonics with Reading Specialist too. I thought the issue was my kids. I thought they weren't picking up on what was being taught in the classroom because there was something wrong with them."

Was it possible that the lack of teaching had led to her older son being classified as "learning disabled" and that there was really nothing wrong with him? That thought was too horrible to contemplate, let alone say to this mother, so all I said was, "Go see for yourself. You'll be shocked at what they *aren't* being taught."

And why weren't they being taught how to read? I was going straight to the top to get that answer.

4

Every morning, my son's principal did something truly lovely. She stood outside of the school entrance and gave a warm welcome to each child as he or she arrived.

Her sincere smile, and happy, "Hello!" upheld the school's motto, "Nothing without joy." The school was, indeed, a lovely, joyful, nurturing place. Unfortunately, "nothing without joy" did not apply to my son's experience learning how to read there. That had caused sadness, anxiety, nightmares, and a fear of books.

This well-meaning principal needed to know that. I had traveled up to school with Eric this morning so that I could tell her. As soon as no kids or parents were nearby, I walked up to her and said, "Can I ask you a question?"

"Sure." Her tone was slightly wary. We had never spoken before, other than to say hello. Understandably, she had no idea what I was going to ask her.

"How do kids at this school learn how to read?"

"What kind of a question is that?" she asked.

Taken aback by her aggravated tone, I replied, "It's just a question. I want to understand how the kids are being taught to read."

"It sounds like you're very uninformed."

Ouch. That hurt, but I was hers for the punching. In Manhattan, principals held tremendous power because, in New York City, most children don't just automatically go to their neighborhood public middle school. Every Manhattan neighborhood *does* have a public middle school that all kids who lived in that area could attend, but those schools tend not to be academically strong. Therefore, most children apply to better ones.

At the time Eric was in school, competition for the better public schools was fierce. (Once the pandemic happened, admission changed to being done by lottery.) In Eric's time, grades, absences, and latenesses were part of the admissions process, and the scores kids got on their fourth-grade New York State math and English standardized tests were used to screen the kids in the same way the SAT and ACT are used by colleges. Many of the middle schools conducted admission interviews. (Remember, these were PUBLIC schools.) The process was harrowing, for both children and parents.

If a middle school principal was ever in doubt about admitting a child, she would pick up the phone and call that child's elementary school principal. If the elementary school principal said a child was difficult, or that the child's parents were complainers, that child's chance of admission vanished. Therefore, Manhattan elementary school parents tended to be better behaved than their children were with their kids' teachers and school administrators.

I remained extremely deferential with the principal. Respectfully, I said, "I *am* uninformed. That's why I asked you that question. I need you to inform me."

"Were you at the meeting last year when we explained how kids learn to read?" she asked, impatiently.

She was referring to the meeting I told you about at the beginning of the book, the one where his kindergarten teacher had said she covered up words with sticky notes and told kids to guess what the words could be by looking at the pictures. The one where the teacher had told parents that sounding out words should be used only as a very last resort.

"Yes, I was at the meeting, but I didn't understand the method then, and I don't understand the method now. Eric didn't learn to read in kindergarten. Kindergarten Teacher thought he was reading, but he wasn't. He had memorized all of his books and was reciting them from memory."

"That's not possible."

I wasn't quite sure how to respond. All I could do was continue to tell her the truth. "He did it," I said. "He can recite books while holding them behind his back. Ask him to do it for you. You'll see."

She shrugged. "I suppose he might have a memory that is so amazing, but it's sort of hard to believe he could do that."

Why would I tell her that if it wasn't true? I needed to get her to believe me and, so, I told her the whole story.

I told her that, in kindergarten, Eric had announced that the school wasn't teaching him to read. I told her how anxious he had been that entire year, about the nightmares he'd had about getting lost and drowning, and about how, every morning, he had said that he didn't want to go to school. I told her he had not been able to read anything over the summer, and how he had finally gotten me to understand he couldn't read by "reading" a book while holding it behind his back. I told her he was now at the bottom of his class in reading and that I was teaching him how to read at home.

"It sounds like you're worried," she said.

"I am *very* worried. I love this school. I just have questions about how the kids learn to read."

The principal visibly relaxed. I realized she had taken my initial question as criticism. I was glad she was no longer on the defensive, and I knew what I was about to say would make her relax even more. Online, I had read that if kids complained about a book you were asking them to read, that meant the book was too hard for them. It meant you needed to take things down a notch.

If I knew this—and I was "just a mom" at the time, and not yet someone who had done her Ph.D. dissertation on how kids learn to read—then the principal must know this too. I would give her a chance to tell me what Eric's behavior meant. In the telling, she would come across as an expert who knew what she was talking about. That would make her feel better and would make her more receptive to what I was telling her.

And, so, I said, "When I tried to get Eric to read with me over the summer, he wouldn't do it. He would moan and groan, and move away from the book, and say he hated reading."

Instead of telling me that the books I had asked Eric to read had been too hard for him, the principal replied, "There is something going on in your relationship with him. Some kids don't want to read with their mothers. He just doesn't want to read with you."

I was stunned.

Do you know how harmful those words would have been if they had been uttered to someone who didn't know why children refused to read certain books? Or to someone who had a difficult relationship with her child? Or was less confident in her parenting skills?

Totally unaware of how ignorant she was being, the principal continued: "I used to be a first-grade teacher. A mother came to me and said her child wasn't reading at home. She wanted me to tutor him. I sat with him, and he read just fine. I told the mother he didn't need a tutor. He just didn't want to read with her."

That poor mother. I wonder how she had handled that comment. I hope she had stepped up to the plate and taught her child how to read.

"Trust us," the principal said to me. "If there is a problem, we will find it and we will fix it. I want parents, more than anything, to take a deep breath and trust us. There's no need for you to worry. He's only in first grade. Reading is developmental. He'll read when he's ready. We'll keep an eye on him and see how it goes."

I was not going to sit back and trust the school.

I had trusted the school in kindergarten and look where that had gotten Eric.

And I didn't want the school to just "keep an eye" on Eric. I wanted his teacher to teach him how to read. "Eric is reading with me at home now that I'm teaching him phonics," I said. "He's making great progress, but I'm worried that he's not getting any phonics in school. I went to Reading Workshop last week and I didn't see any phonics being taught and I was just wondering if the kids get any phonics."

"We do phonics, but we don't do worksheets. We don't do any of that."

"So how do kids learn if the phonics rules aren't reinforced with worksheets?" I asked. "Or with books that allow them to practice the phonics rules they are learning? And how can kids learn to read if words are covered up with sticky notes in the stories they are reading?"

She sighed and began walking towards the school's large metal doors. "We do Whole Language," she said over her shoulder. Google 'Whole Language.' You'll find everything you need to know online."

> **Lesson to be learned**
> Never tell someone to google a topic
> unless you have previously googled it yourself.

5

What is Whole Language?

The answer to that question is so crazy, so unbelievable, so downright whacky that you will think what I am about to tell you can't possibly be true.

You will say: There is no way anyone could be using that method to teach kids how to read. There is no way a theory so absurd could have fully infiltrated colleges of education, become the predominant way of teaching reading in the United States, Canada, Australia, and Britain, and fueled a dispute so bitter that it regularly made the front pages of newspapers across the country and came to be known as the "Reading Wars."

One side of the reading wars consisted of cognitive scientists, reading researchers, parents whose kids were struggling with reading, and informed teachers who were doing a great job teaching kids to read. That side believed children needed to be taught how to sound out words in order to learn how to read. This process is referred to as phonics. They also believed phonics should be taught in an explicit, step-by-step way, starting from the easiest rules and progressing to the hardest.

The other side of the Reading Wars consisted of professors of education and the teachers they had trained in Whole Language approaches. In the United States, their leaders were two education professors—Ken Goodman and Frank Smith.

What did Whole Language proponents espouse?

Since the answer to the question is so hard to believe, let me answer it with a direct quote from Frank Smith: "My own recommendation for how reading and writing should be taught is perhaps radical: they should not be taught at all."

Yes, he really said that.

And he meant it.

Let me explain: Proponents of Whole Language mistakenly, and quite tragically, believe learning to read is as natural as learning to speak. The root of their belief lies in the fact that our brains are wired to learn spoken language. When we were babies, no one ever needed to drill us on letter sounds. They simply talked to us. We learned the meaning of words being spoken all around us and, in time, began speaking them ourselves. As prominent linguist Noam Chomsky stated, "Babies learn to speak and listen through a natural process of imitation."

Whole Language proponents believe children learn to read in the same way—by imitating what a reader does. Of course, no teacher in his or her right mind will let a classroom of kids figure out how to read completely on their own. A teacher's role in the process came to be reading stories out loud to children, pointing to the words as she went. She would read the same story over and over again to her students until they had memorized the words. She would also teach them to guess what words could be by using pictures, context, and just the first letter of a word. At some point, a developmental switch would turn on and the child's brain would begin absorbing written words the way a vacuum cleaner absorbs peanuts. That is nature's way.

There is just one problem with that theory: It is not true.

But try telling that to the believers.

For more than 50 years, reading researchers have been trying to get Whole Language proponents to see the error of their ways. "Reading is not a natural activity!" reading scientists cried from lecture podiums and print and online platforms all over the world. They cited decades of empirically sound, scientifically proven, replicable evidence proving their point.

The alphabet and written words were created by humans, just like skyscrapers were, the scientists said. Calling reading natural would be like calling the building of skyscrapers natural—something you can learn by simply watching someone build a few. Since reading is not natural, systematic instruction in how individual letters combine to form words is required in order for children to grow up to be fluent readers. (Systematic means that phonics rules must be taught in sequence, with each rule building on the one that came before.)

But Whole Language proponents refused to give up their belief that phonics was bad.

Know what Frank Smith told teachers about phonics? He said: "Meet the enemy."

He also declared, "Phonics does not work."

Whole Language proponents believe that teaching the individual sounds in words turns the joyous process of learning how to read into a tedious chore. (To be clear: It is not PHONICS that they are against. They are against the TEACHING of phonics They want children to be able to discover phonics rules on their own, as they read and write.) Whole Language proponents also believe that if children focus too much on sounding out words their reading comprehension will suffer since they will not be focusing on the meaning of the story. In Whole Language approaches, the meaning of the story matters more than reading a word correctly. As long as the child produces a word similar in meaning to the actual word—for example, "horse" instead of "pony"—the teacher will accept that word as correct.

How did something so nutty come to be the predominant way of teaching reading? It all started when one of Whole Language's founding fathers, Ken Goodman, came up with a theory about how people read and never stopped to ask himself what might be wrong with his idea.

*Whole Language took the education world by storm after Goodman presented a paper called "Reading: A Psycholinguistic Guessing Game" at the 1967 American Educational Research Association conference. He believed reading was a "guessing game" because of strategies he had observed children use when they read: they guessed what the words could be by looking at the pictures; they used context clues to decide what type of word would work—a noun, verb or adjective—and they used the first letter of a word to take wild stabs at what the word would be. The kids definitely did **not** sound out every letter in a word. Goodman noted that when the children guessed from the first letter, they made the most mistakes. Ergo—or so his flawed thinking went—sounding out words was the least effective strategy of all.*

*Unfortunately, Goodman did not stop to ask if the children he had observed were good readers, or if they were struggling ones. He never investigated whether the kids had ever been taught **how** to sound out words. If those children had been taught using an earlier type of whole word approach to teaching reading—called* "look-say"—they would not know how to sound out words and would be forced to resort to guessing what words could be.

The whole word "look-say" method was, in fact, the predominant way of teaching reading at the time Goodman conducted his observational studies and wrote his paper. Look-say used different methods of teaching than Goodman's later Whole Language approach, but it shared the idea that phonics was "bad." Look-say thought phonics was **so** bad, that it did not teach kids the alphabet, and the fact that letters even existed wasn't mentioned in the first few years of school. (We will look at this method in more detail in Chapter 21.) Instead of looking at the letters that comprised a word, kids were taught to recognize words according to their shape and size, as if they were symbols. They were taught to memorize whole words and to recognize them "on sight" as if each word was a picture.

The look-say method had been introduced into U.S. schools in the 1920s and, for the first time in our country's history, a huge number of kids began struggling with reading. Before that, the vast majority of kids had been taught using phonics, and they had been reading just fine. A neuropsychiatrist named Samuel Orton saw the connection between the fact that phonics wasn't being taught and children's sudden struggles with reading, and he wrote an article about it for the February 1929 issue of The Journal of Educational Psychology. The name of the article was "The Sight Reading Method of Teaching Reading as a Source of Reading Disability."

The title says it all.

Children were being labeled learning disabled not because there was something neurologically wrong with them, but because they were being taught to memorize words "on sight," as opposed to sound them out. "The sight method not only will not eradicate a reading disability," Orton wrote, "but may actually produce a number of cases."

Orton's article was ignored by the education establishment. To help the children schools were harming, he went on to co-create the Orton-Gillingham method of teaching reading. Today, that method is universally considered the gold standard for teaching reading to children who are struggling with it.

As Dr. Orton had observed, many children taught by a whole word method were bound to be struggling readers. Astonishingly, Goodman never stopped to *think that, when conducting observations for his paper, he had been watching struggling readers, as opposed to kids who could read well.*

The result?

He went on to spend a lifetime refining a theory that taught children to read the way struggling readers did.

It took completing a Ph.D. dissertation, and 17 years of reading mountains of material for me to learn what you just read. If I had known what you do now, I would have taken different steps with Eric's school. But I did not. Back when Eric was in first grade, I did not find details about why Whole Language was preposterous, but I found enough to let me know it was definitely bad…

As I surfed the internet back then, I found post after post detailing the disastrous effects Whole Language had inflicted on children. A post by Robert Sweet, former director of the National Institute for Education, and founder of the National Right to Read Foundation, was particularly disturbing: Because of Whole Language, "two to three million young people are placed in Special Education simply because they haven't learned to read, not because they have any…physiological problems or emotional problems."

Not a single post—not one—said phonics had ever prevented a child from learning how to read. But post after post lamented that children were not learning how to read because of Whole Language. And this was happening on a massive scale all across the country.

Let's take California as an example. In the early 1980s, California had been teaching children phonics and its reading scores on the National Assessment of Educational Progress exams had been near the very top of all the states. In 1987, California switched to Whole Language. Nine years later, its reading scores plummeted to being dead last. Only the territory of Guam scored lower.

Realizing that Whole Language had been a huge mistake, the California state legislature "passed, without a single dissenting vote in either house, two bills mandating the use of instructional materials that teach reading through phonics," I read in an *Atlantic Monthly* article called "The Reading Wars."

That article had been published in 1997. That was three years before Eric was born, and 11 years before he entered kindergarten. If the California debacle was so well known, why in the world was Whole Language still being used?

That question became even more urgent as I kept clicking and reading. A year after California's disastrous reading scores were released, Congress asked the National Institute of Child Health and Human Development to identify which elements of reading instruction were most effective. A group of experts known as the National Reading Panel spent the next three years reviewing over 100,000 studies on reading. Their findings were conclusive: Research definitively showed that phonics was a necessary part of teaching kindergartners and first graders how to read. (Phonics was one of five necessary components, and it was a crucial starting point. Without phonics, kids would never get off the ground.)

Headlines all across the country trumpeted that the reading wars were over, and phonics had won. The general public assumed Whole Language would immediately vacate the classroom.

It did not. Whole Language was how teachers taught, and it was how professors of education were teaching teachers to teach. Those professors had devoted their professional lives to teaching Whole Language, and a few of them were making lots of money creating curriculums based on Whole Language methods. It would be a huge professional embarrassment, and a massive financial loss, for them to say they had been wrong.

Instead of admitting defeat, Whole Language proponents fought harder. They said the research disproving Whole Language was flawed. (Fake news!) They said there was nothing wrong with their way of "teaching." (It was the best. It was HUGELY effective!) There was something wrong with the children who were not able to read using that method. (Blame the victim!) Whole Language proponents also criticized every possible aspect of the panel—who had been chosen to be on it; the studies that had been reviewed; and the panel's conclusions.

To finally put an end to the nonsense, in 2001, the federal government said it would pull federal funding from any school district that did not teach phonics.

Schools were forced to change. Unfortunately, they did so in name only. Instead of slinking away into the dark night ashamed of the damage they had wrought, proponents of Whole Language changed the method's name to Balanced Literacy without changing the substance of what they were doing.

Balanced Literacy was presented as a mix of the best of both methods—phonics and Whole Language. "We teach phonics," teachers told parents, and they were not lying. But those phonics lessons were sporadic and infrequent. Over and over again, when parents complained that their children did not know a particular phonics rule, the response they got was, "Oh. Your child was absent the day I taught that lesson." Very few children are able to pick up a phonics rule in just one short lesson.

Parents thought things had changed, but they had not done so in any meaningful way. One of America's most prominent education researchers, Louisa Moats, Ed.D., summed up the situation best in an article called, "Whole Language Lives on: The Illusion of 'Balanced' Reading Instruction." The article described how, even though reading instruction was now being presented as "balanced," Whole Language's original methods still pervaded "textbooks for teachers, instructional materials for classroom use, some states' language-arts standards and other policy documents, teacher licensing requirements and preparation programs. As a result, many (teachers)…continue to misunderstand reading development and to deliver poorly conceived, ineffective instruction."

Not only did teachers continue to deliver poor instruction, but they were actively urged to do so by their thought leaders. For example, Ken Goodman, Whole Language's founding father, praised teachers who continued to teach children to guess, instead of sound out words. He wrote: "I want to give a shout out for all those teachers who…have quietly nodded their heads as they were told what to do and how to do it—and then closed their classroom doors."

And kept on doing what did not work.

6

What would you have done? Would you have printed out all the negative articles you found about Whole Language, brought them to your child's principal, and asked her to change the way her school taught reading? Or would you have continued teaching your child yourself?

It was already clear that Eric's principal was not a rocket scientist. Look at how she had told me the reason Eric wasn't reading at home was because there was something wrong in my relationship with him. Or how she had said it wasn't possible that Eric had memorized all the books he had seemed to be reading in kindergarten even though the school taught—and expected the kids to—memorize stories. Or how she had sent me to the internet to learn about Whole Language, unaware that the teaching method had been so discredited that its name had been changed to Balanced Literacy.

Given how prickly she had been when I first asked her how the school taught reading, I knew that a request for systematic phonics in the classroom would fall on deaf ears, alienate her, and label me a trouble-maker mom—a death knell for my son when the time came for him to apply to public middle schools. And, so, I decided to say nothing and simply continue teaching Eric at home.

Every night, Eric made progress in his phonics work with me. He was now able to easily read short /a/ and /i/ words and was currently learning words with short /u/.

Every night he felt a little better about himself and about reading.

Not me.

I was worried.

Scared.

Not sure of what I was doing.

But at least I was doing something and, slowly, what I was doing was working.

My son was, clearly, learning how to read.

I wasn't going to say anything more to the school about what I was doing, but then…

Turning points happen at unexpected times

Let me introduce you to "It-was-Nothing-Mom." She was a slim, sweet, stay-at-home mother who had always wanted to be an elementary school teacher. Her parents had discouraged her from getting a college degree, and she had ended up with an associate's diploma instead.

She channeled her unfulfilled dream of being a teacher into being a school's dream class parent. Whenever Hallowed School asked for volunteers to help with a school event, or to supervise a field trip, It-was-Nothing-Mom was the first to sign up. She treated all of the first-graders as if they were her own, constantly zipping jackets, wiping runny noses, giving sips of water, and handing out homemade banana bread in the playground. She always gave of herself, yet any time someone thanked her for her kind deeds, she would respond, "Oh, it was nothing."

Today, at Friday dismissal, It-was-Nothing-Mom approached me as I waited for Eric. She had been part of my conversation the other day in the playground—the one in which a fellow mom had wondered if the school's way of teaching had caused her child to be learning disabled. Now, It-was-Nothing-Mom handed me an article from *New York* magazine. "I thought you would find this interesting," she said.

Interesting was an understatement. The article, "A is for Apple, B is for Brawl: Why New York's Reading Wars are so Contentious," was a game changer. First, it showed me exactly how kids were taught to read in a Balanced Literacy classroom, something I did not understand at the time. It wrote about a second-grade child guessing words incorrectly—saying "collar" when the word in the story was "collie," then eventually settling on the word "dog"—and the teacher accepting those incorrect guesses. Instead of showing children how to sound out words, the teacher, over and over, would ask, "Does that make sense?" any time a child made a mistake. If the child came up with a word that "made sense"—the teacher would accept it, even if it wasn't the word on the page.

The article also told the story of how Balanced Literacy had come to be the mandated approach to teaching reading in New York City schools. That had happened three years *after* the National Reading Panel had found that systematic phonics was imperative in order to effectively teach kindergarten and first graders how to read.

The mandate for Balanced Literacy had come from Mayor Michael Bloomberg, a well-intentioned billionaire with no experience in education. After his election, he took control of the city's school system and said he should be judged by how much he improved schools. His admirable goal was to root out ingrained, ineffective bureaucracy and favoritism and make the school system more equitable for all. To help him, he hired Joel Klein, a successful anti-trust lawyer, to be schools chancellor.

Those two smart businessmen were well-versed in fixing bureaucracy and ineffective management but knew nothing about curriculums. They dealt with their lack of knowledge in the same way they would have at their hugely successful companies: they hired someone with a lot of experience choosing curriculums and delegated the responsibility to her. The academic fate of hundreds and thousands of children was sealed when a woman named Diana Lam was hired to be deputy chancellor for teaching and learning.

Lam, who would resign in disgrace two years later over charges of nepotism, was a huge proponent of Whole Language-based teaching. Her very first move in her very new job was to toss out Success for All (a curriculum with strong systematic phonics that had recently raised reading scores in dozens of New York's low-performing schools) and replace it with Balanced Literacy.

In the article, I learned that, just days after Bloomberg and Klein announced the new curriculum, they received an open letter from seven of the world's top reading experts saying the reading program was "woefully inadequate;" lacked "a research base" and "the ingredients of a systematic phonics program;" and put "beginning readers at risk of failure in learning to read."

Bloomberg and Klein ignored the letter.

They also ignored the scathing articles and op-ed pieces about Balanced Literacy that instantly appeared in the media. The articles carried the same message as this one from education writer Sol Stern: "Many of the programs and methods now being crammed down the teachers' throats have no record of success and are particularly ill-suited for disadvantaged minority children. In fact, (they were chosen) ... in total disregard of what the scientific evidence says about the most effective teaching methods—particularly in the critically important area of early reading."

All of that was disturbing, but it would not have caused me to say something to the school. I already knew Balanced Literacy did not work.

But then I read about why Chancellor Klein loved Balanced Literacy in the first place—he loved it because it was how "successful school districts on the Upper West Side and the Upper East Side and ... most of the city's elite private schools" taught kids how to read. "In a system where so many great schools coexist with so many horrible ones. Klein is convinced that the solution is...to export the best practices of the successful ones and end the educational apartheid," the article said.

That made my heart pound. Those "elite private schools" and public schools in the wealthy Upper East Side and Upper West Side neighborhoods were not successful *because* of Balanced Literacy. They were successful *in spite of* Balanced Literacy. Many of the kids in those schools knew how to read because their parents, or tutors, had taught them how to do so.

The *New York* magazine article did not come right out and say that but, if you read between the lines, the message was there. For example, the article said, "Everyone stands to gain from phonics, but no one stands to benefit more than children from low-income families who—unlike, say, the kids at elite private schools, most of which use a whole-language approach—often can't get the extra tutoring in the basics." (That meant kids at those "elite" schools **were** getting "extra tutoring in the basics," which, of course, was phonics. And their parents were paying for those private lessons. And that's why the kids at those "elite" schools were doing so well.)

I thought and thought about what I had just read: Klein liked Balanced Literacy because it was being used by elite private schools, and at top public schools like Hallowed. But kids at those schools were successful because their parents could afford to pay for tutors to teach them how to read. Or because the parents had taught their children how to do so themselves.

How could there be such a vast disconnect between what was really happening and what the schools chancellor thought was happening?

The article also stated that Carmen Farina (the person Bloomberg and Klein had chosen to replace Diana Lam as deputy chancellor for teaching and learning) was more amenable to phonics than Lam had been. Farina called herself a "centrist" when it came to phonics. Under her, the article stated, phonics was "coming into the classroom … not with every child, but in targeted ways to get specific results."

Phonics had *not* come into Eric's classroom.

And people who knew a lot more than I did at the time said it hadn't come into most classrooms. "How many schools is (systematic phonics) in?" education historian Diane Ravitch, Ph.D. asked in the article. "Has the chancellor made any announcements that (systematic phonics) is going to be a standard … with Balanced Literacy? I would like to hear some evidence that it's in more than just a few schools."

So would I. But, even if it was just a public relations spin to placate parents, the fact that Farina—the current deputy chancellor for teaching and learning—had said phonics should be in classrooms was enough to make me decide to say something to Eric's school. I reached for my laptop and began a course of events that would change my life.

Email from: Me

To: FirstGradeTeacher@schools.nyc.gov

Date: Nov. 22

Can we please meet one morning? I am still worried about Eric's reading. I think his reading skills would solidify much better and faster if there was a way to get him to actually read words in his books, as opposed to talk with Joshua about the pictures or just look at the pictures in the books. From what I see, Eric is not engaging with the words, so he isn't learning to read with the books he is currently using.

I've realized that kids who are reading well in his grade were taught phonics by their parents and that is a big factor in why they are now doing so great. I didn't do any phonics with Eric until this year. Now that I am doing it, he does very well with it and really likes it and that makes me think he would benefit from direct, systematic, phonics-based instruction of reading. Is there any way phonics could be implemented during Reading Workshop for kids like Eric and Joshua and other blue stick dot kids who may benefit from it?

I cannot tell you what a difference phonics has made for Eric. If what we are doing at home could go hand in hand with what he is doing at school, he would progress much more quickly. Is there any way that he could be given more phonics-based books to read in class and to bring home for homework?

I look forward to hearing your thoughts, and I hope we can meet sometime next week.

Thank you and happy Thanksgiving!

Be careful what you wish for

In the meeting, I was going to come right out and say I wanted the school to do more to teach him. I was going to say I didn't want to be the only one doing all the work. I was going to say a lot more, but I ended up saying none of it. As soon as my butt hit the tiny first grade chair, Eric's teacher said, "I talked to our school's reading specialist about Eric's reading and showed her his writing. She said Eric can be labeled 'at risk' and that he would be able to work with her."

At risk?

The only thing Eric was "at risk" of was being in a school where teachers did not teach children how to read. Remember the open letter that seven of the top reading experts in the world had sent to Mayor Bloomberg? They had warned him that, because it did not include systematic phonics, Balanced Literacy, put "beginning readers at risk of failure in learning to read."

I tried to think of a diplomatic way to say that to Eric's teacher.

"It won't go on his record," she said. "She'll work with him in the classroom and see what's going on."

That took my upset down a few notches. Someone certainly needed to see what was "going on." Someone needed to see that Eric was learning how to read at home and wasn't being taught how to do so in school. Maybe the reading specialist would ensure that he received regular phonics lessons in school as well. No harm would come from the "at risk" label, other than me feeling that labeling Eric "at risk" was wrong. It was wrong to put the blame on the child, and not on the school. But my feelings were irrelevant. No matter how I felt about it, I needed to get Eric all the help I could and working with the reading specialist was bound to help him.

"Okay," I said. "When would he start working with her?"

"He has to be accepted into the supplemental teaching support program first, so this has to be reviewed by the principal and some other people. It's not a definite, but the reading specialist said she's going to tell me what to put on the forms, what words to use to make sure he gets accepted, and which writing samples to show." (*The name of the program was actually Special Education Teacher Support Services or SETSS for short. I am sure the teacher did not use the words "special ed" on purpose. Had I known my son was applying to be accepted into a special ed program, I would have had a very different reaction.*)

"Before I say yes, I want to make sure—the reading specialist will do phonics with him?" I asked.

"Yes. She uses the same phonics workbook you are using with Eric at home."

The school had *Explode the Code* under this very roof? Then why didn't the school make it available to all the kids? Why did only "at risk" kids work with it? "Why doesn't the school just teach phonics to everyone in the classroom?" I asked.

"We work in phonics in other ways throughout the day," First Grade Teacher replied. "We do Word Study where we look at words that share a sound." She pointed at a handwritten poster hanging on the wall. The poster listed words that made the long /e/ sound: me, we; Pete; flea; glee.

"Can Eric read those words?" I asked.

"He gets it with e at the end of a word—me, we, free."

But how about the other words? I thought. There was no way he could read words like Pete and flea. Why were those words lumped together? "Pete" and "flea" followed two different phonics rules, and "me," "we" and "free" followed a third. Why not teach one rule at a time so that kids could really master them? And why bother teaching the word "flea" at all? How often does "flea" come up in stories first graders read?

The teacher glanced at the wall clock. It was almost time for her to retrieve her class from the auditorium and start the school day. There was no time for me to question the words being taught in Word Study. It was more important for her to realize how imperative it was for Eric to be accepted into the supplemental teaching program.

"Eric can't read any of the books he brings home for homework" I said, urgently. "He's memorized them. He isn't really reading them."

"That's good," she replied. "We want him to feel confident reading."

OMG.

Did she not hear what I had said?

I spoke louder, the way people tend to do when speaking to someone who does not understand their language. "Eric IS NOT READING. How can he be confident? HE CAN NOT READ THE WORDS."

As if it made all the sense in the world, his teacher replied, "Now we need to take the words out of the book. We need to write them on a piece of paper, cut the words out, and have him put the sentences together."

Speechless, I stared at her.

She returned my gaze, seemingly thinking that what she had said made all the sense in the world. Who had taught this sweet, young, well-intentioned teacher that you needed to "take the words out" of a book, scramble them up, and put them back together in order to teach a child to read? Why not just teach the kid how to read the words in the book?

I sighed. "I know the school uses the Balanced Literacy approach, but what curriculum do you use exactly?"

The teacher sat a little straighter. Clearly, what she was about to say gave her authority and confidence. "We use the Lucy Calkins model from Teachers College."

7

Lucy Calkins is a professor of literacy at Teachers College at Columbia University and the creator of one of the most widely used Balanced Literacy reading curriculums in the country. It was her curriculum that Mayor Bloomberg mandated into all New York City schools, and it is her book—The Art of Teaching Reading (which you read about in Chapter 1)—that tells teachers to have kindergarten and first-grade kids pretend to read.

For decades, Calkins was also the founding director of the Teachers College Reading and Writing Project, a think tank that, according to her publisher, developed "state of the art teaching methods" and provided professional development "to hundreds of thousands of teachers, principals, superintendents, and policy-makers across the country and around the world."

Pretty impressive, huh?

Very impressive until you consider the fact that Lucy Calkins and her "state of the art teaching methods" are the reason millions of children have trouble learning to read or have grown up to be adults who struggle with it.

Professors of education are not usually lumped into the same category as dictators or terrorists, but many people place Lucy Calkins squarely into that category of devastatingly harmful people. The mere mention of her name has triggered fear, anger, and revulsion among literacy advocates, reading researchers, cognitive scientists, and informed teachers and parents for years. In 2012, a blog called South Bronx School called for her to be "arrested, prosecuted, convicted, and sentenced" for "her systematic compliance in ruining the lives of NYC students."

Today, there is an all-out revolution waging against her and her curriculum at classroom and at state political levels.

That revolution was already impotently simmering in 2007. Back then, when I first googled "Lucy Calkins" and "Teachers College," I expected to find facts about how this woman's curriculum was teaching my son to read. Instead, I found opinions. A lot of negative opinions. Most of the blog posts I found had been written by teachers in poor neighborhoods where few, if any, parents were teaching children to read at home.

One teacher, on BlackCommentator.com, referred to the curriculum as an "unproven... motley mess concocted by Lucy Calkins, students and shaggy haired professors at Columbia University's Teacher's College, and other inept 'educators' from the ivory towers of academia."

On TeacherParadise.Blogspot.com, another teacher said he had "lost respect for our mayor, the chancellor, Randi Weingarten (the head of the teacher's union in New York City) and every teacher who sits there passively while the nimwits at Columbia University and that Lucy Calkins idiot recite chapter and verse the bullshit...(that) has now become the norm in our schools."

Today, the internet is flooded with information about Lucy Calkins and her flawed methods of teaching reading. But that was not the case in 2007. Back then, my internet search unearthed lots of anger and frustration, but it did not reveal specific information on what, exactly, Calkins was telling teachers to do.

For every teacher who thought the curriculum was an "unproven... motley mess," another one said it was fantastic. For every teacher who called it "bullshit," another one said the curriculum caused kids to love reading and go on to become lifelong readers. For every teacher who was berating Calkins, another was treating her like a celebrity to be adored and emulated.

Most teachers worshiped her. As a Palo Alto school board member would say on the 2022 APM podcast Sold a Story, "If Beyonce came and gave a private concert in my district, it would not have been a bigger deal for many of my teachers."

What is the Lucy Calkins model?

"The Lucy Calkins model is a workshop model. That means children spend the bulk of their time working independently.

The start of each workshop begins with a "mini lesson" in which the teacher briefly demonstrates the skill she wants her students to learn. The teacher does not explicitly TEACH the kids this skill. Instead, she executes the skill herself. After that, the kids are told to perform the skill that has been modeled for them. If you remember, during Reading Workshop Eric's teacher had retold the story of The Little Engine That Could. That retelling had been the "mini lesson." She had then instructed the kids to go off and retell the story of a book they were reading.

You witnessed how well that went for Eric and Joshua.

While the kids work independently, the teacher works either one-on-one, or with a small group of children. That is when she will have them guess their way through the books in their book baggies, urging them to try to figure out unfamiliar words by using the picture, or context, or just the first letter of the word. If the kids are really stumped, she will tell them what the word is. It is during that reading, that kids begin to memorize those stories. That one-on-one process is what Eric's teacher had meant when she told me the kids are taught to read "on an individual basis."

That is when things begin to fall apart for those poor children.

8

> Here is a multiple choice question: If your child has not been taught how to sound out words, which academic subject (besides reading) will be most negatively affected?
>
> A.) Math
> B.) Science
> C.) Social studies
> D.) Spelling
>
> If you choose spelling, you are correct!

Three days after my meeting with his teacher, Eric came home from school and announced, "I have to work hard on my spelling words because we had a test on them today."

Obviously, the test must not have gone well.

But wait a minute.

Spelling test?

What spelling test?

Just three days ago, Eric's teacher had told me he was being labeled "at risk." She hadn't mentioned that she was going to be teaching spelling or that the kids would be tested on it. Eric had never taken a test in his life. He had no idea how to study for a test, or that he needed to. Had I known he was having a test, I would have made sure he studied for it. After all, not studying for tests was guaranteed to put him even more at risk.

Why hadn't his teacher mentioned that she was teaching spelling? Up until now, the kids had been told not to worry about spelling words correctly. Balanced Literacy believes that worrying about proper grammar or spelling distracts kids from focusing on what they are writing about. It has them use "invented" spelling when they write, which means the kids are told to spell words the way they sound, as opposed to worry about how they are actually spelled. In a Balanced Literacy classroom, "ez" would be accepted as the way to spell "easy." This, of course, gets in the way of kids being able to read words when they see them in a story since the kids have no idea how they are actually spelled.

I would have been thrilled if his teacher had told me she was teaching spelling. Teaching spelling was teaching phonics. After all, in order to be able to spell a word correctly, you need to focus on every letter in it, and know what sound each of those letters makes. Maybe the school was, finally, taking a step in the right direction.

"I will help you learn your spelling words," I promised Eric. "You'll do fine."

Be careful what you promise

The following Monday, Eric brought home these spelling words: right, night, there, their, when.

Those words were much too hard for my son.

Thanks to invented spelling, he still thought "of" was spelled as "uv."

That night, I slept a fitful, restless sleep, trying to figure out how I was going to teach him to spell his class words. By 2 a.m., I had a plan.

In the morning, Cary and my older son, Jamie, were eating toasted waffles at the dining room table. Cary was smiling at something Jamie had said. My husband looked so handsome that I stopped in my tracks.

You haven't seen much of Cary in these pages because I hadn't been seeing much of him. I was so busy with work, and grad school, and figuring out how to teach Eric to read, that I barely had time to talk to my husband. Neither one of us had been smiling or laughing much lately. It was nice to see him smiling this morning. He had such a beautiful smile.

Looking at him now, I realized how much I missed him. Then I realized I did not want my husband to witness what I was about to do. It was embarrassing. And, so, I said to Eric, "Come with me into the bedroom."

I closed the door behind us and said, "I made up a song that will help you remember how to spell 'right.' I want to sing it for you."

Still dressed in his teddy bear pajamas, Eric clambered onto the unmade bed and sat, cross-legged, on the blue and white striped comforter.

He looked so cute.

But there was no time to appreciate his cuteness. We had work to do.

Like a cheerleader, I began pumping alternate arms in the air and chanting:

"R...

"I...

"G...

"H...

"T...

"This is what it means to me. Turn right!"

I jumped a quarter turn to the right. Outside of the bedroom window, I saw sky and rooftops.

"Turn right!" I jumped another quarter turn to the right. In the large mirror hanging on the bedroom wall, I saw Eric's reflection. He looked puzzled.

"Yeah! Right!" I jumped twice and raised both arms in the air in a celebratory V for victory. Facing Eric, I waited for his reaction.

"I don't get it," he said.

I explained: "R-i-g-h-t is how you spell right. 'This is what it means to me' is what the word means—it means you turn right."

I performed the entire chant and the accompanying cheerleader moves again.

Eric frowned. "That's just strange."

I laughed. "It's strange, but it will work. It will help you remember how to spell right. Come on. Sing it with me."

He shook his head no and held out his arms. That was his way of asking to be carried.

I picked him up, opened the bedroom door and—how Cary saw me be dammed—stepped into the hallway. With Eric in my arms, I chanted. "R-i-g-h-t. This is what it means to me. Turn right."

I jumped to the right. We were facing the bathroom. "Oops! Wrong room."

I turned around and jumped into the dining room.

Cary and Jamie had stopped eating. They were staring at me. Neither one of them said a word.

"Turn right." I jumped a few more times until I reached the kitchen doorway and deposited Eric on the floor.

"Can I have chicken noodle soup for breakfast?" Eric asked.

As I opened the can and heated his soup, Eric played with a toy car on the floor. He rolled the car to the right and said, "R-i-g-h-t."

I smiled. My song was "strange" and embarrassing, but it had worked. My kid had just spelled "right."

By the end of the week, "right" was the only word he knew how to spell. He regularly transposed, or got wrong, at least one letter in the other four spelling words. I realized it would be absolutely fruitless for him to continue trying to learn words that were still too hard for him.

On Thursday evening, I sent the following email to Eric's teacher:

From: Me

To: FirstGradeTeacher@schools.nyc.gov

Subject: This week's spelling words

Hi,

I wanted to let you know Eric tried really hard to learn this week's spelling words, but they seem to be WAY over his ability level. I know there are kids in the class who will be able to spell these words but there are also others who won't. Of course, you have to teach everyone in the class, but is there any way you could have two sets of words for the kids—one for the advanced and one for the not

> advanced? It would be great if his spelling words could reinforce the words that appear most often in the stories he reads and could be at a level that will be productive for him. Is there any way that is possible?

I was volunteering at recess in Hallowed School's playground when his teacher told me the news. "Eric's been accepted into the supplemental teaching program. He'll be able to work with the reading specialist."

I should have been happy. After all, I wanted him to work with the reading specialist.

But I did not feel happy.

I felt sad.

In the playground, children laughed and shrieked as they ran and played. On the neighboring sidewalk, a woman walked a golden lab puppy. The large windows of the school glinted in the sunlight as young, sweet teachers exited the building, heading to the yard to retrieve their classes.

All seemed to be so right at this renowned school, yet what was happening to Eric seemed so wrong. It seemed so strange, so wrong, that he needed to work with a reading specialist in order to learn how to read. It seemed so strange, so wrong, that in order for their children to have the privilege of attending this wonderful school—and many things about it *were* wonderful—parents were willing to teach their children how to read at home.

First Grade Teacher cleared her throat. She was looking at me quizzically, waiting for a response.

"I'm glad," I said, half-heartedly. "And sad too. I'm sad that he needs it."

"No," she said, reassuringly "It's a good thing. He'll get the help he needs."

Looking apprehensive, she continued, "I got your email about the spelling. I've been thinking the same thing, but I don't know how to give him different words without making him feel bad."

"Not being able to learn the class words will make him feel bad," I replied. "Learning words that are on his level—and that he really needs to know at this point—will make him feel good."

First Grade Teacher remained silent. She clearly did not agree. Then, I had an idea. "How about if Reading Specialist assigns him his spelling words? That way, the other kids won't wonder why he has different words."

Teacher smiled. "That's a great idea! I'll have Reading Specialist give me his words every week and I'll write them into his spelling notebook."

That made me feel a little better about the supplemental program. Already, having him participate in it had resulted in something positive for Eric.

I don't know who was happier about school being closed for holiday break, my kids or me. My two sons delighted in the joys of their December vacation—sledding, ice skating, baking Christmas cookies, and watching family movies—and I delighted in being able to work with Eric on his reading without school getting in the way.

That was, indeed, how I had come to view his school—it was a place that got in the way of him learning to read. With me, Eric had mastered the short vowels. That meant he could read words like cat, hit, hug, end, and hop. He also knew that /ck/ was pronounced "k," and, so, could read words like "sick" and "pick." He could read sentences like, "The pet cat is on the big mat in the back." That was a big deal for a kid who had been able to read only "the" and "and" just four months ago.

Over the break, I began teaching him blends. Those are words like "stop," "slip" and "king" that begin, or end, with two consonants. And I discovered a great website called TheSchoolBell.com. It was run by a woman named Kathy Gursky who had been a first-grade teacher for 32 years in Brentwood, California. On the site, she had posted many games for teaching sight words. There was Sight Word Bingo, Sight Word Battleship, and Sight Word Concentration. I had never thought of using games to teach Eric, and the website inspired me to make phonics games for him. I started by making Bingo boards with words that began with /bl/, and /cl/, and /sl/, and flashcards to go with each board.

Every day (with the exception of Christmas Eve and Christmas Day), Eric read the words from the flashcards and he and I hunted for those words on our respective Bingo boards. We used pennies as markers and when he won—which he did frequently because I stacked the deck of flashcards in his favor—Eric got to keep the pennies. He loved the game so much that on some nights he actually asked to play it just for fun, separate from his daily reading lesson with me.

Every day, he also worked his way through a few pages in Explode the Code 2 (which focused on blends) and read a few pages in *Are You My Mother*, by PD Eastman. That classic book is about a baby bird who hatches while his mother is out of the nest and approaches all sorts of creatures asking them if they are his mother. At 63 pages, it was the longest book Eric had ever read and was about evenly split between words Eric could sound out on his own (sat, her, egg, will, must, get, went, was, not) words that were new to him (bird, jumped, away, out, down, looked, came, here, eat, could, walk) and one word that gave him frequent trouble. To my continued surprise, Eric often read the word "on" as "no." The book even contained the infamous word "right," which Eric read easily, thanks to the little song and dance I had performed for him. Any time Eric reached a word he didn't know, I read it to him, and we made a flash card for it.

By the end of the break, Eric had made great progress. On the last night of our vacation, he eagerly tackled *Jack and Jill and Big Dog Bill*, a book that contained a lot of blends. He was not at all intimidated when I handed him the book and, beautifully, began reading:

> "Jack and Jill and Big Dog Bill go up, up, up the hill.
>
> "'Pull, Bill!' says Jill.
>
> "At the top, they stop.
>
> "Go, Bill!" say Jack and Jill. So Jack and Jill and Big Dog Bill go down, down, down the hill."

Later, when Eric was out of earshot, Cary said, "Wow, he's really reading, unless he's read that before."

"He hasn't. He's never seen that book."

"He's come a long way since September thanks to you."

Those words were the best Christmas present I could have gotten. ☺

9

Eric and I were in our apartment, about to start working on his reading. He handed me a stack of handwritten flashcards that had been hole-punched and attached to a large metal key ring.

"Reading Specialist gave me these words to memorize," he said. He had had his first lesson with her today. I leafed through the cards, curious to see which phonics rule she was going to be working on with him.

Phonics rule?

Did someone say phonics rule?

These were the words Reading Specialist wanted Eric to learn:

come	some	from
gone	friend	what
done	almost	month
none	was	both
one	want	

I had allowed the school to label my son "at risk" so that Reading Specialist would teach him phonics. But not one of those words followed a phonics rule. In fact, six of them—come, gone, done, none, one, some—*broke* the silent e rule. (That rule says that /e/ at the end of little words like "bake," "kite" and "hope" causes the first vowel to make its long sound, while the /e/ at the end of the word remains silent.)

Why was she giving him sight words to memorize? Avoiding memorization was the whole reason I had allowed the school to label Eric at risk. "Did Reading Specialist begin teaching you the silent /e/ rule?" I asked Eric. "Did she give you these words to learn as exceptions?"

Eric shook his head no.

Why had she chosen those words for him?

She was probably planning to start the silent /e/ rule in their next lesson, and she wanted him to memorize these words as exceptions. Assuming that was the case, I got to work helping Eric memorize those words.

If you remember, Eric's teacher was going to ask Reading Specialist to give her five words to assign him for spelling every week. The following Monday was the first day of implementing that plan.

At home that afternoon, I watched as Eric reached into his backpack and pulled out his spelling notebook. I waited for his face to light up when he saw that five of the words he had been memorizing for almost an entire week were now his spelling words!

Eric opened his notebook, took one look at the words, and slammed the notebook shut. Sounding panicked, he cried, "I can't do those words! No way!"

Again, those words that had never been a part of his vocabulary until his school had begun "teaching" him to read: I can't!

Now he was saying them in relation to spelling.

Why did he think he couldn't spell the words?

He'd been working on those words for days.

I opened his notebook and read the words his teacher had neatly printed:

> could
> would
> should
> one
> because

Not one of those words was from Reading Specialist. What had happened to First Grade Teacher coordinating with Reading Specialist? Reading Specialist had assigned Eric 14 words to memorize and, now, his teacher had assigned him five completely different words to learn how to spell.

> Email from: Me
>
> To: FirstGradeTeacher@schools.nyc.gov
>
> Hi. Eric brought home very difficult words for spelling today. They are should; could; would; one, and because. I thought he was going to get words from the Reading Specialist as his spelling words. What happened?

> Email from: FirstGradeTeacher@schools.nyc.gov
>
> To: Me
>
> Hi Irene,
>
> I am so sorry about the confusion. Eric was supposed to get five of the words from Reading Specialist. It was just a mix-up. I was not at school today because of jury duty and did not have the opportunity to get to his book. I will fix it tomorrow. Hope it did not cause too much of a problem. If you have already chosen words to work with just let me know.

> Email from: Me
>
> To: FirstGradeTeacher@schools.nyc.gov
>
> I picked five words I thought would be the most useful for him and had him practice them tonight. I took the words "some," "come," "one," and "was" from Reading Specialist's list and also added "on" because that word gives him trouble when he reads. I wrote the words into his spelling notebook. Hope that's OK.

Email from: FirstGradeTeacher@schools.nyc.gov

To: Me

Great!

10

Research has shown that when something extremely shocking happens, our brains record that moment with picture-perfect accuracy. That memory is so clear and bright that it is sometimes called a "flashbulb memory."

People remember exactly where they were, and what they were doing, when they learned about terrorist attacks, assassinations, or stock market crashes. I remember how cold the wooden floor felt as I sat on the edge of my bed and listened to my father's grief-stricken voice tell me my mother had died. I remember the events of September 11 in vivid, technicolor detail. Cary had been inside the World Trade Center when the first plane struck. Learning of the attack, fearing he was dead, hours later seeing my husband walk into the lobby of our apartment building and realizing he was alive. Those moments are permanently etched in my brain.

So is my first conversation with Reading Specialist.

She called while I was sitting at a café in a New Age store on lower Fifth Avenue. The scent of curry and cardamon filled the air. At shiny, white tables, people were sipping herbal tea and eating entrees containing tofu. I was putting finishing touches on a blog I had just started called Helicopter Mom. The blog focused on how much work New York City parents had to do to support their kids in school, and the toll it was taking on parents. I hoped someone in power at the Department of Education would read it and do something to change the madness families in New York City were experiencing thanks to constructivist math and Balanced Literacy. It seemed like we were all educating our kids at home.

I had just finished re-reading the first blog post when my cell phone rang.

Flashbulb memory: Two women were browsing through shelves filled with wind chimes and crystals. Enya was playing on the sound system. Reading Specialist said, "In the time I've spent working with Eric, he's made progress, but because the progress has been slower than could be expected I want to refer him for an evaluation."

Translation: Reading Specialist thought Eric had a learning disability.

This could not possibly be happening. My voice caught in my throat as I said, "How can you tell how much progress he's made? You've only seen him twice. He couldn't possibly have made much progress after just two sessions."

"I've worked with him enough to determine that there could be problems," she said. "He's not making progress with sight words or decoding and there are issues with his writing."

He wasn't making progress with her sight words because they were too hard for him. Those were the words she had sent home after her first lesson with him, words like come, done none, almost, and friend.

He wasn't progressing with decoding because she seemed to be working with him on phonics rules he had already learned. After his second lesson with her, she had sent home Explode the Code Book 1½ for him to begin for homework. That book focused exclusively on three-letter words with short vowels in them—words like pan, sit, and pot. It didn't even include any blends—words like stop and clap and king. Eric already knew how to read the most basic short vowel words. How could he make progress working on what he already knew?

And, of course, there were issues with his writing. The kid couldn't spell since he had never been taught any spelling rules.

But I couldn't say any of that. I couldn't offend her. I needed her to be on my side since she was the only person in the school willing to work with him on phonics.

"If Eric isn't put in the pipeline for an evaluation," Reading Specialist said, "I'll only be able to work with him for six weeks, and six weeks isn't enough time. When the time comes for the evaluation, and he's doing great, you can always say you don't want it. But he's young and it's important to catch a problem early. Kids get sent out all the time for services in this school. It's not unusual. You would think it would be, but it isn't.

"There are great services available here," she continued. "You may as well take advantage of them. I'll get you the forms you need to sign. You can think about it. We can't do anything without your permission, but, in the meantime, we'll get the process started."

Because I wanted her to keep working with Eric, I agreed to have her send me the forms. But I'd be damned if I would sign them.

You may be thinking, What's the big deal? What harm could come from having a kid evaluated?

A lot.

First of all, the fact that the school was referring him for an evaluation meant they thought there was a problem with Eric, and not with their teaching methods. They were taking themselves off the hook for the fact that he hadn't learned how to read in kindergarten and he wasn't learning how to do it in his first-grade classroom either. Second, the fact that they thought something was wrong with Eric meant they would expect less of him. And we all know children tend to live up to expectations.

Most worrisome of all—how in the world would I explain to Eric that he was being evaluated? I would need to tell him his school—the people responsible for his academic self-worth—thought there was something wrong with him. The harm that could cause a six-year-old child who was NOT learning disabled was immeasurable.

I spent the next few nights reading anything and everything I could find on the most common signs of a learning disability. They are:

- Slow development of speech
- Difficulty learning new words
- Difficulty following simple, spoken directions.

- Difficulty rhyming words.
- Difficulty understanding questions.
- Trouble memorizing the alphabet or days of the week.
- Poor memory for routine, everyday procedures.
- Difficulty with cause and effect, sequencing and counting.
- Difficulty with basic concepts such as size, shape and color.

None of those difficulties applied to Eric.
Not one.

In fact, he could have been a poster child for kids who did *not* have learning disabilities. He had begun talking early and, once he started, he rarely stopped. He asked so many questions that my jaw muscles would sometimes hurt from answering them. He made up rap songs using rhyming words, followed directions well, and had no problem memorizing the alphabet or days of the week. His preschool directors had told me his vocabulary was off the charts. From the time he was in preschool, he had always counted everything he saw, on his own, with no prompting from me. "One, two, three, four, five, six..." he would say any time he walked up a flight of stairs. And he easily identified size, shape and color.

I remembered how horrified I had been when, after I had recounted what I witnessed in Reading Workshop, a fellow school mom had wondered whether a lack of teaching—as opposed to an actual disability—might have caused her son to be labeled learning disabled. At the time, the thought of that happening to a child had been too horrible to contemplate.

And now it was happening to mine.

11

Believe me when I tell you the weekend was no fun. I felt as if a speeding train was barreling towards Eric, and I was the only one who could safely pull him off the tracks before he was fatally damaged. What his school was doing was absolutely terrifying—taking a perfectly fine boy, not teaching him to read, and then saying something was wrong with him—but I didn't allow myself to feel the depths of my fear. Instead, I channeled that fear into doing what I thought would solve the problem.

On Saturday morning at our weekend house, I sat down at my computer and began researching how to teach Eric the next two phonics rules he needed to learn. They were digraphs—the letter combinations ch, sh, th, wh—and silent /e/.

Book 3 in the *Explode the Code* series taught those rules, but I didn't like the way it did it. I wanted to teach Eric digraphs using only short vowel words like ship, chip, and fish, but *Explode the Code* included long vowel words—like shine and whale—in its digraphs section. I thought about teaching him long vowels first, but I didn't like the way the book approached long vowels either. It lumped all the long vowel sounds together, teaching words like "cake," "bike," and "hope" at the same time. That was not a good idea. I wanted to continue teaching Eric systematically, so that he would focus on long /a/ words in one lesson (ape, cake, bake, fake), and long /i/ words (like, bike, hike, mike, line) in another one, and so on.

I was engrossed in figuring out how to do so when, suddenly, a movement outside caught my eye. Through t he d ining r oom w indow, I s aw E ric standing on the second-floor deck of our upside-down house. (That means the kitchen and living areas are on the second floor a nd n ot o n g round level.) It was an unseasonably warm, gloriously sunny January day, and I had told Eric he could go outside to play. He was now flinging a little wooden airplane into the air, watching it glide to the ground, running down the stairs to retrieve it, then running upstairs and doing the same thing over and over again: glide, run down, retrieve, run up; glide, run down, retrieve, run up.

His blonde hair and red t-shirt were shining in the sun as he played. He looked so beautiful—the epitome of a healthy, happy little boy.

"That is my son," I thought. "My wonderful, beautiful son."

I should be out there playing with him. Or taking him into the village of East Hampton for one of his beloved Dreesen's doughnuts. Or digging in the sand on the beach with him on this unseasonably warm day. The days of him being a little boy were numbered, and I should be doing all I could to enjoy him while he was young.

Instead, I was totally consumed with figuring out how to teach him to read.

But I had to be. If Eric continued to make progress in his phonics lessons with me, the school would have to realize the problem was them, and not Eric. They would call off the evaluation.

And, so, with a pit of fear now permanently lodged in my stomach, I turned away from my son and began writing out a list of short vowel words that could be changed into new words by adding a silent /e/ to the end of them:

can → cane
pan → pane
rat → rate
etc.

That afternoon, Eric was happily looking at pictures in a kids' magazine. I was stacking our lunch dishes into the dishwasher when he brought the magazine over to me and pointed at an ad for the movie *Flushed Away*. "What does this say?" he asked.

"You can read that," I replied.

He moaned and turned away.

"Come on," I urged. "Try it,"

Begrudgingly, Eric read, "Lift the lid and hop into the toilet."

The last word in the sentence was not "toilet." It was "pool." However, the picture was of a toilet. Dear reader, I am sure you know exactly what had gone wrong: Eric had used the picture to guess the word. That is why he had "read" the word "pool" as "toilet."

As it often did, the picture had led him astray. And this was what his school was teaching kids to do. This was how his school was teaching them to read.

"Everything you read is correct except for the word 'toilet,'" I said. "Don't look at the picture. Look at the word."

He sounded out: "P... oooo... ll. Pool!"

"Yes!" I said. "Great!"

"I hate reading," Eric said, but he was smiling.

"No, you don't."

"Yes, I do. I'm good at it, but I don't like it."

At this point, he didn't need to like it. That would, hopefully, come in time. But hold on.

Did you catch what he said?

He said he was *good at reading*.

He was right.

He knew he was good at reading, and I knew it too.

Why in the world did his teacher and the reading specialist not know it?

Once I became a cognitive developmental psychologist and began teaching children how to read for a living, I heard that same question over and over and over again from parents. "My child is reading so well at home," parents would say. "Why is he not making any progress at school? Why does his teacher not realize how well he can read?"

It was because, as I explained in Chapter 3, instead of being leveled according to a progression of phonics rules and frequently used sight words, the pattern books in Balanced Literacy classrooms are leveled according to the size of the print in the book, and the number of words on each page. So the words "My brother wants to be an astronaut" would be deemed appropriate for a beginning reader, as long as the words "My brother wants to be" appeared on most of the pages.

Because the books are not leveled in any systematic way, making progress in a Balanced Literacy classroom is simply a matter of luck for beginning readers—will the child be able to guess the difficult words in the books the teacher was using to assess him, or will he not?

At the moment, Eric was not guessing well.

At the moment, Eric was out of luck.

Later that day, I continued to up the pressure I was putting on Eric. He had set up his painting easel, clipped a large piece of blank white paper to it, and arranged plastic paint cups in their round holders. He took the lid off of one of the cups and saw that it was almost empty. "Can I have more green paint?" he asked.

I got it for him and pointed to the word "green" on the label. "What's that word?"

Eric shook his head no. "I want to paint. I don't want to read."

"Come on," I insisted. "You can read this word."

Eric refused, and I got mad. "Reading is a gift that I can give you," I said. "If you work at it, you will be a very high stick dot soon. But you're not willing to work at it."

"Yes, I am." He looked offended, and I realized he was right. He worked hard, every day, when we sat down to work on reading together.

But I wanted more.

"You are working very hard, and you are doing very well," I said. "But you need to work harder. You need to start engaging with any words you see, not just words in stories. You need to start reading words on labels, on street signs, in the subway, and on the sides of trucks and buses."

"But they move so fast."

I couldn't tell if he was serious. Traffic did not move very fast in Manhattan, and there were plenty of other opportunities to read words on trucks and buses. "Read them when they are parked," I said. "Read them when they are stopped at a red light. Read them any time you are able to read them."

"Okay Mommy," he said. And then, without me having to prompt him again, he sounded out the word "green."

At 5:30 pm, the four of us were inside King Kullen, a very large, brightly-lit supermarket in Bridgehampton. I had made the following deal with Eric: I would pay him five cents for every word he read in the store.

Eric wasn't thrilled with the idea, but he was going along with it.

In the baked goods aisle, I stopped in front of a display of Ring-Dings and Ding-Dongs.

Those pastry names had short vowels!

They had blends!

I pointed at the word Ring-Dings.

Eric's brow furrowed. He stared and stared at the words.

Finally, I said, "Sound them out."

Very slowly, and laboriously, he did so. "Rrrrr ... iiii ...nnnn ... gggg ... Dddd ... iiiii ... nnnn ... gggg ... sss."

Even though he sounded out each letter, he never put the sounds together to read Ring-Dings.

Same for Ding-Dongs. Maybe those words were hard because they weren't common words. He had never heard anyone say Ring-Ding or Ding-Dong. In fact, he'd never even seen a Ring-Ding or Ding-Dong.

But I was worried. We had been working on blends for two weeks now, ever since Christmas vacation. Ring-Dings and Ding-Dongs were blends. He should have known how to read those words. He also couldn't read the word "milk."

"Can we get Go-gurts?" he asked. He clearly did not want to be reading food labels. He wanted to be picking out his favorite flavors of yogurt tubes instead. Maybe he hadn't been able to read Ring-Dings and Ding-Dongs because he was too focused on finishing our game and getting to the yogurt display.

I let him get some of his beloved yogurts, but then we returned to hunting for words Eric could read. By the time Cary and Jamie finished our food shopping, Eric had read 24 words. I handed him $1.20. He was usually very happy when he earned money. Today, he looked absolutely miserable as he tucked four quarters and two dimes into his ski jacket pocket.

I felt terrible.

Life used to be so normal. I used to be so normal.

Now I was acting like a Ding-Dong. I had pushed my son to read food labels in a supermarket when he, clearly, didn't want to.

That was not normal. But our life was not normal anymore. Eric was in the pipeline for an evaluation. Whether he liked it or not, Eric was going to read, and read, and read.

I was not a Ding-Dong.

I was a very scared, and worried, mom.

———

We usually had a really nice time when we went out to dinner as a family.

We talked.

We laughed.

We shared stories.

Not tonight. We had finished our food shopping and were now having dinner at La Parmigiana, a casual Italian restaurant in Southampton. Or, more accurately, all of us were working on reading with Eric as we waited for our food to arrive. After the waitress had taken our order, I had pulled out a large pad of drawing paper and a magic marker.

Eric's class sometimes played a spelling game called Pie Man. This was a politically correct version of Hang Man. Instead of drawing a noose to hang someone, you drew a circle and divided it into sections, as you would a pie. One player thought of a word and then drew as many lines as there were letters in the word. The other players took turns guessing what the letters might be and writing them on the blank lines. Every time you guessed a correct letter, you colored in a section of the "pie." The first one to identify the word yelled, "Pie!" and won the game.

I had been so happy to hear about this game. Pie Man forced kids to think about every letter that appeared in a word, and the sounds those letters made. That meant it was a phonics game. I would welcome, and support, any way the school dished out phonics. It didn't teach it in structured lessons, but a phonics game was better than no phonics at all.

As we waited for our food to come, my family and I played Pie Man.

I had thought playing Pie Man might be fun, but it wasn't.

None of us enjoyed it.

Not me.

Not Cary.
Not Jamie.
Not Eric.

But we kept playing—thinking of words and miserably guessing the letters in them. We didn't talk much, not even after our food arrived and I put the game away. We ate in silence, and I brought most of my food home untouched.

That night, while my husband and children slept, I organized the basement. Organizing helps me gain clarity when things in life don't make sense. The fact that my son was in the pipeline for an evaluation made no sense. Neither did the fact that he was making so much progress at home and none at school.

As I sorted through container after container of baby clothes and toys, I thought of something a child had sadly said in a book I was reading called *Parenting a Struggling Reader*. In that book, a little boy said, "I lost my mother when (his younger sibling) caught dyslexia."

My family had lost me too.

I was different now.

I had vowed that I would never push my kids academically the way my immigrant father had pushed me. ("You got a 97? Why isn't it a hundred?" had been a frequent refrain in my childhood.) His comments had caused my self-worth to become inextricably entwined with achievement, something I struggle with to this day. When my kids were born, and I thought about their futures, I knew with 100 percent certainty that being pushed academically was not going to be part of their life experience.

That was then, this is now.

Now I am pushing.

For a different reason—not because I want Eric to get 100s and be at the top of his class, but because I do not want him to be falsely labeled learning disabled. But, no matter what the reason, I was pushing.

Today, I had seen what a negative impact that had on my whole family.

But there was nothing I could do about it.

If I didn't push Eric to learn how to read, who would?

I organized and organized and organized. After a few hours, the contents of our basement made sense.

How Eric was being taught to read still did not.

No matter how hard I tried, I could see no possible benefit of the method his school used.

I thought of another passage in *Parenting a Struggling Reader*: "Sometimes the methods the school is using to teach your child to read are known to be less effective than another approach or program ... Many parents decide that the most efficient and effective way to help their child is to hire a private reading tutor to work with the child outside of school or to attempt homeschooling with a program the parents purchase on their own."

"But wait, you are likely to say. Why is all this up to me?" the book continued. "Why should I have to hire outside tutors to do what the school should be doing? Many parents expend a lot of emotional energy dealing with this question."

Indeed.

I went upstairs, climbed into bed, cried a little, shuddered in exhaustion, curled up against my husband and, with tears dampening my pillow, fell asleep.

It had been a lousy Saturday, but it had been worth it. At least as far as Eric's reading progress went.

The next morning, Eric was watching TV in the master bedroom. Suddenly, he ran into the living room and yelled, "Come here, quick. What's that word?"

Cary hurried after him, but the word was no longer on the TV screen.

"What do you think it was?" Cary asked.

"Go...ch...aaa," Eric replied, stretching out the sounds.

"Gotcha?" Cary asked.

"Yes!" Eric said.

He did it!

Just yesterday, I had asked him to engage with words in his environment and today he had done it!

He did it only that one time, and with just that one word but, still, that was a big step in the right direction!

12

I have had many blessings in life. One of them is having a Best Friend Forever. Lila and I became best friends in second grade and have been there for each other ever since.

We have consoled each other through the ups and downs of various relationships. We were maids of honor at each other's weddings. We gave birth to our kids at around the same time. We now live 23 blocks away from each other, but rarely see each other because we are so busy. We hardly even talk on the phone. I don't know the names of her bosses or office colleagues, and she doesn't know what classes I am taking, or which journalism project I'm working on. I don't even know how tall her kids are, nor does she know that about mine. But we don't need to know those things. We don't need to talk often. Whenever we do talk, we pick up right where we left off. There is never any awkwardness. It is always just the two of us, sharing whatever we feel is most important. Once a year, we get together to celebrate our birthdays, which are just weeks apart. Today was the day of that annual celebration.

I was waiting for Lila in the lobby of the fancy office building where she worked as a lawyer. I smiled when I saw her exit the elevators. She looked beautiful, as always. Her long blonde hair was pulled back in a ponytail, and she was dressed in a stylish dark suit, white blouse, and high heels. Her face lit up when she saw me, and I felt some of the ever-present tension inside me melt.

We hugged.

"You look good," she said.

"Come on," I said, in the don't-bullshit-me tone I use only with her, my husband, and my kids.

She stopped bullshitting me. "You're tired?"

I nodded.

"You look great to me," she said and, suddenly, I felt myself begin to look, and feel, better.

"Come on," she said, taking me by the elbow. "Let's go." We exited the lobby through one of the revolving doors. We merged into the stream of pedestrian traffic, and our heels clicked on the sidewalk as we walked up Third Avenue.

"How are you?" we both said at the same time.

As always, the one with the most pressing need to talk spoke first. Today it was her. "You know what time I got to work today?" she asked.

I shook my head no.

"Ten thirty."

I didn't know where she was going with this story, but I knew what to do. One of the best things about being a Best Friend Forever is you know when all you're supposed to do is listen.

"You know what time I'm supposed to be in?"

Lila answered her own question. "Nine o'clock. You know what I was doing?"

Again, I shook my head no.

"I was cleaning my apartment. The place was such a disaster. There was stuff all over the place. I had a fit. I said to my family, 'That's it! I can't live like this anymore. You people take such advantage of me. What's the matter with you? Why can't you pick up after yourselves? Why am I the one who always has to do it? Danny (her oldest son) gave me a placating look and said, 'You're really terrific mom.' I yelled, 'Don't give me that you're terrific mom business. I don't want to be terrific. I don't want to be the one always picking up after all of you.'"

She sighed. A taxi honked, and bus fumes wafted toward us as we approached 52nd Street. "I cleaned until ten o'clock and then I went to work."

We reached Houlihan's and pushed through the revolving doors. Lila elbowed her way through the 20-somethings sandwiched together in the dark bar area. The young women looked relaxed and happy. They clearly were not parents of school-age children in New York City. One of them made a "tssk" sound (clearly meant to communicate, "What's up with that bitch?") as Lila pushed past her to the hostess stand.

"How long is the wait?" Lila asked the hostess.

"Fifteen minutes."

Too long.

We headed back outside. As we waited for the light to turn green, Lila said, "I hate who I've become. I don't take shit from anybody. I don't have time to."

"What happened in there?"

"I said, 'Excuse me,' and the girl didn't move so I said, 'Get out of the way.'"

I laughed.

Lila did not. "I wouldn't have done that before time became such an issue. Now, I just don't have time for idiots."

Before I go on, you must know some important facts about Lila's children. Her oldest son attended a well-regarded private school. Her middle child (a girl) was in a private school for kids with learning differences, and her youngest child, who was a year older than Eric, attended public school.

In a coffee shop, Lila put her cell phone on the table. Her oldest son had taken a taxi to school and was supposed to call her when he got there. He had not called. Lila had been worrying about him all morning and was still worried now. She had her cell phone on the table so she would hear it in case he called.

Lila looked at her phone, looked at me and said, "I hate the craziness of my life! I mean, I love the elements of it. I love my kids. I love my husband. But I hate that everything falls on my shoulders."

She took a deep breath and said, "Sorry for doing all the talking. How are you?"

"I'm overextended too, but for different reasons." I told about how Eric's school had failed to teach him to read and how I was now teaching him myself.

"Steve (her youngest child) is still behind his class in reading too," she said. "He's behind because I didn't spend a lot of time working with him on his reading when he was younger. I was too busy supporting Danny with his schoolwork."

Two years ago, her oldest son had made the transition from the less demanding, more progressive lower grades to the much more academically rigorous upper grades at his school. Lila had sat with him every night, helping him with his homework. "His schoolwork took up so much of my time that I couldn't work with the other two, but there was nothing I could do about it," she said now.

"Eric's school thinks there is something wrong with him," I said. "They want to evaluate him."

"Steve's school evaluated him too," she replied. "When he was in kindergarten and first grade, (He was now in second.) I kept telling his school something was wrong, that he wasn't learning how to read. His school kept saying everything was fine, that he would learn to read when he was ready. Then, this year, the school began treating his not reading like a huge problem. Overnight, it went from 'everything is fine' to 'it's an emergency! We have to do something about it!'"

I was shocked that the two of us had this in common too. "Did they find anything wrong?"

"No. The only thing wrong was the way they were teaching reading."

"Did they actually say that?"

"Of course not," she replied. "Schools never think they are doing something wrong."

I told Lila about how I had taught Eric short vowels and blends. Then, Lila and I—two women who used to talk about love, life, literature, and the meaning of life—compared notes on how best to teach kids the silent /e/ rule.

I pulled out the list of words I had made last weekend:

at → ate	hid → hide
can → cane	fine → fine
cap → cape	pet → Pete
fat → fate	cop → cope
rat → rate	glob → globe
mat → mate	hop → hope

Jan	→	Jane	mop	→	mope
mad	→	made	con	→	cone
fat	→	fate	cut	→	cute
sit	→	site	cut	→	cute
bit	→	bite	puck	→	puke
kit	→	kite	mull	→	mule

"Don't show him that!" Lila cried.

I was surprised at the urgency in her voice.

"Seeing that many words might freak him out," she continued. "Show him just two words at a time."

Her advice hit home. "When I first started teaching Eric how to read, he moved to the other side of the couch to get away from a *Bob Book* because it had two lines on the page," I told her. "Before that, all the *Bob Books* had had just one line. I was surprised at how upset that made him."

Her eyebrows pulled together in concern. "You know, he might have a problem. Sarah (her daughter who had learning differences) would always get anxious whenever there were a lot of words on a page."

"Did Steve get anxious too?" I asked.

"I don't know. I learned from Sarah how important it is to present information in small chunks, so I never gave Steve a list to look at."

"Can you recommend any books that would be good for Eric to read at this stage? *Bob Books* were great for short vowels. So was *The Fat Cat Sat on a Mat*."

"Steve and I read that one!" Lila was as excited as she used to be when, years ago, we'd discussed books or movies that we loved. "Dr. Seuss books are good but be careful. Some of them are hard, but some of them are great for beginning readers. They are a good way to practice sight words."

We then talked about how we never had enough time to do the things we would like to. "For the past three days, at some point during each day, I remembered that I have to return a phone call from a mom at Jamie's school," I said. "Then I get so busy that I forget to do it. I feel terrible about it, but I never have even a second to call her back."

Lila nodded empathetically. "I lost two friends because I didn't have time to return their calls. One of them was a single woman I used to work with. She told me, 'I really like you, but I can't take this anymore. I can't deal with the stress of you not calling back and me sitting there wondering if you ever will call back, and when.' And I couldn't deal with the stress of knowing I was stressing her out. It caused a lot of conflict for both of us. I really liked her, and she liked me, but she just couldn't understand my life."

"I don't think anyone without school-age kids could," I said.

Desperate at Barnes and Noble

After lunch, I walked over to the large Barnes & Noble inside the Citigroup office tower in midtown Manhattan. Hockey Mom had told me that she'd bought a bunch of workbooks there.

"They have a great selection," she'd said.

Great selection was quite an understatement.

The very first thing I saw when I entered the children's section was a sea of reading and math workbooks for preschool and elementary school children. Clearly, the successful banking and law professionals who worked in this area were supplementing their children's education at home. Why were so many parents doing that? Was I the last parent on earth to realize that elementary schools no longer teach kids the things they need to know?

I leafed through the phonics workbooks, but didn't find any that did a solid, systematic job with digraphs or silent /e/. Then I headed for the Early Readers section and examined the stories, looking for any that might contain a substantial number of words with digraphs and long vowels.

A young salesclerk approached me. "Can I help you?"

"No thanks." I doubted that she knew the contents of these books well enough to help. Then, I thought better of it. Remembering the sea of phonics and early math workbooks the store was selling, I realized that other parents might have been in here looking for the same kinds of books I was trying to find. Maybe she *could* help me. So, I said, "Yes, actually. I do need help. In fact, I'm in desperate need of help."

She smiled. "From no to desperate?"

"That about sums it up. I didn't think I'd need to teach my son how to read. Now I know I need to and I'm desperate."

I told her what I was looking for, and she led me to a carousel labeled "Beginning Readers." Even the Level 1 (preschool to grade 1) books displayed there were too hard for Eric. The words "world," "different," "dinosaur" and "everywhere" appeared on a single page in a book called *Dinosaur Time*. The word "stegosaurus" was on another page and was then also written out phonetically: "steg-uh-saw-russ."

Are you kidding me? Why teach first graders how to read stegosaurus?

"I'll pass on these books," I told her. "They are much too hard for a beginning reader."

Next, she took me to another display where she recommended *Are You My Mother* and *Go Dog Go*. She knew what she was talking about. I told her those books were great but I already had them. *Are You My Mother* was the book Eric had read so well over his December school break. She recommended examining the rest of the books in that area. "These sound like what you're looking for."

I leafed through some Dr. Seuss books, but they were still too hard for Eric to read on his own. I found only one book Eric would be able to read now: *The Cat in the Hat: Cooking with the Cat* by Bonnie Worth. Another book called *Little Bear* contained a lot of beginning sight words and would be good for Eric to read in the near future.

I bought the two books and headed to Hallowed School for our usual Friday routine. Instead of having Eric take the school bus home, I picked him up at dismissal and took him to the schoolyard to play with his friends. On Fridays, we got to simply be mother and son. On Fridays, I was not his reading teacher.

13

Eric and I arrived home from the schoolyard to find that two tragedies had occurred. Cary's Uncle Irving had died, and Jamie's huge stack of Spanish flashcards (which he needed so that he could study for his upcoming Spanish midterm) was gone forever as well.

I have not told you much about Jamie's school experience yet, but the time has come to include that in our story. Last year—the year Eric began kindergarten—Jamie had graduated from a progressive elementary school and had entered sixth grade at a very rigorous, traditional middle school called New Explorations in Science and Technology Plus Math (NEST+m).

As you have seen at Hallowed, progressive schools do not actively teach kids very much. In a progressive school, kids are expected to construct their own knowledge from materials and experiences the teacher provides them with. The teacher is considered "a guide on the side," someone who helps kids learn on their own. Most of the work is project-based and tests are rarely administered.

In traditional schools, the teacher is seen as a "sage on a stage." He or she imparts a set of predetermined facts to every student in the room and regularly administers tests to assess whether children have absorbed those facts.

Going from a progressive school where kids assembled their own knowledge to a traditional school like NEST+m—where you were expected to regurgitate facts on difficult tests—had been brutal for Jamie. It was like suddenly needing to walk on your hands instead of on your feet. A total change of orientation. The first time he took a test at NEST+m Jamie got a 51. When he showed me the grade, I said, "I didn't know you were having a test. You know, when you have a test, you have to study for it."

His totally honest response had been, "I do?"

Academically, NEST+m was very hard. The quantity of material the kids had to memorize was mind-boggling. And most of the teachers were harsh. Unrelenting. Unbendable in their demands. But they were also unbelievably dedicated. They were available almost around the clock to answer questions the kids emailed them. They met with the kids all the time to sort out any confusion. They had the remarkably difficult job of taking young brains, many of which had not been previously subjected to anything resembling academic rigor, and turning the owners of those brains into outstanding thinkers. But they were not touchy-feely in the way they went about it.

Didn't do your homework? No problem. You got a zero and the zero counted towards your grade.

Didn't show your work on the math test even though the directions said to? You got half credit off for each instance of not following directions. Result? Instead of the 100 you would have gotten because you got all the answers right, you got an 80. (True story. Happened to Jamie many times.)

The school's harsh grading policy drove fear into parents' hearts because, in New York, admission to public high schools is done on a competitive basis. (There are no zoned high schools in Manhattan that kids who live in a particular neighborhood area can automatically attend.) Every single child has to apply to various high schools. The only grades high schools look at when deciding whether to accept, or reject, a child are the ones kids get in 7th grade, which was the grade Jamie was in now. Kids with 90 averages were regularly denied admission to the high schools they would have liked to go to. Therefore, it was imperative for Jamie to do well in seventh grade. (At the time Jamie was in 7th grade, to even be allowed to continue on to NEST+m's own high school, the kids needed to maintain an 85 average which, because of the school's academic rigor, was like maintaining a 100 average at most other NYC middle schools.)

At home, NEST+m students yelled and screamed and moaned at the harshness of the school. And then they started rising to its expectations. The only other options were to fail or to transfer to other public middle schools, places where parents complained that their kids hardly learned anything. Places where kids took open notebook tests on a regular basis. Where words were spelled wrong on the teacher's word wall. Where teachers said they understood the children may be too busy to exceed standards and that was O.K. They could simply meet them.

Kids at NEST+m took their gym teacher's frequent refrain to heart. Whenever the kids complained that he was pushing them too hard, the gym teacher would bark, "You don't like it? Go home!"

They stayed in school but, at home, their parents spent the bulk of their evenings helping their kids with the high-level academics or hiring tutors to do so. (At the beginning of sixth grade, the middle school principal had given a list of recommended tutors to every sixth-grade parent. None of us had asked him for such a list and few of us realized tutors would be necessary for most of the kids.)

As you know, we could not afford a tutor and I had been the one who helped Jamie transition to that school. To say that took a lot out of both of us would be quite the understatement. This year was a little better, but Jamie had been out sick last week with a stomach flu and had missed a lot of schoolwork. Next week, he would be having extremely challenging midterms. He needed me to help him catch up on the work he had missed and also to quiz him on the vast quantity of materials he had to know for his exams.

Last Sunday (Ding-Dong weekend) I had told Cary I could not teach Eric how to read *and* help Jamie learn all the material he had missed last week. I had asked Cary if he would take on the responsibility of helping Jamie prepare for his midterms.

My wonderful husband had said, "Sure."

Things did not appear to be going well.

The minute Eric and I walked through the door, Jamie said, "I can't find my flashcards."

He rolled his eyes at me. I knew what that meant. Cary—who was experiencing midterm duty for the very first time—had been yelling at him, probably quite loudly, about the nowhere-to-be-found flashcards.

I couldn't help Jamie. Knowing how important it was for him to become an independent learner, I took every possible opportunity to help him be one. Part of that independence involved organizing all his school materials himself. Jamie had put the flashcards away. Not me. So, I had no idea where they were.

Cary was talking on the phone across the room. He was consoling his cousin who was very upset about his father's death. Uncle Irving had been 92 years old. He had been very ill, and we had known his death was imminent. But any death, even an expected one, hits hard. Although Cary had not been close to his deceased uncle, I knew he was literally feeling his cousin's pain. Uncle Irving's death must have been bringing up Cary's sadness about his own father recently dying. I was glad I was home to support him.

Cary hung up. He told me the funeral would be on Sunday, which was the day after tomorrow, which was the day before Jamie's Spanish midterm. Cary and I briefly talked about how sad it was that Uncle Irving was gone. Then Cary's gaze fell on Jamie. His expression changed from sad to furious. "HE LOST HIS FLASHCARDS!!!" my normally calm and loving husband yelled. "HOW THE HELL COULD HE HAVE LOST HIS FLASHCARDS? DO YOU KNOW HOW LONG I WORKED ON THOSE FLASHCARDS?"

Jamie had gotten a late start in Spanish. The school began having all the kids study a foreign language in seventh grade. Jamie had chosen to learn French but, after a few months, he realized Spanish was spoken everywhere in New York and felt he'd made a mistake choosing to study a language he would never really need. Luckily, the middle school director and the Spanish teacher had allowed him to switch to Spanish even though the school year was already well underway.

We had promised we would do all we could to help Jamie get up to speed on what he had missed. To live up to that promise, Cary had made a tremendous stack of flashcards of all the Spanish words in the first few chapters of Jamie's textbook. This was no easy task because the textbook did not have the English definitions of any of the words (!). There were hundreds of words for Jamie to learn and, because Jamie had so much other schoolwork to do, Cary had been the one who looked up the definitions for all of them.

Now, Jamie needed to review those words for the midterm. Now, those flashcards were gone. Cary was having such a fit about it that I, who had just been full of love and a wish to support him, now wished he would just shut up. But I let him rant. I have ranted about the demands of NEST+m plenty of times myself.

Cary continued tearing the apartment apart, looking for the flashcards even though he had already looked in every conceivable place they could be. The contents of Jamie's school backpack had been dumped onto the floor. Contents of drawers had been emptied and replaced. The cards were nowhere to be found. Cary ranted louder.

Then, he said, "How the hell are we going to go to the funeral? Do you have any idea how much material Jamie still has to study? (He was referring to the five midterms coming up next week. Not just Spanish.) There's no way he can go to the funeral."

"Jamie will go to the funeral," I said, reassuringly. Last year, one of Jamie's classmates did not go to his *grandmother's* funeral because he had so much schoolwork. The boy was not doing well in school and, rather than talking about how to support him, the school administration was talking about throwing him out. Luckily, Jamie was not in that position, and I was sure he could both study and properly mourn his uncle.

Poor Cary, who had put in hours and hours of work on those flashcards, continued ranting. Finally, I said, "I can't listen to this anymore. Eric and I are going out to dinner."

Jamie piped up. "Hey! What about me?"

"You can come too."

Cary looked at me, hurt.

Oh God. What was I doing? Who was I becoming? What was the stress of Jamie's rigorous schoolwork, and of Eric's school not teaching him how to read, doing to us as a family?

"I'm sorry," I said to Cary. "I know how much work you put into those flashcards."

Today, I was observing Cary live through what my life had been like for the past year-and-a-half. I was watching Cary experience what had totally fried me—juggling the demands of work, life, and a child's schoolwork. (And he was handling only one of the kids' school demands, not both of theirs the way I usually did.) There had been many days over the past year and a half that I had been sorry we had sent Jamie to such a rigorous school.

But Jamie had blossomed at that school. He stood taller. He was more self-confident. He was remarkably articulate and could hold a conversation with anyone about almost any topic. Before he had entered NEST+m he hadn't thought he was smart. (That's because his elementary school had never administered tests, except for the mandated standardized state tests. He had no way of knowing what he knew.) Now he knew he was smart. He had been hand-picked to attend one of the most selective schools in the city. He had seen that if he worked hard and studied in a certain way, he would ace his tests.

Now that they were seventh graders, things were a little less grueling for NEST+m students. They walked and talked a little bit like Marines who had made it through boot camp. They were proud that they were being tested by NEST+m and were surviving. Only we, and the other parents, were stressed to the max because of how much parental support our kids' survival at that school entailed.

Was it worth it?

I don't know.

Would we choose it again?

Long pause.

Given the other options out there, I would have to say yes. We would. And so, I bucked up.

"Okay," I said. "Let's move beyond this. The flashcards are gone. Jamie, go make new ones."

He shook his head no. "I don't need to make flashcards. I needed them when I first started learning Spanish, but I know the words now. I just need to review my book."

One more step towards being a totally independent learner.

"Okay," I said. "Go do whatever you need to do to do well on your midterm."

He sat down on the couch and began studying his Spanish textbook. Cary looked relieved and went into the bedroom to change out of his work clothes. I ordered Chinese food delivery, set the table, and even lit candles. My mission for this upcoming week of midterms was to make our life as normal and nice as possible while my wonderful husband shouldered the bulk of Jamie's midterm prep. When the food arrived, we sat down and ate as a family. It was the last time we would do that until Jamie's midterms were over.

To give you an example of what was expected of them, here is Jamie's rubric for his science midterm. Keep in mind that he is 12-years-old and this is just ONE of five midterms he will be taking next week...

Physical Science   Name_____
NEST+m   Date_____
~~[redacted]~~
7th Grade

Physical Science Midterm Study Packet

** The midterm will be held on Tuesday, January 23, 2007

** So far, we've studied chapters: 1, 2, 3, 4, 5 (section 1 only), 15, 17, 19, and 20 _9 Chapter_

** The four main topics that we've covered are: Atoms and Bonding, Forces, Motion, and Energy/Work. _4_

** When studying, it is important to make the connection between these three topics as well as understand the topics individually.

Chapter 1: The Nature of Science

- The Scientific Method
    - Experiments
    - Hypothesis
    - Independent variable (input)
    - Dependent variable (output)
    - Constants (keeping everything else constant allows us to make sure that *only* the input is affecting the output)
    - Qualitative vs. Quantitative observation
- Measurement
    - The Metric System (SI)
    - Prefixes (milli, centi, kilo…)
    - Instruments
    - Mass
    - Density
    - Volume
    - Length
    - Temperature
- Graphing results
    - Proper components of a graph
    - Scaling the axes
    - Independent variable on x-axis and dependent variable on the y-axis
    - Plotting the data

Chapter 2: Motion
- Describing motion
    - Distance
    - Displacement (distance from beginning and distance)
    - Speed ($s = \dfrac{d}{t}$)
    - Velocity (speed and direction)
    - Instantaneous speed
    - Graphing speed vs. time
    - Using slope
- Acceleration
    - Change in velocity (speeding up, slowing down, turning)
    - $a = \dfrac{\Delta v}{\Delta t}$
- Forces
    - Net force
    - Inertia
    - Balanced vs. unbalanced forces
    - Acceleration caused by unbalanced forces
    - Newton's 1st Law

Chapter 3: Forces and Motion
- Newton's 2nd Law
    - $a = \dfrac{F_{NET}}{m} \rightarrow F_{NET} = ma$
    - Friction
    - Air Resistance

> Note: We use ($a = F/m$) to see that acceleration is caused by a net force. We use ($a = \Delta v/\Delta t$) in order to describe the motion of the object caused by the force.

- Gravity
    - Gravitational force between two objects with mass
    - g – gravitational acceleration of objects near Earth's surface ($g = 10 m/s^2$)
    - Weight = mg
    - Projectile motion – all objects fly through the air in a curved path because of the pull of Earth's gravity on the object (the only force acting on it is gravity, so it accelerates downward)
    - Centripetal force – a force that causes an object to turn
    - Centripetal acceleration – the turn (change in direction) caused by the centripetal force (this is not speeding up or slowing down – but just a change in direction)

- Newton's 3rd Law
    - Action – Reaction: when you push on an object it pushes back with equal force but in the opposite direction
    - The action and reaction forces do not cancel out because they are acting on <u>different objects</u>.

Chapter 4: Energy
- Nature of Energy
    - Energy – an object's ability to cause change to itself or its environment
    - Types:
        - Kinetic – motion – ability to collide with an object ($KE = \frac{1}{2} mv^2$)
        - Gravitational Potential – ability to fall ($GPE = mgh$)
        - Elastic Potential – ability to snap back from stretched position
        - Chemical Potential – ability to break bonds and release thermal energy (fuel)
        - Thermal – heat
        - Electrical – ability to power electrical devices which turn it into other types of energy such as kinetic (blender) or light (light bulb) or heat or sound (speakers)
        - Light – energy from the sun
        - Sound – noise, music, vibrations
- Conservation of Energy
    - Law of Conservation of Energy
    - An object's energy can only be:
        1. Transformed from one type to another
        2. Transferred from one object to another by imposing a force on another object and causing it to move (doing work on it)
    - Total Mechanical Energy: $TME = KE + GPE$
        - An object's total ME will not change unless it gives it away by imposing a force another object (through a collision).
        - Some examples: a falling object's GPE turns into KE, a vertically thrown object's KE turns into GPE as its height increases.

Chapter 5: Work
- Work
    - $W = Fd$
    - In order to have done work on an object, you must have: (1) caused it to move and (2) it must have moved in the same direction as you pushed on it
    - If you don't give the object any more energy, then you didn't do work on it!
    - Power: the rate of doing work on an object (the rate of transferring energy to another object)
        - If you do the same amount of work on an object an it takes a lot longer, you didn't use as much power to do that work
        - $P = W/t$

- $P = E/t$ (E is the energy transferred which is the same as work)

Chapter 15: Classification of Matter
- Pure substances vs mixtures
- Compounds (bonded atoms)
- Homogeneous vs heterogeneous mixtures
- Physical vs. chemical properties
- Physical vs chemical change
- Law of conservation of mass

Chapter 17/19: Atoms and the Periodic Table
- Atomic structure – protons, neutrons, electrons
- Electron cloud
- Charge of atoms – depends on how many protons and electrons
- Mass of atoms – comes from sum of masses of protons and neutrons
- Isotopes - atoms with a different number of neutrons (resulting in different masses)
- Ions – charged atoms (either missing or has extra electrons)
- Stability (full outer shells) vs neutrality (equal protons and electrons)
- Organization of the Periodic Table
    i. By atomic # (# of protons)
    ii. Families (same outer shell configurations)
    iii. Metals vs. non metals
- Octet rule – atoms are stable when they have 8 electrons in their outer shell (that's why they bond)
- Electron dot diagrams – shows electrons in outer shell only (we know that inner shells are full)
- Oxidation number – tells you how many electrons it wants to gain or lose

Chapter 20: Bonding
- ionic – transferring electrons
- covalent – sharing electrons
- using oxidations number to determine how many of each atom will be in a bond

After the kids were in bed, Cary panicked again. "There is no way he is going to be ready for those midterms. When we took midterms in college, we had time to study for them. He has Spanish on Monday, science on Tuesday, English on Wednesday, social studies on Thursday, and math on Friday. There is no way in hell he is going to have time to study for everything. He can't go to Chelsea Piers tomorrow."

Jamie had been looking forward to golfing for a few hours tomorrow with Cary at Chelsea Piers (a huge athletic complex alongside the Hudson River) while Eric and I attended a classmate's birthday party at the bowling alley there.

"We can't take that away from him," I said. "He needs a break. Otherwise, he'll resent all this schoolwork. Going to Chelsea Piers will motivate him to focus and study. It will be his reward."

Cary said nothing. I knew that meant he did not think Chelsea Piers was a good idea, but that he would let him go.

14

The problem with raising school-age children in a small New York City apartment is that you can't get away from the studying. Everywhere you turn, there are books, or papers, or a computer, or a child working on his schoolwork.

When I woke up on Saturday morning, Jamie was already sitting at the dining room table. He had gotten up early and had completed the online review tests for the topics his science midterm would cover. Now, Cary was reviewing the wrong answers with him. I made coffee and walked into the bedroom, closing the door behind me. Even with the door closed, I could still hear:

Cary: Oxygen has 8 what?

Jamie: Mumbled something in a low voice that I couldn't make out.

Cary: The molecular (mumble) of oxygen is 15.99. So how would you find out how many neutrons?

Jamie: Mumble

Cary: Not 15. 15.9.

Jamie: Mumble mumble.

Cary: Always protons first. You gotta remember that.

Better him than me, I thought. I was very aware of how lucky I was to have a husband who helped. Because I had a husband who helped, today I was going to get my hair cut. I hadn't had time for a haircut since July when I was working at *InStyle* and needed to look nice. That had been six months ago. When I thought back to those days of working in an office, it was like remembering a blissful vacation. When you work in an office you get to take the subway to work and read magazines until you get to your subway stop. At work, you get to sit at a desk and do work that you love.

At Time, Inc. there is an employee cafeteria where the food has been cooked by someone other than you. The M&Ms they sell there are fresh and not left over from last Halloween like the ones at home. You get to b-s with other grownups.

In the summer, once I had been done working for the day, I had nothing to think about other than how I would enjoy my husband and my kids. We had gone for bike rides. We had watched movies. We had gone out to dinner. My home had been neat and clean! My neck muscles had been relaxed. They did not crack the way they did now when I moved my head.

I would have loved to work in an office again, but I couldn't. Not until school was closed for the summer. During the school year, I needed to be home in the afternoon to teach my kids what they should have learned in school. (If Jamie had learned how to study for tests and use a textbook in elementary school, my work with him would have been cut in half.)

And, so, I worked full-time from home. The minute the kids left for school, I started writing freelance articles, or papers for my grad school courses and kept working until the kids returned. Then I became a cook, a teacher, and, of course, their mother, talking to them and helping them with any needs they might have.

I was always so busy that I didn't even have time to go to the doctor. I had a suspicious-looking mole on my back that a dermatologist really should take a look at. I couldn't remember the last time I saw my gynecologist. My eyeglass prescription had changed, so I had a hard time reading. But Jamie had gotten a 100 on his last science test!

That had happened a few weeks ago. I had been so proud of him that I had posted that test on the refrigerator.

He had taken it down and stuck it in his science folder. When I asked him why he didn't want his test hanging on the refrigerator, he had said, "I don't want to be reminded of school when I'm home."

As I prepared to leave for my haircut, I told Cary I was putting chicken nuggets in the oven for Eric. Without looking up from Jamie's science notes, Cary said, "375 degrees for 10 minutes."

I stopped in my tracks and stared at him. Just last weekend—Ding-Dong weekend—I had asked Cary to make chicken nuggets.

"How do you make them?" he had asked.

I had not been in the best of spirits last weekend. Not very politely, I had told him to read the directions on the box. Now, I hugged Cary and gave him a kiss. "A week ago, you had to ask me how to make chicken nuggets. Look at you now! You are a changed man."

He was. He was exhausted. Disheveled. Grumpy. All because he was helping his son prepare for midterms. By helping our son, he was helping me.

I felt overwhelming love and gratitude towards Cary. Because of him, I was, finally, able to do something for myself. I walked out the door and felt like a human being for the first time since September.

That afternoon, Eric and I went to his friend's birthday party at Chelsea Piers, and Cary and Jamie golfed at the facility's driving range.

It was Eric's first time bowling. I was looking forward to watching him do it and to hanging out with my mom friends from his school.

But then I noticed a mother I rarely ran into. Her son was in the other first-grade class at Hallowed. Eric had told me her son was being pulled out of class for phonics work. I was always on the lookout for the opportunity to find out how other kids at the school were learning to read. So, instead of joining my mom friends and enjoying my son, I introduced myself to that mother. I told her Eric was also working with Reading Specialist. We bonded instantly, found a private place to sit, and compared notes for the rest of the party.

Guess what? She also hadn't known that other parents were teaching their kids how to read when our boys were in kindergarten. I told her our kids would be doomed if we did not teach them phonics. We compared notes on what we are doing to help our kids. As we talked, I trusted the other mothers would make sure Eric did not clobber anyone with a bowling ball and vice versa. I would do the same for them if they needed to prove to the school that their kid did not have a learning disability.

Talking to that mom exhausted me. Being reminded of how endemic it was that parents were teaching their kids at home was depressing. When we got home from the party, I was sooooo tired.

I hated being tired, but I knew I needed to tend to my fatigue. I didn't need to fight it since my beloved husband was working with Jamie on science.

And, so, instead of asking Eric if he was ready for "reading time," I asked him if he wanted to watch a movie with me.

His answer was a surprised, and joy-filled, "Yes!"

He and I lay down on the bed together and watched *Lassie*. Eric lay right next to me the entire time. I was so aware of his little-boyishness and of how much I was missing of his childhood by being so focused on teaching him to read. I was so aware of how happy he was to be watching TV with Mommy. I was so happy we had the opportunity to do this.

Ten minutes into the movie, Jamie walked in to get some scrap paper. He lingered in the doorway, looking at the TV screen. I knew how much he wished he, too, could lie down and watch TV, at least for a little while. I didn't say a word, and neither did Jamie. Jamie knew that if he sat down to watch the movie, I would tell him to go back to work. He continued standing there, motionless. Finally, I gently said, "Go, Jamie," and he went back to studying.

After the movie, even though schoolwork was the last thing I wanted to do, I said to Eric, "It's reading time."

I had found the perfect series of books for him to work through next: *Dick and Jane*. Remember the mom I had spoken with on the first day of school? The one whose daughter had been tutored in kindergarten and was now reading at a third-grade level? She had recommended those books.

"I found them very effective for my daughter," she had said. I also thought they were great because they had a lot of short vowels, blends, and a few silent /e/ words like "Jane." The series also repeated early sight words over and over again: "See Jane go down. Down, down, down. See Jane go down." That repetition would definitely help Eric learn his sight words.

I showed Eric the *Dick and Jane* book he would be starting with. It was called *Go, Go, Go*. I told him he would be working through Dick and Jane books now, the way he worked through the *Bob Books*. I told him the *Dick and Jane* books had some words that would seem weird because he hadn't learned the phonics rules for them yet. I told him I would teach him two rules today. "You don't have to remember the rules, just know that they exist so that these words will make sense to you. We will do more work on these rules in the future."

I wrote "my" and "Sally" on a piece of paper.

I pointed at "my" and asked, "What's that word?"

"My," he said.

"Good!" Then, I said, "When y is at the end of a two- or three-letter word it makes the sound we say for /i/ in the alphabet," I said. "The /y/ sounds like the word I. When y is at the end of a long word, like Sally, it makes..."

Eric cut me off and said, "the eee sound."

"Good! How do you know that? Did you learn it in school?"

"No. I just know it."

He always wrote "mommy" on birthday cards that he made for me, and on many of the pictures that he drew. He may have doped the phonics rule out from that, but I hoped he had learned it in school. I would really like to think he had learned *something* about reading in school.

I wrote another word on the paper. "This word is 'Jane.' The /e/ at the end of it doesn't make any sound. It makes the /a/ say the sound we say when we recite the alphabet. Ay."

I knew Eric wouldn't remember those rules from such a brief summary, but I thought that giving him that brief introduction would make the book seem less intimidating.

"Okay. Let's read Mommy," he said.

He read the first little story in the book. It was just three pages long and each of the pages had five lines of print on it. Here is what the first page said:

> Come, Spot.
>
> Come and go.
>
> Jump, jump.
>
> Jump up, Spot.
>
> Jump up."

The little story was absolutely magnificent for practicing blends, and Eric did a great job with it. He then completed three pages in *Explode the Code*, and we turned to my goal for today—I wanted to evaluate Eric's knowledge of sight words.

Reading Specialist had said Eric wasn't making progress with sight words and that was partly why she wanted him evaluated for a learning disability. Yet the sight words she was having him memorize were too hard for him—come, friend, almost, month—and did not appear often, if at all, in any of the stories he was reading. I wanted to teach him the sight words systematically, starting with the easiest, most commonly used sight words and working our way up from there.

Luckily, I had a great resource to help me. Remember that website I had found over Christmas break? The one run by the woman who had been a teacher in California for 31 years? That site had listed the 220 most common sight words in order of their frequency of use. "The" was the most common word in the English language and, therefore, was the first sight word on the list. "The" was followed by "to," which was the second most common word, followed by "and," which was the third most common word, and so on.

Every other sight word list I had come across—including the one Eric's teacher had sent me to at the beginning of the year—listed sight words in alphabetical order. That meant that teachers all over the country using the pre-K list of sight words were teaching kids the words "funny" and "little" before the words "the" and "up" since /f/ and /l/ come before /t/ and /u/ in the alphabet.

The website I had found divided the 220 most common sight words into 11 lists consisting of 20 words each. I had printed out the 11 lists and was using them now to see which words Eric already knew and which ones he needed to learn.

Heeding Lila's advice about not showing Eric too many words at once, I covered the last three columns in List 1 with a blank piece of paper and had Eric read the first column. The words were so easy that I was sure he would know all of them.

List 1

the	I	was	for
to	you	said	on
and	it	his	they
he	of	that	but
a	in	she	had

In the first column of the very first words a child should know, Eric paused when he reached the word "he." Then he read it correctly.

His teacher had told me that children were supposed to read sight words instantly, without any hesitation. If Eric hesitated, it meant he hadn't fully committed the word to memory. That meant he needed to still work on it.

We moved on to the second column. Instead of reading "of" he said "for." In the third column, he did not know "his."

I was shocked that Eric did not know those very easy words. I stood up and Eric began playing with a toy plane. Thinking he wasn't paying any attention to what I was doing, I retrieved a pink highlighter and circled the words that had given him trouble. I then turned the page and had him read:

List 2

at	look	out	out
him	is	as	am
with	her	be	then
up	there	have	little
all	some	go	down

Much to my surprise, Eric was not able to read the words "with," "is," "her," "out," "be," "little," or "down."

That didn't make sense.

Just three weeks ago, over Christmas break, he had easily read the word "down" in *Are You My Mother*. He had also read it without faltering in *Jack and Jill and Big Dog Bill*: "Jack and Jill and Big Dog Bill go down, down, down the hill."

Just a few minutes ago, he had read "down" beautifully in *Dick and Jane*. The third page of that story had included these lines: See Spot jump **down**. See Puff jump **down. Down, down, down.**

The word **down** had appeared *five times* and Eric had read it perfectly each time. How was it possible that he did not recognize it on the sight word list?

He had also read "is" and "with" without any problem in many stories, and "is" was a word he should have been able to sound out. Clearly, reading words in isolation was harder than reading them within the context of a story. But if he couldn't read them in isolation, it meant he hadn't committed them to memory.

I reached for the pink highlighter, but Eric said, "Let me do it Mommy."

"Do what?"

"Circle the words I don't know so we can make flashcards for them." Eric knew exactly what I was up to and was all for it. On his own, he circled every word he had not recognized immediately. He knew exactly which ones they were. There was no intimidation on his part. No worry. Just matter-of-factness. He was totally with the program.

We moved on to...

List 3

do	what	get	my
can	so	them	would
could	see	like	me
when	not	one	will
did	were	this	yes

On List 3, Eric did not know "do" and "so." He also did not know "would, yes, were" and hesitated over "when, what, see, will." He circled all of those words with the pink highlighter.

There was a lot of pink on the page.

I was beginning to worry.

Next, he read...

List 4

big	now	very	ride
went	long	an	into
are	no	over	just
come	came	your	blue
if	ask	its	red

This time, Eric kept the highlighter in his hand. On his own, he circled every word he hesitated over, or did not know. He hesitated before reading "went, an, its, into, red." He said "come" instead of "came" and did not know "now, very, ride, just, blue." As he circled, I became more and more worried. Those were very easy words. Those were words he had seen before and, definitely, should have known.

"I don't know a lot of them, huh, Mommy?" he said.

"You'll learn them soon," I said, feigning cheerfulness even though I certainly didn't feel cheerful.

I was very, very concerned.

15

Today was the day of Uncle Irving's funeral. At 9 am, Cary and Jamie were sitting side by side at the dining room table, doing a final review for Jamie's science midterm. In the living area of our apartment's living room/dining room, Eric was on the couch, watching TV with headphones on.

Although Cary was shouldering the bulk of Jamie's midterm prep, I was helping Jamie with his English exam. I grabbed Jamie's vocabulary book, *Simon's Saga for the SAT 1 Verbal*, went into the bedroom, and started looking up definitions for the 20 SAT vocabulary words Jamie would need to know for the midterm.

That's right.

SAT vocabulary words.

The kid was in seventh grade. His elementary school had not taught spelling. Therefore, he didn't know how to spell words like "sentence" and "toilet," and mixed up when to use "there" and "their." But, thanks to NEST+m, he can tell you what "perambulate" means.

Researchers and policy makers are very busy looking at why so many kids struggle in middle school and high school. No one seems to realize it is because basic skills have not been imparted to these children in elementary school. Even though Jamie, and many of the other kids at NEST+m, had gaping holes in their educations, the teachers at that school were not taking the time to fill those holes. Instead, they were plowing straight ahead through the rigorous curriculum. It was up to the parents to make sure those holes got filled AND that the kids kept up with what the school was teaching. That's why, today, I was looking up the definitions of esoteric words most Americans will never need to know, except to ace the SAT, which Jamie and his classmates will not be taking for another five years.

If Jamie had a sane amount of schoolwork to do, he would have been looking up his own definitions to SAT vocabulary words. He WANTED to look up his own vocabulary definitions. Plus, I knew how important it is for kids to do their own schoolwork. I knew that when researchers looked at why kids from a high-performing suburban school district did terribly in college, they found that those kids' mothers had done their homework, and projects, for them all the way through middle and high school. Because of that, those kids had never been able to develop as learners. I knew how important it was for Jamie to be an independent learner, but he had been out sick all of last week and his midterms were breathing down his neck. He was running out of time, and we were banding together as a family to help him. I knew he would reciprocate in any way he could when midterms were over.

Jamie was a really nice and helpful kid. He was the one who fixed the computer when it crashed and changed the batteries in the computer mouse when they ran out. He emptied the dishwasher, carried bags in from the car without being asked to do so, and made pancakes on the few Sunday mornings that were not crammed full of homework. He was very capable. He knew he could look up his own definitions. He also knew he was not super-human and that it was OK to accept help when it was offered.

Suddenly, Eric padded into the bedroom.

Instead of being happy to see him, I was annoyed. We needed to leave for Uncle Irving's funeral in two hours. I still needed to feed the kids, pack their dress clothes for this evening's shiva call (a traditional Jewish mourning visit with the deceased's family), prepare pasta salad for the visit, make sure Jamie had all the books and notes he needed so that he could study at his grandma's apartment (we had realized he still had much too much to learn and, so, could not go to the funeral although he would go to the shiva), dress myself... and more.

Before I could do any of the above tasks, I had to finish typing up the definitions of Jamie's vocabulary words. Eric was going to slow me down.

I stopped typing as Eric climbed into my lap. "Huggie mommy," he said.

I hugged him and he hugged me back. For a loooooooonnnnnnggggg time......

Instead of relaxing into his warm little body, I impatiently waited for the hug to be over. When he finally pulled away, Eric said he wanted to type his name.

I wanted him to go away so I could finish Jamie's vocabulary list.

But he clearly needed to spend time with me. I let him sit on my lap and type his name. Then—*eureka!*—I thought of a way to spend one-on-one time with Eric and finish the vocabulary words at the same time.

"Hey, you want to learn some very big words?" I asked. May as well kill two birds with one stone and teach him some advanced vocabulary. It would be one less thing to do with him when *he* was in seventh grade.

"Sure," he chirped.

Earlier this school year, Jamie had toured nationally renowned Stuyvesant High School with one of his classmates to see if it was a high school he would be interested in attending. Their tour leader had said the homework load at Stuyvesant was "daunting." At the exact same time, Jamie and his classmate had recited the definition of daunting out loud: "Frightening, intimidating." They had studied daunting for that week's vocabulary test. They had certainly learned it well! Maybe because they were struggling under their own daunting load of homework.

I taught Eric the definition, and he scampered off to show his newfound knowledge to Jamie and Daddy. Instead of listening, they yelled at him for interrupting.

Eric returned, deflated.

I hugged him and said, "Jamie's midterms start tomorrow. He has a lot to get done before then. You can show him what you know when midterms are over. Go play so I can finish this and start getting ready."

I finished, printed out the definitions, and headed for the kitchen to make the pasta salad. As I walked by the dining room table, I heard Cary ask, "What's the formula for momentum?"

Jamie: "P equals m times v."

Cary: "What's the formula for acceleration?"

Jamie: "Delta V over Delta T."

I marveled that my kid actually knew, and liked, that stuff. The last time we had gone bicycle riding, he had said that every time he pedaled fast, or turned, he kept thinking about the concept of acceleration and how various forces were changing in his bike and his body. He had wanted to know if there was a way you could make a living using that kind of information. We had told him engineers use those concepts. So do pilots, which was what Jamie wanted to be when he grew up. At least at this point in his life.

I thought it was great that science related to the things Jamie loved. At the moment, Cary was less pleased about it. He was yelling at Jamie because, instead of regurgitating formulas, Jamie was talking about how speed and acceleration would apply to the go-cart he was saving up for.

Normally, Cary would have found a way to use Jamie's interest to further what he was reviewing with him. But Jamie was running out of time. So, Cary yelled, "Will you please stop going off on tangents? Focus! We have 45 minutes left before we have to leave for the funeral, and I haven't even showered yet!" He also hadn't eaten and neither had I.

The rest of the morning moved at a frenetic pace. I tried to be a normal mom to Eric while rushing around getting myself, and the kids, and assorted belongings ready to go.

Eric was sitting on the couch, quietly working on a Disney sticker book Santa had brought him. It had no educational value whatsoever and I didn't care. Even though his school thought there might be something wrong with him, I was still determined to let my kid be a kid.

Holding a snowman sticker, Eric said, "Mommy, I need your opinion. Where do you think the snowman looks better? On this page or this page?"

I knew him well enough to know that he didn't really want my opinion. He had asked that question only to connect with me. I walked over and kissed the top of his head. I said nothing about the snowman and watched as he placed it on one of the pages.

"Looks nice," I said and walked away. I was always walking away from him. I never, ever, had the chance to spend the time I would have loved to spend with him. And, too often, I was yelling at both of my kids to hurry up. Now, I needed to hurry too.

Working quickly, I finished making the pasta salad.

Cary jumped into the shower.

Watch how I became snippier and snippier as I felt more and more rushed and got more and more stressed.

"We can't be late for the funeral!" Cary yelled from the shower.

"I know," I yelled back.

I told Jamie to try on his dress shirts, which he hadn't worn since the summer. He owned two, and he tried on both of them. They were both too small. The only dress shirt that fit him was from his school uniform. Unfortunately, it had the NEST+m logo on it. "You have to wear this," I said as I folded the shirt and put it in the large tote I was taking with us.

Jamie shrugged and went to get the khakis and belt that were also part of his uniform. Thank God my son was easygoing. Thank God he didn't care he would be going to the shiva call looking like he was performing in a school assembly. He was totally comfortable with our cousins. He knew they loved us, and we loved them. Our cousins have seen Jamie dressed to the nines. They have also seen him in jeans and t-shirts and a bathing suit. They will overlook the fact that I didn't have time to run up the street this morning to the Gap and buy my kid a dress shirt. They will overlook the fact that he joined them to sit shiva for their father in his school uniform.

Won't they?

"What is Jamie wearing tonight?" Cary yelled from the shower.

I was in the bedroom. I didn't have time to walk to the bathroom to answer Cary. In order for him to hear me from the bedroom, I had to yell really loud: "I've taken care of it. I'm packing his clothes now."

"Does he need khakis?" Cary yelled.

"Yes," I yelled back. "He has them."

"Khakis?" Cary yelled louder.

I walked into the bathroom. My tone was terse. "I said I've taken care of his clothes."

Cary peered out from behind shower curtain, squinting and wiping shampoo from his eyes. "Why are you yelling at me?"

"Because I said I've taken care of it, and you keep asking me questions."

"I didn't hear you."

"Well, stop talking to me from the shower. Wait until you can hear my answers. Otherwise, I have to stop what I'm doing and come in here to talk to you, and I don't have time to do that."

Cary's head disappeared behind the shower curtain.

Shit.

I couldn't believe I had just yelled at Cary. I was not usually a yeller. And Cary certainly did not deserve to be yelled at. He deserved a medal and a back rub for everything he was doing with Jamie. I walked back into the bathroom and apologized.

Cary turned on his delicious, dry humor. "Funerals are a pain in the neck."

That was his way of saying he knew I was stressed and that he had forgiven me for yelling at him.

I smiled. I loved the way Cary and I reconnected by using humor. Fights rarely turned into a big deal with us because one of us almost always tried to repair any damage we'd caused by making the other laugh. That was our way of apologizing to each other.

"Yes," I said. "Funerals are a real pain."

That was my way of saying, I realize you've forgiven me. Thank you.

Cary and I then talked at the same time.

He said, "Couldn't he have died at a more convenient time?"

I said, "Couldn't he have waited to die until midterms were over?"

We both laughed.

In the time it took Cary and me to reconnect, the kids had started fighting. Eric had come up with an idea for another one of his construction projects. He wanted to make a plane using one of Jamie's rectangular erasers for the airplane body. Jamie was refusing to give him an eraser, even though he had two, and even though he was not using either one of them right now, and even though he had gone back to studying and should be worrying about that instead of about an eraser we could easily replace.

"It's mine," Jamie said about the eraser.

"Let him use it," I said.

"But it's mine."

"Let him use it," I said, louder.

"But it's mine."

I watched myself erupt in anger as if I was a third-party observer. "GIVE HIM THE ERASER NOW!!"

This was how stress affected people, I thought. It made them unable to cope with squabbling children. It made them yell at times they, normally, wouldn't. I took a deep breath and handled the situation the way I should have from the very beginning. Calmly, I said, "I need you to give Eric that eraser. He is patiently hanging around while you study and while Daddy and I get ready and if he wants to build something using that eraser you will let him. Okay? Uh... uh... uh... "

I wanted to say my son's name.

My son was looking at me, waiting for me to finish my sentence.

Much to my dismay, I realized I could not remember his name.

Studies have shown that stress affects your memory. Last year, my best friend Lila was so over-burdened and stressed because of the time and effort she put into supporting her older son in school that she was constantly forgetting things. It happened so often that she was afraid she had early Alzheimer's and went to see her doctor about it.

The doctor told her she did not need to be treated for Alzheimer's.

He told her all she needed was a vacation.

The doctor had misdiagnosed her.

What she needed was a tutor for her kid.

Finally, my son's name came to me. "Jamie!" I said, laughing.

Jamie looked at me, wondering why I was laughing.

"I forgot your name!" I was laughing so hard that I doubled over. "I can't believe I forgot your name!"

Jamie turned back to the computer. "That is not funny, Mom."

Usually, Jamie was the first one to share a laugh. I looked to see if he was smiling, which would have meant he'd said, "that's not funny" in a joking way.

He was dead serious.

But I couldn't stop laughing, even though I also didn't think it was funny. My pent-up fear and frustration were being released as laughter, and I could not control it.

Jamie looked at me again and said, "Mom. That is not funny at all."

Of course it wasn't funny.

None of this was funny.

If I wasn't laughing, I'd be crying. My kids hated it when I cried, and, so, I let my stress, frustration, and fear out through laughter.

Get your own box

Jamie and Eric did not attend their great-uncle's funeral. We felt Eric was too young to attend a funeral. Before you judge us about Jamie not going, please remember how competitive the public high school application process is in New York. In order to get into a good high school, Jamie's grades needed to be as high as possible this year and he still had tons of material to review for his midterms. Therefore, he and Eric stayed alone in their grandmother's apartment while Cary's mom, Cary, and I went to the funeral. Afterwards, Cary dropped me off at the apartment where I stayed with the kids during the burial, preparing material I would review with Jamie closer to the time of his English midterm.

After the burial, Cary came to take us to the shiva call. As Cary was double-locking the apartment door, Eric glanced at the box of Cheez-Its I was holding. His gaze zeroed in on the words on the back of the box.

I froze.

His forehead furrowed.

Was he going to do it?

Was he going to read the words on the box?

Was he going to engage with words in his environment once again?

Slowly, pausing between each word, Eric read, "Get... your... own... box."

Cary and Jamie—preoccupied with thoughts of death, and sadness, and midterms—were walking towards the elevator, completely unaware of the momentous step Eric had just taken. It was the first time he had engaged with words in the environment outside of our home.

Eric shifted his gaze from the box to me. He was waiting to see if the words he had read were correct.

"Yes!" I said, smiling. "That's exactly what it says. What great reading! Good for you!"

In the Jewish religion, it is customary to mourn a death for seven days. That time of mourning is referred to as "sitting shiva," and it is done communally, with friends and relatives coming to the family's home to support them in their time of sadness. We were now sitting shiva with Cary's two cousins and their families.

Sitting shiva is a bittersweet occasion. Everyone brings food or drink, and many people share their memories of the deceased. Often, the stories they tell are funny, and people spend much time laughing and reminiscing about the wonderful times they had shared with the departed.

Unfortunately, Cary's uncle had lived in Atlanta for many years and few of the people gathered in his cousin's living room knew him. This shiva felt more like a subdued dinner party and, like all dinner parties, you sometimes need to make small talk with people you didn't know. Cary and I were sitting on a piano bench in his cousin's living room doing just that.

Across from us, two women who looked to be in their 30s, were oohing and aahing over Eric. "He's so cute!" said one.

"How old is he?" asked the other.

"Six," I replied.

"What grade are you in?" the first woman asked Eric. He did not hear her. He was too busy trying to convince me to let him eat another cookie.

"First grade," the other woman said. "I can tell by how many teeth he's missing. (His top two.) My daughter is in first grade too."

Okay. By now you know me well enough to know exactly what I did.

I sent Eric off to get a cookie, put down my half-eaten plate of food, and sat down next to the woman whose daughter was in first grade. "I've been talking to everyone I can about this," I said. "How does your daughter's school teach reading? Do the teachers use a phonics approach or Balanced Literacy?" I hoped she wouldn't think my question too odd, given that I didn't know her name, or even who she was.

"Balanced Literacy," she said. "Why do you ask?"

"My son's school uses Balanced Literacy, and it's completely failing to teach him how to read. Last year, he memorized all the books his kindergarten teacher gave him. He was reciting them, not reading them, but his school had no idea that he wasn't reading. He lost out on a full year of reading instruction. Now, I'm teaching him how to read."

"That's terrible" she said. "The school should have noticed that. I'd be all over them. They should be doing everything they can to teach him to read. You shouldn't be doing it. How could they have missed that?"

"I don't know," I answered. "I honestly don't know."

The woman waited for me to say more, but I didn't want to waste time criticizing the school. Blaming the school would not help anyone, but getting information would.

I cleared my throat and asked, "Your daughter learned to read with Balanced Literacy? Did her school do any phonics?"

The woman did not give me a direct answer. Instead, she said, "My daughter couldn't read in kindergarten, but her friends could. She wanted to learn. She was competitive. Competition can be a good thing. She learned to read over the summer."

Okay. Last time I checked public schools were not in session in the summer.

So, who had taught this child to read?

Her mother?

A tutor?

I was dying to ask those questions, but Eric had returned. He begged me to go down to the basement with him to help bring up some Power Rangers figurines. I looked at Cary to see if he could take him. Cary was talking to his bereaved cousin. That conversation was more important than mine. "Excuse me," I said to the woman and went on a Power Ranger hunt with Eric.

When I returned, the woman gave me the cold shoulder. She obviously did not want to continue our conversation, so I let it drop.

A few minutes later, Cary pulled me aside and said, "Don't believe a word she says about how her kid is reading now. People lie. No one ever wants to admit that they have a problem, or that things are not going as smoothly for them as they are for other people."

"What happened?" I asked.

"I told her that a few of the kids in Eric's class are so advanced in reading that they are reading *Harry Potter*. She said, 'Oh, my daughter reads *Harry Potter* too.'"

I was puzzled. "Her daughter wasn't even reading last summer. How could she be reading *Harry Potter* now?"

"She couldn't be. It's bullshit. But that woman didn't like hearing that other first graders were."

Later that evening, the woman walked right by us as she was leaving. She did not make eye contact. She did not say goodbye.

"That's strange," I said.

"What I told her bothered her," Cary replied. "Now she has to go home and teach her daughter how to read *Harry Potter*."

That shiva call took place in Westchester, a well-off suburban county just north of Manhattan. Specifically, it took place in a town called New Rochelle.

In American Public Media's 2022 podcast *Sold a Story*, reporter Emily Hanford interviewed a Black woman named Lacey Robinson who had been a teacher in the New Rochelle public schools. Here is Robinson's story:

When she was in first grade, Robinson's school in Ohio failed to teach her how to read. "I remember my mother being extremely worried," Robinson told Hanford. "My mother was like, wait a minute, she doesn't know her letters? She doesn't know her sounds?" The school was planning to promote Robinson to second grade, but her mother insisted that she be held back. The following year, the school placed Robinson with a different teacher—one who taught her how to read using systematic phonics.

That summer, little Lacey Robinson helped her grandmother learn how to read. "I just watched her come alive," Robinson said. As she got older, she learned that she had other relatives who had also never learned how to read. "That's when Lacey Robinson knew that she wanted to be a teacher," Hanford reported. "She was going to teach children how to read. And, in particular, she was going to teach Black children how to read."

Robinson's initial foray into teaching was not successful. It was at an elementary school in Marietta, Georgia where the students were poor and half of them were Black. They were not being taught phonics, and they were not learning how to read. Robinson became frustrated and she made a plan: "Her plan was to go to wealthy schools in the suburbs, learn everything she could about how the kids were taught, and come back to schools like the one … in Marietta. She wanted to give poor Black children what rich, white children were getting," Hanford reported.

In order to be hired by schools in wealthy white suburbs, Robinson needed more training. She got it by earning her master's degree at Teachers College, where she ended up working for Lucy Calkins. Yes, **that** Lucy Calkins. The Ivy League professor whose curriculum is being used in one in four elementary schools across the country, including Eric's. The one who thinks it's fine for kids to pretend to be reading and whose reading "lessons" consist primarily of having kids read independently and guess what words are by looking at pictures or from context.

Robinson overcame her initial skepticism of Calkin's approach and went on to embrace the Reading Workshop model. She rose from being an administrative assistant at Teachers College Reading and Writing Project, to training teachers on how to conduct Reading Workshops. She came to believe that if kids followed Calkins' approach they wouldn't need phonics. They would be getting something better.

After graduating, Robinson was hired to teach reading by the New Rochelle school district. That district used the Teachers College curriculum and it sure seemed to be working. Most of the students in New Rochelle were good readers who knew how to decode (sound out words). But then Robinson noticed something, something Hanford said, "was kind of a secret…Something no one seemed to be talking about."

This is what Robinson noticed: "Those white, affluent students weren't learning how to decode in school. They were learning how to decode at home with tutors. I know because I became one of them."

"As a tutor, she did a lot of direct and explicit instruction," Hanford reported. "The kind of instruction that had helped her when she was a little girl. The kind of instruction that had helped her grandmother."

Robinson eventually left New Rochelle for a suburban school district in Montgomery County, Maryland. That is just outside of Washington DC. There, according to Hanford, "she saw the same thing she'd seen in New Rochelle. Private wealth taking care of the problem when schools weren't teaching children how to read. Lacey Robinson wanted it to be true that there was something in rich, white schools that she could take and give to poor Black children... But what she ultimately discovered is that a lot of rich white kids weren't getting what they needed in school either."

Robinson's friends, who were also of color, discovered the same thing. Her friends had "worked tirelessly to shift the trajectory of their family for their kids," Robinson told Hanford. They scrimped and saved and were, finally, able to move into middle class neighborhoods.

What happened? "They send them to the neighborhood schools under the assumption that if I'm in this area, my kid will learn," Robinson said, "Only to find out ... I gotta hire a tutor."

Being a genius isn't all it's cracked up to be

When we got home from sitting shiva, Jamie disappeared into the bedroom to finish reviewing Spanish for tomorrow's midterm. I pulled out *Go Go Go* for Eric. Yesterday, he had read the first story in that *Dick and Jane* book and had read it very well.

Tonight, however, he took one look at the book and began acting the way he always acted when he felt a book was over his head.

He moaned.

He squirmed.

He said, "I don't want to read that."

"Why not?" I asked. "You did a great job last night with the first story in here."

"I want a *Bob Book*."

"But this is the next level of book you need to read. You're ready for the next level."

"Why don't you buy the next level of *Bob Books*?"

It's tough having a smart kid. His questions were always good ones.

I was switching Eric to *Dick and Jane* because I believed those books would bring him to a higher reading level faster than the *Bob Books* because they included more sight words. Speed was of the essence for us, but I could not tell him that since I did not want him to know about his pending evaluation.

"*Dick and Jane* books are good because they have a lot of the sight words you've learned," I replied. "More than the *Bob Books* do. It's important to practice your sight words."

But Eric stood firm. He wanted a *Bob Book*.

I thought of what the mother up in Westchester had told me a few hours ago. Competition could be a good thing. It could motivate kids to do something hard. All the kids in Eric's school were competitive. They were all aware of each other's stick dot levels. Playing to Eric's sense of competition, I said, "You can read a Bob Book, but you're the one complaining about your stick dot level. I don't care what color your stick dot is, but if you want to move up to the next stick dot level these are the books you need to read."

My 6-year-old, son of a journalist and a lawyer, knew all about the importance of credible sources. He looked at me now and said, "How do you know?"

I answered as seriously as if I was on the witness stand before the Supreme Court. "I am studying child development in school. Soon I am going to be a Doctor of Psychology. Doctors of psychology know about stuff like this."

The part about the doctorate was true, but the part about how I knew which books kids need to read was not. I had not even started my dissertation yet. I knew what kids needed to read because of all the research I had recently done online and from talking to other mothers who had taught their kids how to read. And just from common sense. He should read books that contain the words he is learning how to read.

Eric accepted my credibility. He looked at the *Dick and Jane* book. He had accepted that he would read it tonight, but he was still squirming.

I didn't understand the problem. "What do you like about the *Bob Books*?" I asked. "What makes them different from *Dick and Jane*?"

"I don't like reading all those pages."

"The *Dick and Jane* books are too long for you?" I was surprised. They were very slim books.

He nodded.

"You like the feeling of accomplishment you get when you finish a *Bob Book*?" He nodded again.

"You don't get that feeling from a *Dick and Jane* book, even though you know you've finished a story?"

He shook his head no.

I flipped through the pages of *Go, Go, Go*. If I could have torn the book apart and stapled the stories together as single stories, I would have done so. But the stories were very short. One story led into another, and the stories shared front and back pages. I had to find another way to give Eric a sense of accomplishment.

I tried this angle: "You know, *Dick and Jane* books are like chapter books. No one reads a chapter book in one sitting. When Jamie reads a book, it sometimes takes him weeks to finish it. Think of these Dick and Jane books as chapter books."

That made him sit up a little straighter.

I kept going: "How about if I put a big yellow sticky note at the end of every story so you know what you need to read up to? Will that make you feel better about it?"

He nodded and headed into the bedroom to retrieve sticky notes from my desk.

I inserted the sticky notes, then opened the book to the same *Dick and Jane* story he had read last night. I knew it would be easy for him. We'd had a long day. It was 8:30p.m. and I wanted to leave him with an all-important feeling of accomplishment.

Eric read every word in the story with no problem. I thought he will be happy, but he complained, "I don't like re-reading. I wish I'd read a new story."

I was having Eric read these little books solely so that he could practice sounding out words. He, on the other hand, always read for the sake of the story. I can't tell you how many times I had no idea what the book he was reading was about, while he had stopped and questioned something about the action the book was describing. Even though he was working so hard at sounding out, he was also closely following the story he was reading. I knew that was very good. His teacher had told me that some kids who are fluent readers at this age often have no idea what they had just read. At least Eric was with, or ahead of, the curve when it came to reading for meaning.

I said, "Okay. We can read new stories from now on. We won't re-read anymore. I thought maybe you were too tired to see new words in the next story."

Eric read the next story, called *Come*. I pointed to, and read him, the words I thought he did not know. One of them was "funny," which I had just introduced to him yesterday, and another was "mother." (I had forgotten that he had read *Are You My Mother* over Christmas break.)

"I know 'mother,'" said Eric. "Mother is in *Baby Owls*." He was referring to one of the pattern books he had brought home to read a few times for homework. He then went on to recite all the lines in that book that included the word "mother."

"Mother Owl is looking for moths," he began chanting in a monotone voice. "Mother Owl sees a big moth. Mother Owl comes to the tree."

I watched him in amazement. He hadn't read that book in weeks. How could he remember exactly which of the 15-or-so books he'd brought home to read for homework included the word mother? And how could he remember every single word in the story?

I knew the kid was gifted, but maybe he was a genius.

These days, it seemed that everyone wanted their kid to be a genius. However, I can tell you from what I have witnessed that being a genius isn't all it's cracked up to be. It is not easy to be six years old and to be smarter than your teacher, and your mother.

It is not easy having a mother who did not listen when you came home in kindergarten and said, "My school is not teaching me how to read." I am not sure I will ever be able to forgive myself for that.

16

Later that night, I slowly and quietly cracked open the bedroom door and peered into the living/dining room of our apartment. It was dark, and it was quiet. I listened for any stirring coming from the two bunk beds lining one wall of the living room. There was none. Good. That meant both boys were asleep. I did not want them to see what I was about to do.

Following the ray of lamplight coming from the bedroom, I tiptoed towards the small entrance foyer where my kids' school backpacks lay on the floor. I retrieved Eric's backpack, carried it into the bedroom, and, gently, closed the door behind me. I unzipped the bag, pulled out his black and white composition spelling notebook, and tucked a folded piece of paper inside the front cover. On that piece of paper, I had written five of the sight words he had not known when I had checked his knowledge of the most frequently used sight words. Those five words would be his school spelling words this coming week.

I know this will come as a surprise to you, but I—and not Reading Specialist—was now in charge of selecting Eric's school spelling words. Unbeknownst to Eric, I had been assigning him his spelling words for three weeks now, ever since the spelling mix-up had happened when his teacher was on jury duty. Eric had learned his words well that first week and, since the reading specialist's sight words were too hard for Eric—they were words like friend, month, and some—I had asked his teacher if I could keep choosing Eric's spelling words. She had said yes, but I had kept the fact that I was doing so a secret from Eric.

He already knew I was teaching him how to read. I wanted him to believe his teacher was educating him in every other subject. Otherwise, my smart little boy might ask a very reasonable question: Why bother going to school?

At this point, I would not have a very good answer.

Don't get me wrong. I was grateful that his teacher had agreed to use my words. She could conceivably have said, "Go to hell. This is my class, and this is what kids in my class are expected to know." That happens regularly at academically rigorous public and private schools. That was certainly what would have happened at Jamie's middle school. At NEST+m, tremendous pressure was put on the kids to keep up with the class curve. Kids were expelled when they could not do it. Even in first grade.

Eric's school was not like that, yet I was the only parent taking advantage of the teacher's willingness to work as a team. Some kids in his class learned the spelling words for each Friday's quiz and then forgot how to spell them the next week. Other kids were having a hard time learning them at all. One mother told me she got so frustrated that her kid wasn't nailing the spelling words that she took her child by the arms and shook him out of frustration.

Can you imagine? Shaking your child because he could not learn his spelling words?

I had told that mother to ask the teacher to give her child easier spelling words, but she did not want to do that. She thought that would make her child feel bad. She believed her child was capable of keeping up with the class and she wanted him to do so.

My child could not keep up with the class. Not yet. I knew that frustrating him and pushing him beyond his current capability was fruitless and would backfire. So, he was the only child in his class who was getting his own personalized set of spelling words. He was aware of that but did not seem to mind. Even though he didn't complain about it—and seemed to welcome having words he could actually learn and retain—I had told him that the only reason his teacher was giving him individualized spelling words was because I had not taught him to read at home when he was in kindergarten, the way other mothers had taught their children. I told him his late start in reading was affecting his spelling and assured him that he would be caught up to the other kids by second grade.

I was looking forward to second grade.

Hopefully, at that point, my spelling charade would be able to stop. But, for now, every Sunday I would secretly tuck a list of five words into Eric's spelling notebook. For the past couple of Mondays, his teacher had written my words into his spelling notebook. At home on each of those Mondays, Eric had opened his spelling notebook and read his spelling words. He had made flashcards for the words and, every day, I had drilled him on them and had him write each word five times.

For the past couple of Fridays, Eric had aced his spelling quiz. He had spelled the words correctly any time he used them in his writing and had been able to read them without hesitation in books and on flashcards. That meant he had permanently stored those words in his memory. That meant he KNEW them.

My spelling subterfuge was working!

Where's The Spelling?

By the time Cary came home from work that Monday, I had fed the kids dinner. Jamie had even showered already, so he wouldn't have to take the time to do it later. His Spanish midterm had gone well, and he was ready to buckle down and study science for the rest of the night.

Cary and Jamie disappeared into the bedroom to finish their science midterm review. I cleaned up the kitchen, then sat down to work on spelling and reading with Eric. I ate a cold, quick dinner - pretzels, cheddar cheese and green grapes—while I worked with him. I don't know what Cary ate. I don't think he ate anything. Neither one of us had the energy to even order in anything resembling a real meal.

And to think that in my former life as a magazine editor, I had assigned and edited articles on the benefits of families eating dinner together.

These days we were lucky if we ate, period.

Eric opened his spelling notebook and looked at the page where his teacher should have secretly printed the spelling words I had smuggled into his spelling notebook last night.

Eric looked at me, puzzled. "Where's the spelling, Mommy?"

I examined his notebook. The lines where my words should have been written were blank. On top of the page, his teacher had written "chose 5 words for this week."

Chose?

Chose was past tense. If she had chosen five words for this week, where were they?

Had she meant to write "choose"? If yes, she, herself, could use a spelling lesson.

Had her note had been meant for me, or for the assistant teacher? Had the assistant teacher forgotten to write the words in Eric's notebook?

"Did your teacher say anything to you about which words you should learn this week?" I asked.

"No."

I took a deep breath. Maybe his teacher had had a hard day. I didn't say anything to Eric but he, apparently, had a similar thought. He told me his teacher had been so mad at the class that she had allowed only four of them to go to music class. "The rest of us had to sit on the rug and keep on doing what we had done that got her so mad," he reported.

I laughed. Then I picked up a pencil. There was no way to hide my involvement anymore.

"These are the words your teacher was supposed to give you." I printed the following words into his notebook: down, do, so, yes, were. Much to my surprise, Eric didn't ask how I knew what his spelling words should be. *(BTW, his teacher had, indeed, meant to write "choose." Her note was meant for me. From that day forward, for the rest of the year, I would openly write Eric's spelling words into his notebook every week.)*

He got right to work and began making flashcards for the words. That seemed to remind him of something because, suddenly, he stood up and ran to his backpack. "Reading Specialist gave me new words to memorize."

He pulled out a new set of flashcards. They were hole-punched and attached to a large metal ring just like his first set of words had been.

I read the flashcards and sighed.

Once again, the words Reading Specialist wanted Eric to memorize were much too hard for him.

It was time for us to talk.

"Throw my words in the garbage," Reading Specialist said on the phone the next day. I had just told her that her words were too hard for him since he had not yet been taught many of the easier most frequently used sight words. I told her I was teaching him those words.

"He should do the words you've been doing with him," she said. "Mine will overload him. Tell him I told you to throw them out."

"You throw them out," I replied. "I don't want to be the one throwing out your words. I don't want him to know how much I'm steering what he's doing in school."

"Fine," she said. "Send my flashcards in with him. Tell him I told you to do that. I'm not going to do sight words with him anymore. I'm going to focus just on the phonics aspect of things. I'll tell him we're working just on phonics from now on."

One step in the right direction. I tried for another one: "Speaking of phonics," I said. "Is it all right if we stop working in *Explode the Code 1 ½*? Eric knows the words in there, and he really hates the book. Book 1 was great, but in Book 1 ½ we both have a hard time figuring out what a lot of the pictures are showing. For example, the illustration for 'pan' looks like a tray, so he kept looking for the word 'tray.' Since he knows his short vowels, that book seems like a waste of time for him and he doesn't have time to waste."

"He should still do *Book 1 ½*," she replied. "If kids don't have repetitive practice with short vowel sounds when they are younger, they will be in trouble in second or third grade. The more practice they get with short vowels at the beginning stages of reading, the better."

How could the reading specialist at his school be saying repetitive practice with short vowels was imperative, while the kindergarten and first-grade teachers at the same school were telling kids to ignore the vowels?

"I need to share this with you," I said. "A lot of parents at the school taught their kids how to read at home. I was talking to (one of the other first-grade moms) about that the other day. She said reading 'hadn't worked' for her son in kindergarten and she taught him how to read using Hooked on Phonics. She said, 'We should let the school know how much work we had to do with our kids. It's too late for us but, if we tell the school, parents in upcoming years won't have to go through what we did.' I told her I would tell the school."

"Yes," Reading Specialist said. "You should definitely tell the school."

"I just did. I told *you*. Isn't telling you the same as telling the school?"

"Oh no. They already know I believe in phonics," she replied. "Teaching phonics is what I do. If I told them the parents all taught their kids phonics, the school would think I was just pushing what I already know. Kids need direct, systematic instruction that builds off of what they've already learned. To get to the next level of it, you need to have the foundations of the earlier level. The Teachers College curriculum, which is what the teachers do in the school, doesn't do that. It doesn't build off of things."

She paused. "Erase that," she said. "I will get in trouble for saying that. Eric should be doing phonics five days a week, but I don't have time in my schedule to see him more than twice a week. What you're doing with him at home is great. It can only help. He's so lucky he got picked up this early. Most kids don't get picked up until fourth or fifth grade."

"Picked up for what? What do you think is wrong with him?"

"I don't know. We need the evaluation to see what's going on."

The evaluation.

She had just told me "Kids need direct, systematic instruction" in phonics. She knew Eric had spent a year and a half at the school without receiving direct, systematic phonics instruction. Now that I was teaching him phonics, in a direct, systematic way, he was making great progress.

Logical conclusion: the problem was with the curriculum, and not the child. So why did she still think he needed to be evaluated?

What, oh what, was I going to have to do to get the school to realize that blaming the child for what they were doing wrong was beyond inexcusable?

It was a crime.

17

It was standing room only in a drab conference room, in a drab building, on a drab stretch of Seventh Avenue. After a long day of work, about 200 parents had left their children at home and trudged through the cold, dark January evening to attend a Community Education Council (CEC) meeting.

CEC meetings gave families a chance to meet with the superintendent of their school district. The purpose of those meetings, according to the New York City Department of Education (DOE) website, was to "solicit and encourage public comments on issues important to families."

CEC meetings for District 2—the largest, and wealthiest New York City school district, and the one Hallowed School was in—were usually sparsely attended. Tonight's meeting was different. Tonight's meeting was on "differentiated learning and special education." The subject of the meeting had clearly struck a nerve—it was standing room only. Every folding metal chair was occupied and parents were standing shoulder to shoulder, lined up along the walls.

"Differentiated learning" was a hot buzzword in education these days. It meant using various instructional methods to make sure the learning needs of all children were met. I had come to this meeting to see if anything was going to be said about the need for phonics.

The superintendent of District 2 was a woman named Daria Rigney. Oddly, Rigney opened the meeting by spending 10 minutes reading an entire children's book out loud. The book had nothing to do with the topic of the meeting. The story was about how a child learned what it meant to be wise. Ten minutes is a LONG time to spend listening to someone read a children's book when you are tired and hungry and would really much rather be home with your family. Ten minutes is a LONG time when you are bursting with questions about how a school is teaching your child to read and why he or she is not learning to do so. But every parent sat motionless and silent, imprisoned by the need to help his or her child, waiting for the meat of the meeting to be presented.

Finally, it was.

Rigney told parents that District 2 schools "were not one size fits all" and that "there was now a push to pay attention to the individual needs of each child." That sounded good, but, as the meeting went on, I realized that, for the most part, this differentiation was not happening inside the classroom. It was happening via "pull out" services for kids who were struggling. But, hey, at least their needs were being met in one way or another.

Or not.

Parent after parent stood up and, choking up with emotion, spoke about how their children were struggling to learn how to read in spite of extra help the kids were getting in school. (*Much of this extra help was being done using a Whole Language-based program called Reading Recovery. That program did not teach systematic phonics, but the parents did not realize that, and neither did I at the time. By 2022, Reading Recovery would be soundly discredited. Although it is now banned from some school districts, many schools still use it.*)

Rigney did not react to, and did not even seem to register, the pain and worry these parents were expressing. However, to her credit, Rigney did answer parents' questions honestly. Some of her answers made my head spin, but at least they were truthful. For example, when a mother from a well-regarded downtown elementary school asked why the school no longer had Reading Recovery, Rigney said there were many struggling readers in that school.

The school used to employ one Reading Recovery specialist to work with those struggling readers. But, Rigney said, the demand for that specialist's services became more than one person could handle and the school did away with the program completely. It seemed that since the school couldn't meet the needs of **all** the students who were struggling, it wasn't going to meet the needs of **any** of them.

Her response befuddled parents.

Rigney went on to explain that having extra help for students "came down to money." She said Title 1 (high poverty) schools "get a big pot of money" which they can then use to buy programs like Reading Recovery. When schools are not Title 1, they don't get that federal money and, often, don't have any extra money in their budgets to pay for supplemental programs.

My heart went out to the parents who had talked about their children's struggles. Those parents were clearly leaving it up to their children's schools to teach their kids how to read.

I wanted to help those parents.

I also wanted to help the schools.

It seemed to me that if the DOE realized that the only reason so many kids were not learning how to read was because they were not being taught systematic phonics, then the DOE would do what any reasonable body of educated people would do—it would fix what was wrong. If every teacher taught phonics, then every child would learn how to read with no need for any expensive supplemental programs.

And, so, I stood up and shared our story. I spoke openly, honestly, and constructively, without a trace of blame or anger. I told everyone how my teaching Eric systematic phonics had enabled him to read. I then said to Rigney, "If so many kids are struggling with reading, and your goal is to provide differentiated learning, wouldn't it make sense to teach phonics in the classroom? Clearly, a lot of kids need it and isn't that simpler than pulling them out for supplemental services?"

Rigney was stone faced. She made direct eye contact with me but did not say a word.

Surprised at her reaction, I turned to the parents in the room, "If your child is having a hard time learning to read, I really recommend getting a series of workbooks called *Explode the Code* and working with your child at home." I turned back to Rigney. "Teachers should really let parents know how to help their children at home."

Rigney looked at me with such disgust that you would think I had told her to eat her dirty socks. "*Explode the Code* is old," she said.

"But it works," I replied.

"Hallowed School teaches phonics as part of the Balanced Literacy curriculum," she said.

"It teaches phonics but in a very cursory way. It does not teach it in a systematic way."

"Yes, it does," she said.

"No, it doesn't."

"Yes, it does."

"No, it doesn't."

Not very productive, huh? And very confusing. Systematic phonics was definitely not part of the Teachers College curriculum. Maybe Rigney didn't know what systematic phonics was. Maybe she didn't realize it was a step-by-step, sequential approach to the introduction of phonics rules, with each step building on the step that came before. Maybe she didn't know that the teaching of phonics was supposed to be supported by decodable books children could read to practice the lessons they had learned. My son's school definitely did not teach systematic phonics.

"Yes, it does," Rigney said. "The kids get phonics in small groups in Balanced Literacy."

Was that really what she thought? Or maybe that was supposed to be happening. It certainly was not happening in my son's school. He was being pulled out of the classroom and working with a reading specialist in order to receive systematic phonics instruction. His school thought *there was something wrong with him* because he needed systematic phonics instruction. If my son's school had dropped the ball and had not taught him phonics in small group lessons, this woman (who was responsible for all the schools in my son's school district) should want to know about it. But she was not interested.

Realizing I was not going to get anywhere with Rigney, I sat down.

A woman sitting in front of me stood up and said, "My son goes to Hallowed School. That school does not teach systematic phonics."

Rigney did not respond.

A few months later, that same mother would tell me Rigney had a reputation for not listening to parents. "She thinks everything is perfect in her schools and, if you think something is wrong, then there is something wrong with you or with your child."

In the book Rigney had read at the start of the meeting, a child had learned that being wise meant being curious and asking lots of questions.

Rigney's lack of interest in what parents told her made her earlier reading of the story even more puzzling. Her behavior defied the very definition of wisdom she'd put forth. Unlike the protagonist in the children's book she had read to the parents, Rigney had not been curious. She had not asked a single question about the problems parents had presented to her. Instead, she had glossed over those problems, or had explained them away as being caused by a lack of federal funding for schools in wealthier school districts, or had simply said the problems did not exist.

Using her own definition of wisdom, I leave you to deduce whether or not Rigney was wise. I leave you to deduce what it meant that someone like that was in charge of District 2 schools. Rigney needed to get out of her office more and see what was actually happening in the schools she was responsible for. Maybe then we could have a real conversation about how to effectively teach children to read. Until then, I was going home.

A man stopped me as I headed for the elevator. During the meeting, he had passionately spoken about his daughter's struggles with reading. In first grade, his child had had trouble learning how to read and had been pulled out of class to work with a reading specialist. At the end of the year, his daughter's school had told him the work had been successful, and that his daughter was reading fine. But she continued to struggle in second grade. The family paid for an independent evaluation and the psychologist diagnosed dyslexia. "The school completely missed the fact that my daughter had dyslexia," this man had told Rigney. (*The psychologist may have completely missed the fact that the girl had not been taught systematic phonics and, so, was suffering **not** from neurologically inherent **dyslexia**, but from **dysteachia**—reading problems caused by incorrect teaching methods. But that is water under the bridge that, tragically, cannot be recovered at this point.*)

Rigney had not responded to what this man had told her.

Not even a nod of the head to acknowledge the pain that had been so clearly audible in his voice.

That father now told me he was the head of District 2's newly formed Committee on Special Education. "You are an eloquent speaker," he said. "Would you become involved in the committee? We need parents like you."

"You need us for what?" I asked. "To talk to people who won't listen? I'm sure you're trying to do valuable work, but I don't have time to waste talking to people like Daria Rigney. I barely have time to talk to my kids—or get their meals on the table—because I'm so busy trying to get everything done and also teach them what their schools didn't."

"I'm very busy too," he said. "I don't have time for this either, but it needs to be done. It's important for parents to get involved and start making a difference." He handed me his business card.

I took the subway home, feeling totally deflated. I had thought that if the DOE recognized how easy the problem was to fix, it would fix it. All it had to do was put some phonics workbooks and stories in the classrooms. But Daria Rigney didn't even want to admit—or hear—that there was a problem. How long would parents keep on speaking the truth when no one at the DOE would listen?

On the subway, I wondered how a woman named Elizabeth Carson had maintained the stamina and energy to put together a website called nychold.com. HOLD stood for "Honest, Open, and Logical Discussion" about math. The website presented articles and research detailing all the reasons constructivist math curriculums were a disaster. In addition to spearheading the website, Carson made frequent media appearances and testified before various educational committees about the need for math reform.

Someday, I'd love to meet Elizabeth Carson and ask her what made her keep on fighting when so many other parents never bothered. Most parents simply hired math tutors and focused on their own children and not on an extremely flawed public school system that didn't want to be fixed. When I had tried to speak to Jamie's elementary school principal about the problems with the constructivist math curriculum at his school, she had told me that if I didn't like the way the school taught math, I should send him to a different school. (I couldn't do that since the other public schools in our district taught math in the same way and we could not afford private school.) Her words made me shut up and focus on teaching only Jamie, and not on getting the school to change its methods.

Was that going to happen with me and Balanced Literacy too?

Was I going to try to help fix things for all children, or was I going to simply focus on Eric's needs?

I knew which type of parent I wanted to be—a crusader, an activist, a fighter-for-the-right-to-read-for-all. But I didn't know which type of parent I could be. I had only so much time and energy to divvy up among working, going to school, being a wife and mother, housekeeper, cook, and educator of my children.

At home, I put the father's business card on my desk. Maybe, someday, I would email that dedicated, crusading parent, but right now my own kids needed me.

I want to read this!

Eric had had his night-time bath. He was dressed in his cozy footsie pajamas, and I had read him a bedtime story. Before climbing into his bunk bed, he asked, "Can I pick out a book to read?"

He did this often, but when he "read" in bed he always just looked at the pictures.

"Sure," I said. "Pick out a book and stay in bed. I'll be out in a few minutes to turn out the light."

I went into the bedroom where Cary and Jamie were sitting at the desk by the window. Cary was checking some of Jamie's answers on a review packet his teacher had handed out for his upcoming math midterm. As Cary and Jamie worked, I tackled some of the clutter that always accumulated on my dresser, no matter how hard I tried to keep up with it.

A few minutes later, the bedroom door opened, and Eric walked in. He was holding a very slim book called *Bye-Bye Mom and Dad* about a hedgehog named Little Critter.

Thinking he was just delaying going to sleep, I said, "Get back into bed."

"I want to read this," Eric replied.

The world stood still.

"You want to read that book?" My voice was a little too high pitched, my excitement a little too obvious. But I couldn't help it. I would let Eric stay up until midnight if he wanted to read a book.

"I want to read this *page*." He opened the book to an illustration of a fast-food hamburger place called "Critter Burger" and pointed at the letters written on a take-out drink cup. "I can't tell what that word is." He sounded out "s- l- u."

"Those are the first three letters of slurpy. A slurpy is a thick, cold drink with a lot of ice." Together, we read the rest of the words in the picture. He tried to sound out the words "Critter Burger" and I simply read him "drive-thru," (sic) and the crooked, hard-to-read letters on an arrow that said, "Arrow Gas. The Best."

In the past, whenever he did not know a word, Eric would always say, "Can you read this to me?" or "What does this say?" He had never tried to figure out the word on his own.

The fact that he'd tried to sound out "Critter Burger" and had said, "I want to read this" showed that he was ready to take a more active role in his learning.

He wanted to read and, when Eric wanted something, he found a way to make it happen.

18

If you're ever looking for an evening of sheer boredom, I highly recommend attending a talent show at a Gifted and Talented school.

For hours, you will watch children perform musical solos. The vast majority of them will either sit alone at a piano or stand alone in the center of the stage with a violin tucked under their chins. One after another, they will perform technically sound, if uninspired, pieces. One after another, they will receive tepid applause from everyone except their parents, who will be cheering wildly. Except for the brief time when their own child is performing, no one will seem to be enjoying themselves. Not the parents, and not the children.

Last year at Hallowed School there had been one exception to the mind-numbing parade of similar performances. Last year, one child had actually brought down the house. Parents and children had smiled with delight as she performed, and she had received a heartfelt standing ovation.

What had been her instrument?

A hula hoop.

What had been her skill?

Swirling, twirling, and whirling one, two, and even three hula hoops around her body and in midair!

Can't put that on your college application but—OMG—it was fun.

Fun was not the word that came to most parents' minds when the date of this year's talent show was released. That's because not every child at Hallowed School played a musical instrument or was proficient with a hula hoop. Some of the kids were quite talented in other ways, but it was hard to paint a picture or write a story onstage. And some of the kids weren't particularly amazing at anything; they were plain old ordinary, smart kids.

Eric couldn't have cared less about not participating in the show, but other children were bothered by it. To make them feel better, a few first-grade moms had, kindly, choreographed a performance to the Beatles' tune "Yellow Submarine" that any first-grader could participate in.

That's how a group of 20 or so "gifted and untalented" (☺ Eric's words, not mine) children came to be sitting in the front rows of Hallowed School's auditorium on this Friday afternoon. Because many of his friends had signed up to be in the skit, Eric had signed up too. He figured he and his buddies could hang out together in the auditorium and then go play in the schoolyard when the rehearsal was finished.

From the back of the auditorium, I watched as one of the moms in charge passed out lime green sheets of paper to the children. "Okay, first graders," she said. "Let's read the lyrics out loud."

My heart sank.

My son could not possibly read the lyrics to "Yellow Submarine."

Could all the other first graders read them?

The children looked at their lime green lyric sheets and began reading, "In the town where I was born, lived a man who sailed to sea…"

I looked around for Reading Partner's mother. She was standing across the auditorium looking at me. Our eyes met and she rolled her eyes as if to say, "Look at what these kids can do. Look at what our kids can't."

I looked at Eric's reading partner. Joshua was looking at his lyric sheet and his mouth was moving. His mother and I knew he couldn't read those words, but no one else would have been able to tell. From all outward appearances, he appeared to be reading fine.

Eric was not.

Eric was aimlessly looking around the auditorium.

My heart broke for him. I felt the way any parent would feel if they watched their child be left out of something, such as not being picked to participate in a game, or not being picked to be on a team. If I felt this bad, I could only imagine what he must be feeling.

I wanted to run to him and pick him up and tell him it was okay.

I wanted to carry him out of here, away from the sense of exclusion and difference.

The reading of the lyrics seemed endless.

It was torturous to watch.

I didn't know how I would make it through.

I didn't know how Eric would make it through.

Suddenly, Eric took his lime green sheet of lyrics and folded it in half.

Was he getting ready to leave?

If so, we would turn our backs on the reading of the lyrics and exit together.

I picked up my jacket and got ready to stand, but Eric remained seated.

He folded his lyric sheet in half again.

And again.

Tears sprang to my eyes as I realized that, while his classmates were reading the lyrics to "Yellow Submarine," my little boy was slowly, methodically, transforming his lyric sheet into a paper airplane.

The first graders finished reading "Yellow Submarine" and scampered onto the stage to learn their dance moves. Eric scampered right along with them, joking and laughing. He didn't seem at all upset by what had just happened.

Seeing he was fine, I headed to the main office to finalize Eric's participation in Extended Day. In that program, every Monday, Tuesday, and Wednesday afternoon, kids got an extra 45 minutes of time with their classroom teachers to work on whatever they needed help with, be it reading, writing or math.

I knew, in my heart of hearts, that signing Eric up for Extended Day probably wouldn't help him, and might even hurt him, since he would be too tired to work with me on reading when he got home. So why was I walking up the school steps with a heavy heart, about to lock him into a program where he would be working with the same teacher, using the same methods that didn't teach him to read in the classroom?

Because, at this point, with the school thinking something was wrong with Eric, I would give anything a chance.

In the main office, I ran into the principal. She froze, like a deer in headlights. Someone from her staff had been at the CEC meeting and had heard me tell Daria Rigney, and a room full of parents, that Hallowed School did not teach systematic phonics. I hadn't noticed the staff member until the meeting was over and was worried about what she had said to the principal. But the principal did not mention the meeting.

Instead, she pulled me aside and said, "I looked over Eric's file from kindergarten. He wasn't at the bottom of the class in reading then. He was towards the bottom, but there were kids who were lower than he was. All the other kids moved ahead in the summer."

Excuse me, but did she not see the irony in what she had just told me?

Wasn't school closed in the summer? Remember that first grader in Westchester who had learned how to read during the summer? Was this a new trend in education? Kids learn to read best when school is not in session?

This news made me even more conflicted about Extended Day. But I had to exhaust all possible avenues of help for Eric. If it ended up not being useful, I could always pull him out of it.

Things were even worse than I thought

Back in the auditorium, I unzipped Eric's backpack and pulled out the report card I knew Eric had received that day. I opened the 8 ½ x 11 yellow envelope with happy anticipation. I knew his reading grades would not be great, but I was sure the rest of his report card would be as stellar as his kindergarten report cards had been.

It was not.

Eric was below grade level in writing, which was not surprising since writing well went along with reading well. But I was stunned to see that some of his math grades also stunk, as did some of his grades in behavior.

Eric had always loved math. His kindergarten teacher had identified math as a "real strength" for him. Last summer, Eric had constantly asked us to give him math problems to solve, and he had solved them well. And he had always gotten the highest grades possible in behavior. How could his math ability have dropped and his behavior have changed so much from one school year to another?

It wasn't possible.

There had to be some mistake. Maybe another child's report card had been accidentally placed into the envelope with Eric's name on it. I checked the name on the front page of the report card. It was, indeed, Eric's.

The report card had his name on it, but it did not correlate with the child I knew and loved. I examined his math grades more closely. He was below grade level in being able to count by 2s, 5s, and 10s and in knowing doubles to 20.

Last year, in kindergarten, he had been at grade level in counting by 2s, 5s and 10s. How could he have gotten worse in that? Kids were supposed to learn more as they progressed through school, not forget things they already knew.

As for doubles, this was the first mention of his needing to know doubles. And what were doubles, anyway? Counting by 2s? Was counting by 2s so important that it was listed in two different places on his report card?

Eric had never received homework that would allow him to practice counting by 2s. His most recent math homework had consisted of tracing two shapes at home and bringing those tracings in to school so that the other kids could guess what they were. Eric had traced an action figure and a banana and that had been the end of math homework for the night. If homework consisted of tracing bananas and Power Rangers, how was he supposed to know how to count by 2s, 5s, and 10s?

I had been in constant communication with his teacher, and she had never, ever, hinted that there was a problem with his math performance, or his behavior. If I had known he was having trouble counting by 2s, 5s, and 10s, I would have helped him with it. And I would have talked to him about his behavior.

I put Eric's report card back in his knapsack. There was one benefit to the fact that Eric could not yet read big words—he would not know what was written on his report card, and I would not tell him.

At age 6, he did not need to be devastated.

I was devastated enough for both of us.

On the subway ride home, Eric sat on my lap and exclaimed, "I got my report card today!"

He was so happy! So excited!

"I know," I replied with false enthusiasm. "I looked at it. You did great!" I was not going to tell this very smart boy that, in addition to being below grade level in reading he was below grade level in some areas of math and behavior.

"Let's look at the report card, Mommy!" he exclaimed.

No way.

"Let's look at it at home," I said. "It's really special. Let's sit down and do it together when we can really focus on it."

"Okay." He snuggled back against me.

At home, I told Eric he could watch TV while I made dinner. Surprised, he grinned and scurried off. TV was generally off-limits during the week, but I made an exception tonight because I wanted a chance to talk to Jamie privately.

Once Eric had closed the door to the bedroom, I turned to Jamie, who was doing his homework at the dining room table. "Eric got a lot of 2s on his report card," I told him. "It doesn't make any sense. Please don't tell him. I'm hoping he won't ask to look at it. If he does, I want you to know why I don't want to show it to him."

Jamie was as shocked as I was. "Eric got 2s? But he's so smart."

"I know. I don't understand it either. Please don't tell Eric."

"How could he have gotten 2s?" Jamie asked.

I sent an email to Eric's teacher, asking her the same question.

19

The next morning, on the way to Eric's roller hockey game in East Hampton, I asked Cary to stop at the IGA so that I could buy dried pinto beans and small baggies.

At the hockey rink, I sat on a bleacher and began putting 10 pinto beans into individual baggies.

The sister of one of Eric's friends sat next to me.

The 8-year-old looked at the baggie I was filling with beans.

Then she looked at me.

"What are you doing?" she asked.

"Eric is learning how to skip count by 10s in school. I'm putting 10 beans into each bag to help him learn how to do it." ("Skip count" is what schools call counting by a certain number, such as counting by 2s, 5s, or 10s.)

"Oh," she said. "My brother is learning how to skip count by 2s. He can do it up to 12." Her brother was also in first grade and attended a Catholic school in a nearby town called Sag Harbor.

The little girl's father was divorced. His live-in girlfriend came over now and told the child that they needed to go and get something at Brent's, a local general store. Girlfriend was a teacher at a private school in East Hampton. She was teaching her boyfriend's son how to read. The fact that we were both teaching boys we loved how to read had been the first deep root of our budding friendship.

"Can I go with you?" I asked. "I really need to talk to you about something."

"Sure," she replied.

As we drove to Brent's, I swallowed hard and said, "I need your help."

Suddenly, I started to cry. All the fear and worry I had been so valiantly repressing bubbled to the surface. No matter how I tried to stop them, silent tears kept flowing down my cheeks. I was so worried about Eric. So scared of what the school was doing—blaming him for not reading, instead of examining their flawed teaching methods. I felt so betrayed, not just because his school had failed to teach Eric how to read, but also because his teacher had allowed his performance in other areas to slip so much without ever reaching out to me. How was I going to teach him math and writing in addition to reading and spelling?

Girlfriend was a very nice person. She listened empathetically as I told her about Eric's report card and how stunned I was by it.

"All of his grades going down probably has to do with the fact that reading is an issue for him," she said. "Reading issues affect everything else. I don't know how the school could have missed that he'd memorized all his books and couldn't read a word of them. Why don't you pull him out of there and send him to the Amagansett school until you can find a good school for him in the city?" (She wanted to pull her boyfriend's son out of his school as well, but the boy's mother would not agree to it.)

I shook my head no.

"Why?" she said. "You are homeowners in Amagansett. You have a right to go there."

Cary had to be in Manhattan for work, and I needed to be there for graduate school. Moving out of the city to find a good public school—and by that I mean one that taught all the kids in a classroom how to read and do math—was not the solution for us.

"We can't move, so Eric has to stay where he is," I said. "The other public schools in Manhattan use the same reading curriculum, so moving to another public school in the city isn't an option either. I have to teach him myself. Will you help me find some books to help me do that?"

"Sure," she said.

I told her I was about to start teaching him digraphs. I had asked his teacher and Reading Specialist if they could recommend any books that would help him practice those sounds and they didn't know of any. "Does your school have any books I can borrow that would help him?"

Girlfriend promised to ask the reading specialist at her school. She also said, "Go to the library and look for books that have a lot of sight words in them. The more he can practice actually reading words he is supposed to know, the faster he will learn them."

Now it's my turn to listen…

Girlfriend told me her boyfriend's son was able to read on his own, but he didn't want to. She thought he was afraid of reading. (*Do you hear that? Schools have made children afraid of reading.*) He always wanted her to sit next to him so that she could read him any unfamiliar words in the story.

Girlfriend was trying to show the little boy that he didn't need her for that anymore. She did that by saying she had to go to the bathroom when they were reading together, even though she didn't need to use the toilet. "Keep on reading out loud," she would tell him.

As her boyfriend's son read, she would stand behind the bathroom door and listen. Every time he finished reading a page out loud, she would say an excited, "Yes!" under her breath.

Every time she did this disappearing act, her boyfriend's son came one step closer to being a more confident, independent reader. And she was by his side with every ounce of her mind and heart, if not body.

As we returned to the hockey rink parking lot, I remembered something I had read in *Parenting a Struggling Reader*: "It is our experience that children with reading problems who ultimately catch up to grade level often have at least one parent who played a major role in this success story."

It didn't have to be a parent, I thought. It could be a girlfriend too.

That afternoon, Cary and I drove to the East Hampton Library. Like most busy parents, we typically used any rare moments we had alone to catch up and talk about what was most important to us. Today, I told him there was a tremendous void in the children's book market for books that would allow kids to practice their digraphs.

It was hard to imagine that digraphs were what were most important to me. Just one month ago neither Cary nor I had any idea what a digraph was. From the blank look on his face, I realized Cary still didn't know what a digraph was. I had been so consumed with teaching Eric how to read that I'd forgotten Cary was not aware of everything I'd learned along the way.

I explained that digraphs were the /ch/, /sh/, /th/, and /wh/ letter combinations.

"I'm sure we'll find books with digraphs in the library," Cary said.

We did not. But we did find one of the most wonderful, caring children's librarians on the planet.

After I told her why I was teaching Eric to read, she pulled out all stops to help me. As Cary and I paged through page after page of Dr. Seuss books looking for digraphs and early sight words, the librarian searched the library's computer system for decodable readers. She did not find any.

The only other people in the children's room were a young mother and her child, who was about two years old. The mother had overheard my conversation with the librarian. She introduced herself to us as a first-grade teacher at the East Hampton Elementary School.

I used to think that being a first-grade teacher was sort of a cute, not very important job. Now I knew it was one of the most important jobs in the world. First-grade teachers set the stage for success, or failure, for the rest of a child's academic career. A child either learns to read in first grade and is set to then learn other school subjects (since they all require reading), or a child does not learn how to read, misses much of what is happening in the classroom, and is on the road to disaster.

I asked this teacher how she taught her students to read.

"We use a curriculum called Success for All. It takes the best of both reading systems. It teaches sight words, but it also teaches phonics in a systematic way so that all kids can learn to read. Whole Language-based curriculums like Balanced Literacy are an old way of teaching kids how to read. The theory behind Whole Language is that kids are somehow supposed to absorb words by being surrounded by them, and that just doesn't work. I'm surprised at how many schools still use it. All kids absolutely need some exposure to systematic phonics. If they don't get that, they struggle."

She told us the following story: "My friend came over to my house with her son. He's in first grade. I had early phonics readers laying around the house and her son picked one up and read it out loud. I was shocked when my friend started to cry.

"I asked her why she was crying, and she said, 'That is the first book he has ever been able to read on his own. His school sends home really hard books and expects the kids to guess what the words are from the pictures and that's impossible for him. So, he's started to think he can't read.'"

That was my son's story.

It was Lila's son's story.

It was Girlfriend's son's story.

It was the story of millions of other children.

And of millions of other mothers, most of whom are at a loss for how to help their children.

I walked out of the library with the phone number of that first-grade teacher in my pocket and a huge stack of sight word-filled books—mostly Dr. Seuss Bright and Early readers—in my hands.

"It's amazing how many people have come into our lives because of my needing to teach Eric to read," I said to Cary as we loaded the books into the car. I marveled at the conversation we had just had with the first-grade teacher. And Cary and I discussed how we had seen that librarian for years but had never talked to her before.

"It's like we've entered a new world," I said. That made me remember a wonderful essay called "Welcome to Holland" that I had recently read in grad school. I told Cary about it. The essay was written by the mother of a child with Down Syndrome. It is so beautiful, that I want to share it with you in its entirety…

Welcome to Holland
by Emily Perl Kingsley

I am often asked to describe the experience of raising a child with a disability—to try to help people who have not shared that unique experience to understand it, to imagine how it would feel. It's like this……

When you're going to have a baby, it's like planning a fabulous vacation trip—to Italy. You buy a bunch of guidebooks and make your wonderful plans. The Coliseum. The Michelangelo David. The gondolas in Venice. You may learn some handy phrases in Italian. It's all very exciting.

After months of eager anticipation, the day finally arrives. You pack your bags and off you go. Several hours later, the plane lands. The stewardess comes in and says, "Welcome to Holland."

"Holland?!?" you say. "What do you mean Holland?? I signed up for Italy! I'm supposed to be in Italy. All my life I've dreamed of going to Italy."

But there's been a change in the flight plan. They've landed in Holland and there you must stay.

The important thing is that they haven't taken you to a horrible, disgusting, filthy place, full of pestilence, famine and disease. It's just a different place.

So you must go out and buy new guidebooks. And you must learn a whole new language. And you will meet a whole new group of people you would never have met.

It's just a different place. It's slower-paced than Italy, less flashy than Italy. But after you've been there for a while and you catch your breath, you look around.... and you begin to notice that Holland has windmills....and Holland has tulips. Holland even has Rembrandts.

But everyone you know is busy coming and going from Italy... and they're all bragging about what a wonderful time they had there. And for the rest of your life, you will say "Yes, that's where I was supposed to go. That's what I had planned."

And the pain of that will never, ever, ever, ever go away... because the loss of that dream is a very very significant loss.

But... if you spend your life mourning the fact that you didn't get to Italy, you may never be free to enjoy the very special, the very lovely things ... about Holland.

Copyright 1987 by Emily Perl Kingsley.
Reprinted by permission of the author

By not teaching Eric how to read, Eric's school had set us on the metaphorical path to Holland. Because the school thought Eric was learning disabled, I had interacted not just with the East Hampton librarian and first grade teacher, but also with many parents at Eric's school and in my neighborhood whose kids were also struggling with reading. It was also why I had befriended Girlfriend. Those people had all shown me that Holland was a warm and nurturing place. But, no matter how supportive Holland was, it was a place we did not belong.

We did not belong because Eric did not have a learning disability.

I was determined to get us to Italy.

20

As soon as Cary and I returned home, Eric and I went into the master bedroom to work on reading. He had our reading routine down pat. Sitting cross-legged on the bed, he reached for the pile of flashcards I had made for him last Saturday. Without me needing to tell him what to do, he began reading the sight words he had not known a week ago out loud.

"I know 'of,'" he said. "We don't need that card anymore."

He took that card and placed it next to him on the bed.

"I know 'his,'" he said. "We don't need that one anymore either." He put that flashcard on top of the other one.

He hesitated briefly over "do" and then read it correctly. "I don't need that anymore."

He was about to put that card aside, but I said, "Leave that one in. You hesitated just a little bit. It will be good to review."

He left it in.

One by one, he made his way through the stack of flashcards. He knew 29 of the 30 words he had not immediately recognized just last weekend. That was not as big a deal as it sounded because the words were easy, and he had been exposed to them before. But I was very happy that he was now able to read them right away. That meant he really knew them.

"I need some new sight words, Mommy," he said.

"I know," I replied. "I'm so proud of you."

I retrieved our master list of frequently used sight words and the pink highlighter. Eric took them from me. He uncapped the highlighter and, without me telling him to do so, used it to cross out 29 of the 30 words he and I had circled last weekend. He radiated confidence as he did so. It must have felt very good for him to be able to see, and mark, his progress like that.

When he was done, he turned to the next list of 20 words and began reading them out loud. Unprompted by me, he circled every word he did not know on sight.

It was fascinating to watch him assess his own knowledge.

At this point, my six-year-old was a better reading teacher than his teacher.

After he had circled 10 words, I told him to stop.

I pointed at his "we-don't-need-this-anymore" pile and said, "Look at all the words you learned in such a short time! That's amazing!"

Eric looked justifiably proud of himself, but he didn't say anything about what he had just done. Instead, he asked, "What am I going to read today?"

"I have a new Dick and Jane book for you." The book was *Go Away, Spot*. The first story, "Jane and Puff," was three pages long. The action consisted of a cat licking up milk that Jane had spilled. Multiple lines appeared on each of the pages, but that no longer intimidated Eric. Happily, he read:

> Oh, Jane.
> I see something
> Look, Jane, look.
> Look here.
>
> Come, Puff.
> Come here.
> Jump, little Puff.
> Jump, jump.
>
> Look, Baby Sally.
> Come here and look.
> See Puff.
> Puff can help.
> Puff can help Jane.

That was the whole "story." Not exactly a page-turner, but perfect for a kid who needed to practice his blends (jump, help) and early sight words (look, see, come).

When he was done, I closed the book and said, "That was great."

I needed to start getting dinner ready and assumed Eric wanted to go play. I stood up.

Eric did not.

Instead, he eyed a box of his beloved Tic Tacs that was lying on the dresser. "If I read another story, can I have a Tic Tac?"

Instantly, I sat back down.

"Sure!" He could have anything he wanted (within reason) if he read another story.

He popped a Tic Tac into his mouth and began reading:

> Come here, Dick.
>
> Come and see Puff.
>
> See Puff play.

As he read, the Tic Tac kept sliding through the space between his top teeth where his center two baby teeth had once been. Over and over again, the little white candy fell out of his mouth and landed on the quilt.

Each time it happened, Eric stopped reading, giggled, and popped the candy back into his mouth.

This slowed down his reading significantly, but I didn't care.

I didn't care if his reading took a long time.

I didn't care if the quilt got sticky.

I didn't care that my kid was having candy before dinner.

All I cared about was the fact that he was reading.

Perfectly.

When he was done with the story, I hugged and praised him and waited to see if he would ask to read another story.

He did more than that. He asked if he could read the whole book. It was 25 pages long. Longer than anything he'd ever read in one sitting.

"The *whole book*?" I said, surprised.

He nodded and kept reading. He read easily, and well, until he reached the last story. At that point, he started reading more slowly, and he looked tired.

"You can stop, you know," I said. "You've read so much already. You don't have to read the whole book."

He flipped through it, seeing how many pages were left. After seeing it was just four, he perked up again and went back to reading. When he reached the last page, he took the Tic Tac out of his mouth and read really, really fast—as if he was sprinting for a finish line:

> Oh, oh, oh.
>
> Spot can find Dick.
>
> Spot can find Jane.
>
> Oh, oh.
>
> Spot can help Sally.
>
> Spot can play.

That was the end of the book.
I applauded him.
I praised him.
I hugged him.
"Wow!" I said. "I can't believe how much you read! You are Super-Reader!"

Eric flexed his little arms and struck a Super-Hero pose. Then he said, "Stay here, Mommy. I'll be right back."

He walked out of the bedroom and closed the door behind him.

Normally, I would have used that time to make a new set of flashcards or to clean up some ever-present clutter.

Not today.

Today, I just sat and thought.

Eric was reading these beginner books beautifully. Not only that, but now that reading was clicking in, he was teaching HIMSELF how to read! On his own, he had identified which sight words he knew, and which ones he needed to learn next. There was nothing wrong with this kid that a good reading teacher couldn't have fixed—and totally prevented.

Suddenly, the door opened so fast and hard that the doorknob made a loud BANG! as it hit the wall.

Eric charged through the doorway, shouting, "Super-Reader to the rescue!"

His baby blanket was tied around his shoulders like a Super-Hero cape. I laughed and laughed.

But it was not his words, or the blanket, that cracked me up.

What made me laugh was what Eric brandished in front of him, like a warrior's shield that would protect him from all harm: A *Bob Book*.

My six-year-old was fully aware that systematic phonics—as represented by the *Bob Books*—had empowered him. It was astonishing that a six-year-old recognized how important systematic phonics was and that his school and the New York City Department of Education did not.

21

The beautiful illustrations in Dick and Jane reflect the seeming innocence of a bygone era. In the illustrations, Dick and Jane and their baby sister, Sally, frolic in their sunny neighborhood and in their lovely home. Unsupervised, they play with water hoses, cats, wagons, puppies, and balls. They roller skate and ride bikes without helmets.

Not a single safety measure is taken or appears to be needed.

The same can be said for the books themselves.

Back in 1930 when they were first published, those books seemed perfectly harmless.

They were not.

They were great for Eric because of the way we used them—to practice early phonics rules and sight words. But they had not been great for the 85 million children who learned how to read with them from the 1930s to the 1970s. In fact, those books caused such harm that we should take a moment of silence to mourn the millions of children who ended up with severely curtailed lives thanks to Dick and Jane. The teaching methods used with those books ushered in the reading crisis that exists in our country today and turned children into *The New Illiterates*—the title of an excellent book by literacy advocate Samuel Blumenfeld about that horrifying period of reading instruction. Horrifying really is not too strong a word. Wait until you hear how children were taught to read using Dick and Jane...

The story of the Dick and Jane debacle begins with a little bit of history about reading instruction in our country. If you think history is boring, I promise this will not be. It reads a bit like a who-dun-it, full of characters with good intentions gone wrong.

The first character I need to introduce you to is Horace Mann. He is the father of public education in our country, and he also established the first state-run school for training teachers. Mann was a good man who cared about kids and about education. He cared so much that, in 1837, he gave up his job as president of the Massachusetts state senate and took a 50 percent pay cut—from $3,000 to $1,500 a year—to become the first State Secretary of Education in Massachusetts. He and his very tolerant bride spent their honeymoon visiting public schools in Europe to see how children were taught there.

Mann believed that educating all people was imperative because it would help the United States avoid the rigid class system that existed in Europe. But he knew from first-hand experience that going to school in the United States was pretty dreadful. In the early 1800s, only a few schools existed, and they were private. That meant schools charged tuition. Most families were poor and could not afford to pay tuition, so not many children went to school. When they did, they encountered dull, joyless places where they sat on hard, slab benches, where dunce caps were a thing, and where learning to read meant reciting boring phonics drills.

That's what Mann had done as a young boy. His parents had struggled to pay for his schooling, and he had hated the experience. He was determined to set up free, public schools and he was determined to have them teach in a way that was not mind-numbingly dull.

On his honeymoon, Mann was very impressed with public schools in Germany. The German way of teaching had its roots in the educational theory of the Swiss philosopher Jean-Jacques Rousseau. Rousseau believed children learned best when they were given challenges to solve on their own, as opposed to being lectured at by a stern and boring teacher. (This is the foundational belief in all current progressive, or constructivist, methods of teaching.)

Germany used this "natural" way of learning to teach reading. Teachers presented sentences as a puzzle. The children would break those sentences down into words and the children would learn those words as whole units. Mann became a vocal proponent of that method when he returned home and was equally vocal about the fact that he abhorred phonics. He said letters were meaningless and called them "bloodless, ghastly apparitions."

At around the same time, a man named Thomas Gallaudet had figured out how to teach deaf children to read. Obviously, deaf children cannot hear sounds and, so, cannot be taught to sound out words. Gallaudet, who was director of a school for the deaf in Hartford, Connecticut, taught his students to read by showing them whole words paired with illustrations: the word "cat" would be presented with an illustration of a cat, and so on. The children memorized the words and learned how to read at a basic level.

Gallaudet believed his method could be used by all children and, in 1836, the Boston Primary School Committee decided to give it a try. They reported good results, and the method was officially adopted for use in Boston primary schools. Mann was a big supporter of this method since it fit in with the German "natural" way of teaching.

In 1839, Mann established the first state-owned teacher training institute, and he asked Gallaudet to be the school's director. Gallaudet declined, but the institute trained future teachers to use his method. "In the very first year of the very first state teachers college in America, the whole-word method of reading instruction was taught to its students as the preferred and superior method of instruction," Blumenfeld wrote in his 1980s essay "The Victims of Dick and Jane": "Thus educational quackery not only got a great running start with state-controlled teacher training but became a permanent part of it."

Educational quackery indeed. That was how the whole word method came to be viewed in Mann's lifetime. In 1844, it came under fierce attack from Boston schoolmasters. (That's what secondary school teachers were called at the time). Those teachers saw that kids who had been taught to read using the whole word method were not able to decipher any words that they had not already memorized and that they were abysmal at spelling. The schoolmasters "who had had enough of the nonsense, published a blistering book-length attack on Mann and his reforms," wrote Blumenfeld. That attack was the first skirmish ever fought in the reading wars.

Mann lost that skirmish. Teachers continued to use phonics to teach kids how to read and every child who did not have a neurological impairment learned how to do so. Even though phonics was the name of the game in classrooms, "the whole-word method was kept alive in (teacher training) schools as a legitimate alternative until it could be (brought into classrooms) by a new generation of reformers in the ... progressive age," wrote Blumenfeld.

Progress is supposed to make things better, right?

The progressive era, which ran from the late 1800s to the 1920s, was a time of great change in our country. Almost every area of life got an overhaul, with many activists making life better for low-level workers, women, and the poor.

Part of making life better was improving education. The number of schools in the country increased dramatically and the way they taught changed drastically. The leader of this change was a professor at the University of Chicago named John Dewey. He was a leading champion of progressive teaching methods. By that time, progressively oriented teacher colleges—including The University of Chicago and Teachers College at Columbia University—had trained many teachers in progressive teaching methods. Dewey said teachers should apply a whole word approach to teaching reading and teachers listened. That whole word approach came to be called "look-say" since children were expected to look at words and say them as whole units, as opposed to sound them out.

Look-say began to be used in classrooms across the country and for the very first time throngs of children with no learning disorders began having trouble learning how to read. Prominent neuropsychiatrist Samuel Orton (co-creator of the Orton Gillingham method of teaching kids to read) was doing a lot of work in Iowa schools and he saw, firsthand, the problem look-say was causing. As I mentioned in Chapter 5, he wanted to get professors of education to realize there was a big problem with how they had trained teachers to teach reading and, so, he published his article, "The Sight Reading Method of Teaching Reading as a Source of Reading Disability," in the February 1929 issue of *The Journal of Educational Psychology*. "The sight method not only will not eradicate a reading disability," Orton wrote, "but may actually produce a number of cases."

Orton's article was ignored. The education establishment whole-heartedly believed that the whole word method worked and they weren't going to listen to anyone who told them otherwise. Their belief was given credence by a psychological theory called Gestalt Psychology that was in vogue at the time. Gestalt Psychology theorized about how our brains process information and espoused that we process visual inputs (including words) as wholes, and not as sums of their parts. The halls of academia were abuzz with these new theories (which were later disproven). That excitement trickled down to publishers, who hired college professors to oversee the production of mass-market look-say teaching materials and books for children.

Enter Dick and Jane.

Dick and Jane was more than just a series of books. It was the name of a very detailed look-say curriculum that used the little books as teaching tools. Like other look-say curriculums, Dick and Jane taught children to read by memorizing whole words according to their shape, size, and overall appearance as if each word was a picture or a symbol, like the McDonald's logo. Those curriculums told teachers that letters served no purpose. Therefore, instead of telling kids to sound out the letters in a word, teachers would ask questions that got kids to focus on the form of the words: "Is it a short word or a long word?" they would ask the children. "Is the beginning of the word tall or small?" Teachers were expressly told to never utter the word "letter."

In fact, the alphabet was not taught to beginning readers.

I repeat: The fact that letters exist—and that they stand for sounds—was not mentioned to children.

Samuel Blumenfeld went through the 1951 version of the Dick and Jane curriculum line-by-line and reported on it *The New Illiterates*. That is where much of the following information comes from. Let's take a look at the shockingly ridiculous way kids were "taught" to read with look-say. You will soon see many precursors to Balanced Literacy.

The very first step in teaching kids to read with Dick and Jane consisted of giving children books that had no words in them. **Sound familiar?** Teachers used the books to introduce children to the characters Dick and Jane and their baby sister, Sally. The children were asked to look at the pictures and describe what was happening in them. "Though he has not encountered a single printed word," Blumenfeld wrote, "the authors tried to give the child the illusion that he has read a story."

After spending weeks "reading" pictures, the children were given their first book that included words. The book was 48 pages long and consisted of tiny little stories that used the same 17 words over and over again. Teachers would introduce each of those stories by telling children to carefully examine the pictures to notice what happened first, second, and so on. (**The same thing is done in Balanced Literacy. Children are told to do a "picture walk" to get a sense of what is happening in the story by looking, first, at the pictures.**)

Within the Dick and Jane curriculum, children were then asked to, individually, retell the story to the class. Keep in mind that nothing has been said about the words yet. The kids were retelling the story from the pictures. "Because the story (told will be) different with each (child), not only will interest be maintained, but the story will grow in zest and detail with each rereading," the teacher's guidebook said. The story was "different" with each child because the kids were not actually reading. They were looking at the illustrations and making up their own versions of what was happening in the pictures.

The next step was to actually teach the children to read words and the very first words children were taught to read were "oh" and "look." Those are pretty useless words. Think about it: How often do you say, or read, the words "oh" and "look"? But children spent weeks learning those words, and the way they learned them is almost beyond belief. They were first introduced to those words by a little three-page story called "Look."

This is the entire story:

> Look, look.
> Oh, oh, oh.
> Oh, oh. Oh, look.

Not much can be gleaned from those words alone, right? In fact, the story literally exists only in the illustrations. The first picture shows little

Sally walking out of the house wearing a pair of her mother's shoes that are much too big on her. Her brother, Dick, is outside playing with the water hose and he has made a big puddle on the sidewalk. Sally says, "Look, look" because she wants Dick to look at her wearing their mother's shoes. She then says, "Oh, oh" because her foot slips out of one of the shoes and she is about to fall into the puddle. On the final page, she says, "Oh, oh," because she is falling and "Oh, look," because she realizes she has fallen, not on the sidewalk, but into the little red wagon Dick has pushed behind her.

Notice that, unlike the pattern books that Balanced Literacy uses, children can't guess what the words in Dick and Jane are by looking at the pictures. You can't illustrate the words. "oh" and "look" the way you can illustrate nouns like "truck" or "apple." Instead of using the illustrations to help them figure out what the words could be, children spent days examining the pictures to understand what the story **was**.

Once they knew what was happening in the pictures, it was time to teach them the first word they would ever read. That word was "look." The teacher's guidebook instructed teachers to help kids memorize the word "look" by asking the following questions: "Do you think Sally can walk in the big shoes when she gets them on her feet? How do you suppose she will have to walk to keep them on? How can you tell that the water is splashing? Is Sally having fun? What makes you think so? What do you think Sally is saying to Dick? You can find out by reading the line under the picture." (That line was "Look, look.")

The teacher would then say, "How do you think Sally feels? Can you read what she says in a happy way?" And that was how children began memorizing the word "look."

The word "oh" was paired with the second picture in the story—that of Sally's foot slipping out of the shoe, causing her to begin to fall backward into a puddle. To "teach" the word "oh," the teacher would ask a little boy to show how he might walk if he was wearing shoes that were much too big and a little girl to demonstrate how she would walk if she was wearing her mother's high-heeled shoes.

The second story in the pre-primer was this:

> Dick.
>
> Look, Jane.
>
> Look, look.
>
> See Dick.
>
> See, see.
>
> Oh, see.
>
> See Dick.
>
> Oh, see Dick.
>
> Oh, oh, oh.
>
> Funny, funny Dick.

In the illustrations, Dick was on roller skates. The word "skate" does not even appear in the book, yet the teacher's guide suggests teachers do the following: "Let the children 'skate' to music. The 'Skaters Waltz' by Waldteufel, played on a piano or phonograph, is particularly suitable... Children quickly get the feel of the waltz and will join in, even though not everyone will move to the same side at the same time.

"As the music continues, ask the children to try to see someone skating slowly and easily down a street. Ask, 'Can you show us how you would skate to this music?'... If the story is reread after this rhythmic activity, pupils' kinesthetic images of Dick's ride on skates will be more vivid."

Can you imagine? This is how children were "taught" to read the word "Dick." By pretending to roller skate.

To learn the word "funny," children were asked to talk about what Dick is doing that is funny in the illustrations and to share funny things that had happened in their own lives.

The entire first year of instruction was similar. "Each additional word is given the same lengthy treatment, ad nauseam, until the children have exhausted every possible idea, thought, and action which Dick Jane, and Sally can possibly have or commit," wrote Blumenfeld. "All this to learn 17 words of no particular distinction by memory."

Besides teaching in an absurd way, the Dick and Jane curriculum had another huge problem—the fact that the books consisted of just a few, not very common, words. If the children ever needed to read words that did not appear in those books, they would not be able to.

Several professors of education—most notably William Dolch, a professor at the University of Illinois—were very aware of this problem. "The vocabularies of most primers contain many words that, though needed at the primer (learning) stage, are later not of general usefulness," he wrote in the February 1936 issue of *The Elementary School Journal*. Once a child reaches second grade, "the child's reading is now chiefly in books other than the series (of look-say readers) with which he started."

Was the solution to teach kids phonics, so that they would easily be able to tackle many unfamiliar words?

You guessed it—of course not!

According to Dolch, (who was a big proponent of the whole word method of teaching) the "remedy (for this) condition (is) drilling on the sight words that will be of most value to these children in their reading." But teachers did not know which sight words were most important for kids to learn.

To give them the answer, Dolch compiled his list of the 220 most commonly used words. (This list came to be known as the "Dolch list" and, today, is ubiquitous in English-speaking classrooms all across the world. It is the same list I had used to check Eric's knowledge of frequently occurring sight words.) Dolch called the words on his list "tool" words. They were verbs, adverbs, adjectives, pronouns, and conjunctions that showed up in every type of book, no matter what the book was about. He did not include nouns because nouns were specific to the topic of a book. For example, a book about dogs will not have the nouns "cow" or "horse" in it.

From the 1930s to the 1950s, teachers, dutifully, drilled kids on the most common sight words but, still, kids continued to struggle with reading. As far as professors of education were concerned, they had done everything in their power to teach kids how to read. They n ever s topped to think that something might be wrong with their methods. They never considered that the parents who were asking teachers to teach phonics might be right. Instead, the professors of education deduced that something must be wrong with all those millions of children! Or their parents.

Take this comment made by Arthur Gates, a prominent professor at Teachers College, Columbia University as an example: "When a mother storms to the school to protest delaying the starting of the child to read or what she imagines is the failure to teach good old phonics, it is likely that things have already happened in the home, which are having a disadvantageous—indeed, sometimes a disastrous—influence on the pupil's efforts to learn." Those words appeared in a pamphlet called *Teaching Reading* published in the 1950s by the National Education Association and distributed to teachers across the country.

Dr. Gates also authored a very popular textbook called *The Improvement of Reading*. In it, he shared the case studies of three struggling readers. He stated that the first reader was having trouble reading because of "sibling rivalry," the second child was struggling due to "parental interference," and the third due to "parental anxiety and family conflicts."

Rudolf Flesch blew the lid off of this nonsense with his landmark 1955 best seller *Why Johnny Can't Read*. It was the first book, ever, to state the obvious: there was nothing wrong with the vast majority of kids who were having trouble learning to read. The problem was the way schools were teaching reading and he raked schools over the coals for it.

"The teaching of reading—all over the United States, in all the schools, in all the textbooks—is totally wrong and flies in the face of all logic and common sense," he wrote. "The teaching of reading never was a problem anywhere in the world until ... the United States switched to the present method."

Flesch then asked: "How do educators explain all the thousands and thousands of remedial reading cases?" You can feel the anger in his words as Flesch, sarcastically, answered his own question: "To (educators), failure in reading is never caused by poor teaching. Lord, no, perish the thought. Reading failure is due to poor eyesight, or nervous stomach, or poor posture, or heredity, or a broken home, or undernourishment, or a wicked stepmother, or Oedipus complex, or sibling rivalry, or God knows what. The teacher or the school are never at fault. As to the textbook or the method taught to the teacher at her teachers college (being the problem)—well, that idea has never yet entered the mind of anyone in the world of education."

Although Flesch's book was an instant best seller and made many parents realize what was going wrong in classrooms, schools dismissed his accusations. But parents and reading researchers did not. As millions of children continued to struggle with reading, parents and reading researchers began a vocal campaign against the look-say method. That was when the Reading Wars between phonics and whole word proponents went from a simmering argument to open warfare.

At that time, the Dick and Jane curriculum did not introduce phonics until the second grade. And it did a bad job of it. Instead of teaching phonics in a step-by-step systematic way, all the possible sounds of a vowel were taught in one lesson. So, for example, the kids learned long /i/ words like bite and fright in one fell swoop. **(As they did in Eric's classroom.)** No wonder so many kids never learned their phonics rules.

To appease furious parents, the Dick and Jane curriculum began teaching phonics in earlier grades in the late 1950s. But it did not do so in a systematic way that first taught letter sounds and then had kids put those letters together to make words. Instead, it continued using a top-down, whole word method. It first had kids memorize whole words and then analyze those words to discover which ones shared the same sounds. Instead of teaching kids to methodically sound out all of the letters in a word, it taught kids to look at the letters at the beginnings of words and use them to guess what the words could be. **That is one of the three strategies Ken Goodman, the founding father of Whole Language observed kids using as they read unfamiliar material. They used the first letter to guess what a word could be. They often guessed incorrectly since they had never been taught how to sound out the rest of the word. But that idea never entered Goodman's mind. Instead, the fact that looking only at the first letter caused those poor children to make so many incorrect guesses led Goodman to wrongly conclude that sounding out words was the least effective reading strategy.**

Even though phonics was now taught earlier with Dick and Jane, it was taught too superficially. Kids were still struggling with reading and the Reading Wars continued. Parents and teachers with common sense wanted systematic phonics, and look-say proponents refused to give that to the children.

In 1962, the Carnegie corporation attempted to use science to resolve the conflict. It commissioned Jean Chall, a reading researcher at Harvard, to analyze studies that had been done on how children learn to read. Her task was to investigate whether scientifically valid studies had found phonics or whole word methods to be more effective.

Unlike the big-name professors at prominent teachers' colleges, Chall had no skin in the game. She was not making any money from authoring, or consulting on, a whole word curriculum the way those other prominent professors of education were. For example, the Dick and Jane books had been written by William Gray, Dean of the College of Education at the University of Chicago. Another whole word series of early readers published by Macmillan had been written by Arthur Gates, the Teachers College professor who, literally, wrote the book on blaming parents for their kids' reading difficulties. Unlike those professors, Chall had no vested interest in her findings. She couldn't care less whether kids learned to read best using phonics or whole word methods. All she cared about was finding out the truth.

And the truth was this: kids learned best with systematic phonics.

It took Chall three years to come to that conclusion, three years in which she meticulously reviewed the research, interviewed leading proponents of both phonics and whole word methods, and analyzed the most popular curriculums. In 1967, she published her findings in her book *Learning to Read: The Great Debate*.

By the late 1970s, Dick and Jane had disappeared from classrooms.

Was it replaced by a phonics curriculum?

Sadly, no.

Why not?

Because, in 1967, the exact same year Chall published her book, Ken Goodman presented his paper, "Reading: A Psycholinguistic Guessing Game," at the American Educational Research Association conference.

The stupidity behind this is almost incomprehensible, but it is true: Instead of moving to systematic phonics, schools embraced Whole Language and began teaching kids to read the way struggling readers do—by guessing from the pictures, using context clues, and looking at only the first letter in a word. This new whole word approach—with whole word's continued disdain of systematic phonics—entered the classroom, where it remains firmly ensconced to this day.

22

Several hours had passed since Eric called himself a super-reader. It was now 5 pm. It was cold and dark outside but, inside, our house felt warm and cozy. The four of us, along with Jamie's best friend, Alex, were scattered throughout our house's open living/dining/kitchen area. There was a nice feeling of being together, even though each of us was doing our own thing.

I was in the kitchen making chicken cacciatore. Directly across from the kitchen island where I was slicing a red pepper, Jamie was doing homework at the dining room table. To my right, Cary was puffing at a fire he had lit in the living room fireplace, and it was beginning to happily crackle. Jamie's friend Alex was on the floor near the fireplace, playing with Eric's toy trucks. Alex was sleeping over this weekend. He had no homework and was waiting for Jamie to be finished with his. Eric was...

Eric was...

Where was Eric?

I walked up the stairs to the loft. Before we had kids, that open, airy loft had been my writing space. Now it was Eric's play area. The golden oak floor was almost completely covered with forts he had constructed out of blocks and Lincoln Logs. Colorful toy knights and tiny, green plastic army men were lined up in meticulous, straight rows and surrounded by miniature horses, wagons, and cannons.

But Eric wasn't playing with his toys. Instead, he was rummaging through the large, blue container tucked away in the corner of the loft. That container held our party supplies—happy birthday banners, party hats, streamers, blowers, and assorted party plates and napkins.

Eric pulled out a big, brightly colored congratulations banner and taped it to the loft rail so that the sign was visible from below. (That was our traditional spot for hanging celebratory banners.) He checked that the sign was firmly secured, then walked back to the container, pulled out a bag of balloons, and began inflating a red one.

I smiled at him. "Are you doing this to celebrate how well you read today?"

He shook his head no. "It's for my report card."

OMG.

I had completely forgotten about Eric's report card.

Report cards had always been a cause for celebration in our house. We had always gotten the kids a special toy as a reward and had a festive dinner together.

We had not celebrated the report card Eric received yesterday.

You know—the bad report card that he thought was excellent.

Eric hadn't complained about what he must have thought was an oversight. Instead, he was simply making sure a celebration happened tonight. He would feel terrible if he knew he was preparing to celebrate something that wasn't true, but I decided that was exactly what we would do. I felt guilty about deceiving him, but I didn't want him to know about his poor grades. I didn't want those grades to affect his perception of himself as a smart kid and an excellent student.

But I was pretty much an open book when it came to feelings and my son was perceptive. If I was not genuinely happy about his celebration, he would sense it. So, I psyched myself up to celebrate—not his report card, but who Eric was as a person. I would also silently celebrate how well he had read today.

As was our custom on winter evenings, we ate dinner at the coffee table in front of the fireplace. We all raised our water glasses in a toast to Eric.

"Congratulations on your wonderful report card," I said.

To the tune of "Happy Birthday" we sang, "Congratulations to you, congratulations to you, congratulations dear Eric, congratulations to you."

He smiled a wide, gap-toothed 6-year-old smile.

He was so happy.

So proud.

My heart broke as I watched him.

He would be so mad if he knew we were lying to him. Again, I felt guilty about deceiving him, but telling him the truth would cause more harm than our deception ever would.

After we finished eating, Eric asked, "Can we make s-mores? Can we make them as part of my celebration?"

"Sure," I replied.

He ran into the kitchen, climbed onto the counter, opened a cabinet door, and retrieved a package of Hershey Bars. He pulled marshmallows out of a lower cabinet and graham crackers from the pantry. He retrieved five plates, lined them up on the counter and started assembling the s-mores.

He split the graham crackers in half and asked me how many squares of chocolate to put on each.

"Two," I told him.

He broke the chocolate into squares and counted, "One, two," as he put two pieces of chocolate on the first graham cracker.

Eric's report card had said he was below grade level in counting by twos, and I grabbed this teaching opportunity. "Let's count by twos as we put two pieces of chocolate on each graham cracker," I said.

Out loud, he and I counted, "Two, four, fix, eight..."

I resented what we were doing. I wanted to be enjoying my son, not doing schoolwork with him. No reasonable mother wants to be counting by twos with her child on a Saturday night as they make s-mores. But Eric had not gotten any homework from school to help him practice counting by twos and, for some reason, he had forgotten how to do it. So, I would teach him. Tonight, and on any other night, and during any other moment an opportunity arose.

That's why, on this Saturday night in the Hamptons, as the fire crackled in the fireplace, and I should have been focusing only on how nice it was to do something fun with him, he and I broke chocolate into squares and skip counted by twos.

After dinner, we all watched the movie *Click*. In it, Adam Sandler plays a man who uses a TV remote to fast-forward through his personal life so that he can give his full attention to his job. In the process, he misses out on precious family moments, and on having a relationship with his kids and his wife. Eventually, his kids become strangers to him, his wife divorces him, and he comes to regret having missed out on all the important moments in his life.

My kids and Alex thought *Click* was hysterical. They laughed and laughed. The movie made me so sad that I had to blink back tears. The experience of fast-forwarding through life—and missing out on children's hugs, smiles and laughter—was all too real for me.

As I watched the movie, I thought about how the weaknesses in my kids' elementary schools, and the rigorous demands of my son's middle school, were causing me to feel like my life was on fast forward too.

I thought about what I remembered most from Jamie's childhood.

Third grade was the year I needed to teach him how to subtract three-digit numbers since his elementary school had failed to do so. His shoulders had sagged with relief when I taught him the traditional column subtraction way of stacking numbers and then subtracting from right to left, as opposed to the constructivist math method of breaking the numbers apart and then subtracting first the hundreds, then the tens and then the ones from the first number. *(Doesn't make sense? Don't worry. You are not alone. It didn't make sense to most parents and kids at Jamie's school either.)*

Fourth grade was the year I prepped him for his state English and math tests.

Every single day. Without fail. Starting in January and ending in April when the tests were administered.

Every day, we would sprawl on the floor, test prep workbooks spread out in front of us. Eric, who was three years old at the time, would either lay on my back and listen, or play nearby, patiently waiting for me to finish so that I could give him some time and attention too.

Was it worth it? I still have the tape recording of the deliriously happy message Jamie left on our answering machine telling me he had scored at the highest level on his exams. Those scores meant he could go to a safe, and good, middle school. The sacrifices Eric and I had made so that Jamie would be prepared for that exam still, to this day, seem like a necessity. But wouldn't it have made more sense for his elementary school to align its curriculum to the test and to simply teach the kids what they needed to know to get into a good middle school? You know, things like math facts, subtraction, and long division.

Fifth grade was the year I prepared him for the New York State Social Studies exam. The review book I bought said the test would be on material every fourth grader in New York State had been taught. Not my son. He had never even seen most of the material. Year after year, his elementary school concentrated on teaching kids about the Lenape people, since they were Manhattan's original inhabitants. Very little else was covered. His elementary school told parents not to worry about the state social studies test, since it didn't count for anything. Translation: the kids' scores would not be released to the middle schools they applied to.

Jamie's school said the same thing about the state science test the kids took that year. The school never even released the grades from that test to the kids, or their parents. (Now, state test scores are released online directly to the parents. Back then, they were sent to the schools and the kids received a paper copy of them to bring home.)

I asked for my son's science grade several times but, again, was told to not to worry about it because "those grades don't matter. They have nothing to do with which middle school a kid gets accepted to." (No, but they have everything to do with knowing whether your kid is learning anything in school.)

Sixth grade was the year of hell as Jamie made the transition from a progressive elementary school to a traditional, academically rigorous middle school. The transition was grueling. There were no playdates, no sleepovers, no dinners with friends on the weekends for the four of us. Purely and simply, there was no life.

There was only schoolwork. (And hockey. The kid needed to do something fun, and hockey was what he chose.)

And now Jamie was in 7th grade. He had risen to the academic challenge and was doing well. Next year he would be applying to high schools.

How did that happen so fast?

It was amazing how sad a funny movie could make you when it strikes close to home. I moved closer to my kids. They were laughing and laughing. I wanted to remember them laughing and enjoying themselves. Otherwise, my memory of their childhoods would simply be a sea of homework and test prep workbooks.

As a mother from Jamie's former elementary school recently said to me, "I expected the sleepless nights of the newborn years and the endless supervision of the toddler and preschool years but nothing prepared me for the amount of schoolwork I would be doing with them. That took me totally by surprise."

It took me by surprise too.

So did the number of curse words in *Click*. They were words I'd prefer Eric not hear, but they seemed to go over his head. And he was having so much fun watching the movie that I let him keep watching.

At one point, Adam Sandler cursed, the older boys laughed, and Eric asked, "What did he say, Mommy?"

It was a word Eric knew, and so—trying to make even this a teaching moment—I spelled, "S-h-i-t."

"Shit!" Eric said.

Six-year-old boys are fascinated with bad words and bathroom language. "Shit" was one of the first words Eric had learned to spell. He had first heard the word on the school bus and had repeated it at home. I told him he couldn't say the word "shit" but he could write it if he spelled it correctly. When you're desperate for your kids to learn to read, and spell, correctly, you'll do just about anything. Teaching him to spell "shit" had been a quick, and very effective, way to teach him the short /i/ sound. Now, I realized it was also useful for the /sh/ digraph.

I had also taught Eric how to spell "ass" after he heard that word on the school bus. He would chortle with glee whenever he found "ass" in other words: class, grass.

Last week, Eric had turned to me and, out of left field, had said, "What does fuck mean?"

"Where did you hear that word?" I had asked, shocked.

"Peter in my class got sent to the principal's office today for saying it. What does it mean?"

"It's really bad," Jamie had said. "Trust me. DO NOT use that word in school. OK?"

"OK," Eric had said. "But what does it mean?"

"It doesn't really have a definite meaning," I had sidestepped. "In a culture people just decide that certain words are bad words, and the f-word is one of the worst words in our language."

I was desperate for him to learn to read and spell, but there were certain lines I would not cross.

And, anyway, he already knew how to sound out short /u/ and that /ck/ made the /k/ sound.

23

Eric's teacher was very hard-working and dedicated. She usually responded very promptly to emails, even on the weekends. But she never responded to the email I had sent on Friday about Eric's report card.

Maybe she was angry? My email had not been very nice. I had been more direct than ever before about how the school was failing him. This is what I had written:

To: FirstGradeTeacher@nyc.schools.gov

From: Me

Subject: Eric's Report Card

Dear Teacher,

I was shocked by Eric's report card. Something appears to be going terribly wrong for Eric in your classroom and I am really wondering what it is.

Regarding the 2 he got in skip counting, he has NEVER brought home any homework to practice skip counting by 2s, 5s and 10s so how is he supposed to know how to do it and how were we supposed to know that he is expected to do it? This was not mentioned during math morning. The only homework for the longest time has been about shapes.

I know the other parents have been doing math workbooks with their kids. Once again, I feel Eric is behind the class because the other parents are educating their kids at home. I feel like we are living in the twilight zone and appear to be the downtown dummies. We always

> thought the school would tell us what Eric is supposed to learn and provide us with the tools to help him learn it.
>
> We will certainly practice skip counting by 2s, 5s, and 10s with him now that we know he needs to learn that, but why in the world didn't you tell us sooner that he was having trouble with it? And why was no homework ever sent home in it so that those of us who do not buy Kumon workbooks on our lunch hours would have some support from the school?
>
> What is upsetting is the fact that Eric was supposed to know something, and wasn't grasping it, yet you never told us about it until now. And we've been communicating so much. I thought I had a total handle on Eric's school performance.
>
> To say I am stunned would be a total understatement.

Maybe there was nothing she could say in response? Maybe she hoped my anger—and I—would go away.

I was not going away. When she hadn't responded by Monday afternoon, I headed uptown to talk to her in person. Dismissal would be the perfect time for us to talk because Eric would not be there. He would be in his classroom, waiting for his teacher to return and start his first session of Extended Day.

When she saw me, his teacher said a pleasant hello and made no mention of my email.

I got right to the point. "His report card shocked me," I said. "Especially the 2s in behavior. In kindergarten, he had all 4s in behavior."

As always, Eric's teacher was gracious. Being accosted by upset parents must have been a regular part of her day because she sure took it in stride. "I know," she said. "I saw his kindergarten report card."

"So what's going on? His preschool and kindergarten teachers had always said Eric was well-behaved. He always followed classroom rules and would even tell other kids to follow the rules when they weren't. Why is he suddenly misbehaving?"

"I think it's the frustration he's feeling about not reading," First Grade Teacher replied. "That frustration is affecting everything."

Tears sprang to my eyes, and I quickly wiped them away. "We have to do more to help him." What I meant was, *she* had to do more to help him. I was already doing everything humanly possible.

In a consoling tone, the teacher said, "Look at how much progress he's made."

I was so happy that his teacher was aware of his progress! He was now able to read short vowels and blends and many frequently used sight words. He now knew the 30 basic sight words he had not recognized just a week ago, as well as many harder ones. That combination of phonics and sight word knowledge was what had enabled him to read so well over the weekend. He must be reading better in class too.

I smiled at his teacher. "I'm so glad you're seeing progress."

"Yes," she replied. "We are having him work with Reading Specialist. And we are having him evaluated."

My hair felt like it was standing on end. She called that **PROGRESS**?

That was not progress. Those were steps the school was taking to fix a problem it had caused. I had to make her aware of how much *real* progress Eric had made. I told her how well he had read over the weekend, how he had transformed his baby blanket into a Super-Hero cape, and how he had called himself "Super-Reader."

"Good," she said. "He doesn't have to know."

He doesn't have to know what?

Every instinct in me was crying, "Beware!"

I hadn't even signed the papers giving permission for an evaluation, and his teacher was already acting like something was wrong with him.

That was bad.

Really, really bad.

If she thought something was wrong, she would expect less of him and that's exactly what she would get.

At home, Eric and I sat down to work on his reading. He pulled out a zippered plastic bag filled with the colorful little pattern books his school used to teach reading. The words "Reading with Susie" were written on the bag.

"Who's Susie?" I asked.

"Susie!" he said, as if the answer was obvious.

"I don't know Susie."

"Yes, you do."

"No, I don't. Is she a new assistant teacher?"

"She's the assistant principal."

"The *assistant principal* is reading with you?"

"Yes."

"Why?"

"I don't know."

"When?"

"In Extended Day."

I had many more questions but, suddenly, the phone rang. Thinking it might be a work-related call, I went into the bedroom to answer it.

"Hi," a sweet, calm voice said. "It's Susie from Eric's school." Susie used to be a kindergarten teacher, and she still looked and sounded like one. Everything about her, including her voice, was gentle and reassuring. I was happy to hear from her.

"Hi!" I replied. "I just saw the book baggie with your name on it. You're reading with Eric?"

"Yes. I'm calling to see if we can have a meeting so that I can talk to you about him."

"Sure."

Just then, Jamie came into the bedroom. He looked upset and desperately wanted to tell me something.

I waved him away. I couldn't listen to him now because I wanted to give Susie my full attention.

Jamie grabbed a piece of paper and wrote, "Eric is writing Jamie is an asshole over and over on his drawing easel."

There was nothing I could do about that now. I shooed Jamie away. Sighing in frustration, he walked out of the room.

In the same gentle tone she must have once used with her young students, Susie said, "Did you know I used to be a kindergarten, first, and second-grade teacher?"

"No," I replied.

"Well, I was."

I wasn't sure why she was telling me this, or what I was supposed to say, so I said nothing.

"Did you know I used to be a reading specialist?"

"No."

"Well, I was."

Again, I had no idea what she expected me to say.

"Did you know the principal was a staff developer?"

At this point I was thinking, how was I supposed to know all this and why did she think it was important for me to know? Was she proving that she and the principal had the credentials to teach reading ineffectively? At Jamie's former elementary school, the principal had trained teachers from the entire district to use Investigations, an ineffective constructivist math curriculum. Had Eric's principal done the same with the ineffective Lucy Calkins/Teachers College curriculum?

Of course, I didn't say that. Instead, I said, "Earlier this year, when I asked the principal how reading was taught in the school, she told me I was uninformed. I must be uninformed about a lot of things because I didn't know that about you or the principal."

"Well, come to the meeting and I'll inform you," she said, sweetly.

"I will. Thank you." I meant that thank you from the bottom of my heart. I was very grateful that she was taking the time to read with my son. He certainly needed all the support he could get. The support had come late from the school, but at least it had come.

I hung up the phone and walked into the dining/living room of our apartment. Eric had pulled out his drawing easel and set it up next to the dining room table. A piece of paper was clipped to the easel. On the paper, in childish print, Eric had written "Jamie is a asshol" five times.

Jamie and Eric were standing next to the easel, glaring at each other. Eric looked at me, and then looked away. He clearly thought he was going to get in trouble.

He was not.

Instead of reprimanding him, I was going to take advantage of this teaching opportunity.

"Hole has an e at the end of it," I said. "It's h-o-l-e."

"Oh," Eric replied. He was momentarily uncertain of what to make of my response. Then he said, "Thank you." He picked up a marker and added an e to the end of each instance of "asshol."

Jamie looked shocked. Then, my usually empathetic, usually extraordinarily kind son grabbed a piece of paper and wrote, "Eric is the stupidest asshole." He handed the paper to Eric and angrily yelled, "I bet you can't read this. YOU'RE SO STUPID, YOU CAN'T EVEN READ!"

Instinctively, I protected the child who would be most damaged by this interaction. "Of course, you can read," I said to Eric. "What did Jamie write?"

Perfectly, Eric read, "Eric is the stupidest asshole."

"Don't ever say Eric can't read," I said to Jamie, sternly. "He reads beautifully."

Eric put a piece of white paper on the dining room table. On it, he wrote, "Jamie is a ass hol." At the bottom of the page, he scribbled, "I am smrt."

"Remember, 'hole' has an 'e' at the end," I said.

In a stunned voice, Jamie said, "Mom?"

His reaction reminded of the passage in *Parenting a Struggling Reader* where the boy said he'd "lost" his mom when his brother got dyslexia. Jamie probably felt he had lost me too. Before our world had been turned upside down by Eric not being taught how to read in school, by his pending evaluation, and by his recent report card, Eric would have gotten in a lot of trouble for what he had written. Now, I would take advantage of any instance to teach him to spell correctly even if the word he spelled was "asshole." Even if he was using that word in reference to my older son.

"Ignore him," I said to Jamie. "You know you are not an asshole, and Eric needs to know how to spell hole correctly."

Jamie turned away, obviously feeling betrayed. I should have defended my wonderful older son. I had not, and he didn't know why not. He knew nothing about Eric's pending evaluation and I couldn't tell him. I couldn't risk having him tell Eric about it in a fit of anger, the way he had just yelled, "YOU'RE SO STUPID, YOU CAN'T EVEN READ!"

Jamie did not know that I often woke up at night in a cold sweat, worrying that the school was about to take a perfectly fine kid and try to find something wrong with him. Worrying that the school would leave no stone unturned to find something wrong, so that they could say the problem was him, and not them. Worrying that Eric would find out his school thought something was wrong with him, and that that would permanently affect how he saw himself as a student. Jamie did not know Eric's teacher was already acting as if something was wrong with him.

Good. He doesn't need to know, his teacher had said.

She had meant: He doesn't need to know he has a learning disability.

Jamie had no idea that—in scrambling to teach Eric how to read and spell—I was, literally, fighting for Eric's academic life. Because of that fight, none of us would remain unscathed.

It seemed like a total waste of time

Eric was tired from Extended Day and, because he was tired, he was stressed and grumpy. I tried working with him on his reading but soon saw that my teaching was not sinking in. He needed to relax and unwind before he could absorb anything.

I felt sorry for him. No kid should have to go to school, go to Extended Day, and then come home to learn how to read. "Go play," I told him.

"Play" for Eric almost always meant building or creating something. Today he inflated balloons, taped them to long streamers, and asked me to attach the streamers to the ceiling. He then taped tiny toy astronauts to the low-hanging balloons and used sheets of construction paper and more tape to create space stations and docking stations. Soon, our living room was transformed into a fantastic scene from outer space. The balloons were planets, and astronauts were either dangling in space, walking on the planets, or docking in the space station.

Eric created and created. With every minute that passed, he became more relaxed. Soon, he was humming and happy.

We ate dinner as a family and, afterwards, both kids did their homework. Eric started by working on the spelling words I had written into his school spelling notebook that week. Next, he quickly and easily did two pages in

Explode the Code 1 ½. His math homework consisted of finding things in our apartment that were shaped like squares. He did so in the blink of an eye. (That was the full extent of the math homework sent home for a kid who was below grade level in counting by 2s, 5s, and 10s and in knowing doubles. Doubles, by the way, are the answers you get when you add two of the same numbers together: 2+2; 3+3; 4+4, etc.) Then, it was time for him to read.

"Susie said to read the books I brought home from her," Eric said.

Yuck.

I hated those pattern books.

Actually, let me qualify that statement.

I hated the way his school *used* those books. If those books had been used to support the teaching of specific sight words, or phonics rules, they would have been fine. Great actually.

But that is not how those books were used. Their repetitive sentences were meant to be memorized and the unfamiliar, difficult words at the end of each of those sentences were meant to be guessed at by looking at the pictures.

The last thing in the world I wanted to do was waste valuable time on pattern books that encouraged memorization and guessing. But I didn't say that to Eric. I wanted him to respect his school and listen to his teachers and the school administrators. So, I let him to do what the assistant principal had told him to do.

The first book he read was called *The Way I Go to School* and it began like so:

> "I go to school.
>
> "I go to school in a wheelchair.
>
> "I go to school on a bike."

By the time he got to the third "I go to school," Eric had stopped looking at the words. For the rest of the pages, he recited, "I go to school," from memory and then looked at the pictures to guess what the word at the end of each sentence was.

On page four, he looked at the picture of a car.

"I go to school in a car," he recited without looking at the words.

On page 5, he read, "I go to school in a taxi," again looking only at the picture and not at the word taxi.

Same thing with the following pages where the pictures illustrated the words "van," "bus," and "boat."

Useless.

The next book was called *The Skier*. Its opening lines described how the skier was getting himself to the ski slope from his home. Each of the following sentences appeared on separate pages:

> "He is going down the ladder
>
> "He is going down the stairs.
>
> "He is going down the path.
>
> "He is going down the steps.
>
> "He is going down the road."

Please take special note of what happened next because it will become very important in the next chapter. What happened was this: Eric read/recited the words "going down" that appeared in the first five sentences in *The Skier*. Then, the pattern changed. In the first five sentences, the skier was going down. In the sixth sentence, down changed to up. But, because Eric was reciting and not reading, he did not notice the change. And, so, he said, "Down."

"It's not down anymore," I said. "Look at the word. "It's not down. What is it?"

He looked at the word and read, "up." Then he read, "He is going up and up and up."

On the next page, the pattern changed again. Instead of repeating the word up, the sentence said, "He is going down the mountain." But, because the previous page had said up, Eric recited, "He is going up the mountain."

"Look at the word," I said. "It's not up anymore. The pattern changed again."

Eric looked at the word and read it correctly: down.

"Reading" the way his school had taught him—by memorizing and reciting, instead of by looking at the words—also initially tripped him up with the next book, called *Cat and Mouse*.

> Page 1: "Mouse ran over the shovel. Cat ran over the shovel."
>
> Page 2: "Mouse ran under the broom. Cat ran under the broom."
>
> Page 3: "Mouse ran over the rake. Cat ran over the rake."
>
> Page 4: "Mouse ran under the wheelbarrow. Cat ran under the wheelbarrow."

As you can see, the pattern changed on every page. But, because the sentence on the first page said over," Eric made a mistake on the next page: He recited over, instead of under.

"Eric, stop memorizing the words," I said. "*Look* at them. Don't assume a pattern exists. The pattern changes on every page in this book."

He listened. He looked at the words and read over and under correctly on all of the following pages. Understandably, he did not know the big words like shovel, or broom, or wheelbarrow. Nor did he need to know them at this stage in the reading process. How often does the word *wheelbarrow* show up in books?

Another harmful book. At least for the purpose of teaching Eric to read. But definitely bookmark what just transpired in your memory for reference in the next chapter!

Eric does what his report card says he couldn't

After he finished "reading" the pattern books, I held up a new Dick and Jane book. It looked different from the Dick and Jane books he'd read so far. The earlier books had been very slim paperbacks. This one was a thicker hardcover.

"I don't want to read that," Eric said.

I assumed it was because the book looked so long. "This book has lots of different stories," I said. "I'll put sticky notes in it so that you will see where each story ends. Read one story in here and I will give you a Tic Tac." He deserved the reward since he had already read more than his quota of stories for the night.

"I want Dick and Jane," he said, suspiciously eyeing the book's cover.

Ah! So that's why he hadn't wanted to read this book; he hadn't realized it *was* a Dick and Jane book. In addition to being thicker, and a hardcover, the illustrations were different. On the cover, Dick and Jane looked a lot older than they had in the earlier books. Not realizing it was a familiar Dick and Jane book must have made this thick book very intimidating to him.

"This *is* a Dick and Jane book,'" I replied. I pointed to the characters' names on the cover. "I wouldn't have recognized them in the pictures either. They look older, don't they?

"Yeah. A lot."

Knowing it was Dick and Jane must have made him feel better because he began negotiating: "Two Tic Tacs for one story."

"One," I said.

"Three," he replied.

"Two," I said. "That's as high as I'll go."

He accepted the deal and read a story. He read it beautifully and was surprised when it ended. "That's it?" he said. "Let's do another one."

"Okay."

"So, I get 4 Tic Tacs."

I sat up straighter. He had counted by twos naturally, without even thinking about what he was doing.

I said, "Right. What comes after four?"

"No more," he said.

He must have known I was testing him. I didn't care. I wanted to see what he knew. "I'll give you two more Tic Tacs if you count by 2s for me. "If you had read another story how many Tic Tacs would you have gotten after 4?"

"Six," he said, instantly.

"And another story?"

"Eight."

"And another?"

He went all the way up to TWENTY-EIGHT without taking any time to think. Then he got stuck because he didn't know what number came after 29. I told him. Then I said, "Go show Daddy how well you count by 2s."

Eric and I walked into the bedroom where Cary was sitting at the desk, helping Jamie with some hard math homework.

"Daddy?" I said.

I called Cary "Daddy" only when I was about to say something important that had to do with the kids. The unspoken message was: "This is important. You need to give this all of your attention."

Daddy looked up.

"Listen to what Eric can do."

Proudly, Eric said, "Two," but then he stopped.

I prompted him. "Another 2?"

"Four," he said instantly.

"And another 2."

"Six."

"Keep going."

He went all the way up to 30.

"Wow!" Cary said. "That's great! You're counting by 2s!"

Eric took my hand and said, "Come on, Mommy. Tic Tacs."

Cary shot me a look and held his palms up towards the ceiling in a gesture meant to communicate, "I don't get it." He was silently asking: If it was so easy for Eric to count by 2 why wasn't he doing it in school?

Because, as his teacher had said, struggling with reading was affecting everything. Struggling with reading had caused him to tune out to school, even to math, a subject he loved.

All the more reason to get him reading ASAP.

My kid can read! I mean really, really read!

Washington D.C. has the Lincoln Memorial to commemorate Abraham Lincoln.
New York City has the Statue of Liberty to commemorate freedom.
To this day, the bookcase in our Manhattan living room holds the book "Little Bear" by Else Minarik to commemorate the day Eric first read a real story.
Bye-bye, Bob Books.
So long, Dick and Jane.
Hello, real books.

That momentous occasion happened on Tuesday, January 30th, four months after I first began teaching him how to read. On that day, Eric had put in a full day of school and then stayed for Extended Day. He took the school bus home, did his homework, had dinner, took a bath, and then played a little bit. Then, it was time for him to read out loud to me.

I handed him *Little Bear*, one of the two books I had found in Barnes and Noble on the day I'd had lunch with Best Friend.

Eric began reading the first story, called "What Will Little Bear Wear?" A lot of the words were sight words he had memorized, but there were also words I thought were new to him. I was prepared to help him with any words he couldn't read. Eric began reading, and he did not stop:

> It is cold.
>
> See the snow.
>
> See the snow come down.
>
> Little Bear said, "Mother Bear,
>
> "I am cold.
>
> "See the snow.
>
> "I want something to put on."
>
> So Mother Bear made something for Little Bear.

There was more to the story and Eric kept on reading. Imagine my surprise when, even though it was late and he was tired and the story was brand new to him, Eric read the whole thing. The only words he stumbled over were "hurray" and "put." He thought "put" was "but." To my knowledge, he'd never seen the word "cold" before, but he read it. He initially read the word "something" as "sometimes" but then corrected himself.

When he finished the story, I was so proud and happy. I gave him a big hug and a kiss. "You are a reader, kiddo," I said. "You did it! You are ready to read real stories!"

His smile and the glow on his face could have lit up the night.

I don't know who was more surprised at how well he had read—me or my son—but I can tell you we were both absolutely thrilled.

24

Imagine talking to a cow.
    Never mind. Scratch that.
    Imagine *pleading* with a cow.
    Begging.
    Doing everything in your power to get the cow to listen to you.
    The result of your efforts?
    The cow stares at you, blankly. It is calm. Unmoved. So serene, that it could be doing a *Saturday Night Live* impersonation of a Buddhist monk.
    You continue pouring your heart out, but your words start to come out more slowly. Your voice becomes quieter as you realize your words are falling on deaf ears. Eventually, you stop talking because the cow, clearly, does not understand you.
    I was in that situation, except I was not talking to a cow—I was talking to Eric's teacher.
    I had been so worried about her calling his evaluation "progress," that I had asked to meet with her. I was trying to communicate my concern with her, but my message was not getting through.
    Sitting on a child-sized chair in her classroom, I decided to try one more time. "I need you to really hear what I'm saying. Eric has made great progress with reading. Just last night, he read *Little Bear*."
    The teacher's long, red, wavy hair gently swung forward and back as she nodded. Her lightly freckled face remained expressionless. Dressed in a plaid shirt and jeans, she could have been manning a cash register at a Vermont farm stand. My news—ERIC HAD READ *LITTLE BEAR*!!—had made as much of an impression on her as my telling a farmer his farm stand sold tomatoes. She was completely unfazed.

I tried again: "Eric has made *huge* progress. He can read *real* stories! Not just books like *Bob Books* and *Dick and Jane*. Are you seeing that progress in class?"

"He's made a lot of progress," she replied. "He's become more confident, and I see him using his strategies when he reads."

Yay!

How great that she was seeing progress too!

"The other day I had the kids talk about the strategies they use when they read," the teacher continued. "Eric told the class that the strategy he finds most effective is looking at the pictures to help him know what the words are."

Can you believe she said that?

Maybe I was the cow.

I simply did not understand.

Why in the world would Eric say looking at the pictures *helped* him when he knew full well that looking at the pictures *hurt* him? He had spent the entire school year trying to break that bad habit. Had he spouted the party line because he wanted to please his teacher? Or because he wanted to fit in?

Here's an anecdote that might help us understand Eric's motivation: The other day, Eric told me his teacher had told the class they were going to be learning how to tell time.

The teacher had asked, "How many of your parents have taught you this at home already?"

Because all the other kids raised their hands, Eric had raised his too. Then he had come home and asked me to teach him how to tell time.

"Why did you raise your hand?" I had asked him.

His response? The kids had once laughed at him when he didn't know who Derek Jeter was and he "didn't want to not know again."

I could understand a 6-year-old who wanted to fit in saying that looking at the pictures was his most effective strategy. But how could his teacher think I would see that as a sign of progress? For months, I had been asking her to teach Eric how to sound out words so that he would *stop* guessing from the pictures.

I didn't know what to say.

I certainly could not say what I really wanted to say, which was: "Are you really such an idiot?"

The only constructive thing left for me to do was find out why, even though my son was reading harder and harder books at home, his reading level in school continued to remain unchanged. "How do you ascertain kids' reading levels?" I asked.

The teacher retrieved a big three-ring binder with the name Rigby on it. Rigby was a publisher of pattern books. She opened the binder to the little book Eric had needed to read in order to move up to the next level. "He needed to score 95 or higher in his reading of this. He got an 85."

"The ability to read just one story determines whether or not a child moves up to the next reading level?"

"Yes."

I paged through the story. It was very easy. My kid should have read that story with no problem. "Eric can read this."

The teacher shrugged. Obviously, my son hadn't read it to her.

"The pictures are throwing him," I said.

I knew it was futile, but I had to say it. If I said it often enough, maybe she would finally listen. "He's guessing what the words are from the pictures. He's probably not even looking at the words. Try covering up the pictures. I'm sure he'll read the words beautifully."

The gentle cow nodded.

I examined the two stories Eric needed to read in order to move up two more levels. He could definitely read the words in those books too. If only he would actually look at the words and stop guessing what they were by looking at the pictures.

I threw my heart and soul into getting through to Eric's teacher. "Please," I pleaded. "Please believe me! Eric can read these books! *Please* try having him read the words with the pictures covered!"

"Okay," the gentle cow said.
She never did.

A miracle happened on East 95th Street

A few hours later, Cary and I were at our much-anticipated meeting with Susie, the assistant principal. Wanting to make sure she was fully aware of the situation, I told her the whole story. I told her how Eric had gotten excellent grades in reading in kindergarten when, in fact, he couldn't read a word; how he had held a book behind his back and recited it to get me to realize that he was memorizing books, instead of reading them; how I had been working with him on phonics at home, and what great progress he had made.

She nodded empathetically.

"It's very important for you to know how proactive the other parents in this school have been about teaching their kids to read," Cary said. "You should make sure the parents of this year's kindergarteners know that so that they won't have to go through what we did. We didn't know how much work was being done at home, and we would have appreciated being made aware of it so that we could have done the same."

I worried that Susie would get defensive, but she simply nodded.

Hoping to smooth any invisible ruffled feathers, I said, "We're not bashing the Balanced Literacy curriculum. Our older son learned how to read with that curriculum, but Jamie also has a very different learning style than Eric. Jamie is a holistic learner while Eric is an analytic learner."

"What is that?" she asked.

I explained a bit about the psychology research I had been doing on how people process new information, research that would soon turn into the topic of my dissertation. "Are you familiar with the Myers-Briggs system of personality typing?" I asked her.

She shook her head no.

"Myers-Briggs is a popular personality assessment lots of corporations use to screen employees. It says everyone's personality is composed of four dimensions, and one of those dimensions is how we take in, or process, information. In that information-processing dimension, people are either intuitive or sensing. In psychological research, intuitive learners are referred to as "holistic," and sensing learners are called "analytical." Each of these processing styles has its strengths and weaknesses and neither one is better than the other. But sensing, or analytical, kids need to learn phonics in order to learn how to read."

"Why?"

"Intuitive, or holistic, learners focus on the big picture. They do not need, or like, to do a lot of work with systematic phonics. They are able to intuit the rules on their own. Their processing style helps them learn to read more easily but, when they get older, they usually have trouble in school because they tend to gloss over many details."

Susie leaned forward, her forehead furrowed in concentration. She was clearly interested.

"Sensing, or analytic, learners focus on the little picture," I continued. "They take in every detail and learn in a systematic way. If they come across a word they don't know, they will stop and not keep going until they figure it out, or someone tells them what that word is. If they can't figure it out, intuitive learners will just guess at, or skip, the word. Sensing kids will not pick up phonics rules on their own. They need to be taught phonics rules in a step-by-step, systematic way and if someone doesn't teach them those rules, they will not learn how to read. That is so sad because analytic learners who are taught systematic phonics usually do very well in school, especially in math and science."

"They do better than intuitive kids?"

"Definitely in math and science and, often, in other subjects as well. They do better on tests because analytic learners tend to read directions and are able to show their work in a step-by-step detailed manner. Intuitive kids tend to skip reading directions and will intuit their way to an answer and then have a hard time showing their work. They are also usually bad spellers and will misread words when they are older. But that doesn't stop them because they are interested in getting the gist of what they are reading, not every exact detail."

Susie reached for paper and a pen. "I've never heard of these processing styles. What are they called again?" She wrote down "intuitive/holistic" and "sensing/analytic," and said, "I'm going to look into this further."

Cary and I exchanged a hopeful glance. If she looked into the research on how beginning readers process information, she would find proof that sensing/analytical learners need to be taught phonics. If she found that, then systematic phonics might actually be put into the classroom. Change might actually happen!!

A miracle!

But you know how miracles sometimes go—the Lord giveth and the Lord taketh away.

Looking, and sounding, very serious, Susie said, "As you know, Eric has been working with me." She opened a three-ring binder filled with Eric's running records. Those are forms provided by publishers of pattern books. Every book has a running record that goes along with it, and that record consists of all the sentences in that book. As the child reads, the teacher uses the running record to track each word. She puts a checkmark over the words the child reads correctly and writes in the word the child said if he read it incorrectly.

Balanced Literacy teaches children to use three main cues when they read and, on the running records, the teacher notes which of these three cues caused him to make mistakes. *Pretty strange, since teachers should not be teaching kids strategies that cause them to make mistakes, but let's just add that to the list of problems with Balanced Literacy...*

The teacher notes those mistakes by writing either M, S, or V on the running record. Here is what each of those letters stands for:

- <u>M is for meaning</u>. The teacher will write "M" if the child made an incorrect guess because he looked at the pictures, or used the context of the story. The M means that he used a word whose meaning did not fit with either what was shown in the picture or said in the rest of the sentence.

- <u>S is for sentence structure</u>. "S" will be written if the child guessed an incorrect type of word—a verb, when the word should have been a noun or an adjective, for example. The "S" means he used the wrong kind of word, given how the rest of the sentence was structured. (Maybe he said "happy" instead of "horse" in a sentence like, The man rode a horse.)

- V is for visual information. In running records, letters are referred to as "visual information." A "V" is written if the child incorrectly guessed a word that begins with the same letter as the word he was trying to read. (Maybe he said "many," instead of "more.")

Teachers also record whether a child corrects his mistakes on his own and how. *This will become very important in a minute…*

Susie examined Eric's first running record. "He read this book, which is a beginning-level book, and he scored 100 percent," she said.

She turned to the second running record. "He read this book and also scored 100 percent."

After examining his third running record, her voice changed. Her tone was compassionate, as if she was delivering very bad news: "Eric got a very low score for this book. He didn't know words he should have known. He didn't know words he had read correctly in the two previous books." Susie clearly felt we should be very concerned about what she had just told us.

"Can I see the book?" I asked.

She stood and retrieved a large, zippered plastic bag full of colorful pattern books.

I held back a sigh. I hated those books. "Those books hurt him more than help him," I said. "Those books taught him to guess what words are by looking at the pictures. They taught him to not even look at the words. They instilled a lot of bad habits."

Susie did not respond. She rummaged through the bag and pulled out a book called *Here is a Bird*. She turned to the first page, which had a cartoon illustration of a bird. The words on that page were: "Here is an eye."

"I can tell you exactly what he read correctly and incorrectly," I said.

She raised her eyebrows. Clearly, she was skeptical.

I continued. "He was able to read 'here,' 'is' and 'an.' He did not know the word 'eye' since he's never seen it before. He probably guessed that the word was 'bird.'"

Susie nodded and turned the page. The first word on that page was "the." Still looking, and sounding, very concerned, she said, "He knew how to read 'the' in the other two books, but he didn't know it in this one."

"Did he read it as 'here?'" I asked.

She consulted the running record. "He said, 'he' but then he corrected himself and said 'the.'"

"I can tell you exactly why he did that."

"Why?" Her tone was gentle and kind, as if she expected me to tell her Eric was afflicted with a heart-breaking memory disorder which I had failed to mention until now.

"Because he thought the words follow a pattern. The sentence on the first page started with 'here,' so he thought the second page would also start with, 'here.' That's why he said 'he.' He was starting to say, 'here' but then realized the word wasn't 'here.' He then corrected himself and said, 'the.'"

Susie examined the page, seeing if what I was saying could possibly be true.

"Something similar happened the other night when he was reading a book he'd brought home from school," I continued. "On the first few pages every sentence began with the words, 'He is going *up*.' Then the pattern changed to 'He is going *down*.' But, because he was reciting the book from memory—and not really reading—Eric said 'up' instead of 'down.'" On the next page, the pattern changed again—from up to down—but Eric said 'down' instead of 'up.' I had to keep telling him to actually look at the words and not assume there was a pattern."

Susie nodded but said nothing. She showed us other mistakes Eric had made. They all had to do with him not recognizing when a pattern had changed. It was obvious that he had been reciting the words from memory and not actually reading them. How could Susie not realize that? "He was getting all these words wrong that he had known the day before," she said, still sounding very, very concerned.

"Cover the pictures next time you read with him and tell him not to rely on the pattern," I urged. "I'm sure he'll read a lot more of the words correctly. When he reads these pattern books, he falls back on using the strategies he's been taught in the classroom. He memorizes the pattern and guesses from the pictures. He's not even looking at the words. If you cover the pictures, he'll be forced to look at the words and he'll be able to read them. I'm positive of that."

Susie went back to the beginning of the binder and carefully examined the errors she'd recorded on his running records. "This is fascinating," she said. "I was taught that children learn to read by looking at the pictures, but what you are saying is fascinating and it makes sense, given the kinds of mistakes I see in his running records."

VICTORY!!!!

I could not believe that finally, *finally*, someone at the school had heard what I'd been saying for months. Now I had to show her that Eric could read much better than she, and his teacher, thought.

I reached into my purse and pulled out *Little Bear*. I opened the book to the first story and handed it to Susie. "Eric read this last night. He read it beautifully."

Susie looked doubtful. "He hadn't read that story before?" That was her way of suggesting that Eric may have memorized the story, and recited it, and that he hadn't actually read it on his own.

"No," I said. "He'd never read that story. And I hadn't read it to him either."

"How is that possible? How could he have read that?" She asked those questions in the same tone a doctor would have used if a cripple at Lourdes had thrown down his crutches and done the polka.

"The pattern books you are having him read are actually much harder than *Little Bear*," I replied. "Eric knew most of the words in *Little Bear*, and the ones he didn't know he was able to sound out. I was surprised too. It was late by the time he sat down to read. He was tired, and the book was brand new to him. But I swear he read it beautifully. The only words that gave him trouble were 'hurray' and 'put.' He thought 'put'; was 'but.'"

Susie opened the book and leafed through it.

She sighed.

I could tell that she didn't know what to think. Was I a crazy, delusional mother, or could Eric read much better than she thought?

"Keep the book," I said. "See for yourself. Have him read you the story and any of the other stories in the book. He hasn't read them yet. You'll see. He'll be able to read them."

She nodded. "I'll do that. And, in the meantime, remember he is being evaluated. We will see what the evaluation turns up."

Oh no, no, no, I thought. Please don't turn into a disbeliever! Don't go back to thinking there is something wrong with my son. What could I do to get her to realize my son could read? Really, really read.

"Listen," I said. "At the start of this school year, I came to you guys and told you I thought something was wrong. His teacher and the principal told me not to worry, but I was worried. Thinking something might be wrong with him, I had his vision and his hearing checked. Both were fine. If I thought there was even the slightest chance Eric had a learning issue, I would want to know all about it, and I would get him all the help I could. I'm getting a Ph.D. in psychology. I am all for testing and evaluating kids who are not making progress and helping those who need help. But I can tell you, as an almost psychologist, and as Eric's mother, that my son is fine. The only problem is that he wasn't being taught how to sound out words. When I taught him how to do that, he learned beautifully and his 'problem' went away."

Susie nodded but remained silent.

"Look." I pulled three Dick and Jane books out of my purse. "He can read these too."

I handed the books to her, and she leafed through a book called *Go Away Spot*. "Why don't the pictures in these stories interfere with his reading?" she asked.

"Because the pictures aren't directly linked to the words, the way they are in pattern books. He can't use the pictures to guess what the words are, so he has to really read them."

She remained silent, but I could tell she had heard me and was thinking about what I had said.

"I'll show you." I opened the book to the first story and pointed at an illustration of spilled milk. "The words don't say, 'Here is spilled milk,' the way they would in a pattern book. The words say, 'Oh, Jane. I see something. Look, Jane, look. Look here.' There is no mention of milk. Because he couldn't guess the words from the pictures, he had to actually read them."

Susie nodded. "Yes, in the books I'm having him read, the text directly supports the pictures."

I held my breath. Was she starting to believe there was nothing wrong with Eric?

"How is his writing?" she asked. "Does he reverse his letters when he writes at home?"

"Sometimes he'll write a 'b' for a 'd' or a 'd' for a 'b' but that's normal for kids this age."

"With me, he reversed his 'f' and 'h.'"

That surprised me. "Never," I said. "Never at home. He writes all the letters, except for b and d, beautifully. In fact, look at this. You will probably refer us to child services when you see this, but look at how well he can write."

I showed her the piece of paper on which he'd written, "Jamie is a asshol."

I told her the story behind those words, and she laughed.

"He wrote the 'h' in asshole in the right direction," I said.

She examined the paper.

"And his spelling is improving," I said. "He left the 'e' off of asshole, but he spelled the other words correctly."

"I was going to ask you if he spelled 'hole' right."

Before this school year, before Eric's school had failed to teach him to read and before his school had put him in the pipeline for an evaluation, if you had told me I would be discussing whether or not Eric spelled "asshole" correctly with *anyone*—let alone his assistant principal—I would have thought you were crazy.

Yet here I was doing exactly that.

"What does that say?" Susie pointed at the words Eric had scribbled at the bottom of the page: I am smrt.

"That says, 'I am smart.'"

She smiled, in a touched way. We were sitting here talking about a child who thought he was smart.

Correction: a child who *knew* he was smart. But instead of discussing his intelligence—intelligence so great that, at age 5, he realized his school was using incorrect methods to teach reading—we were dancing around the fact that Susie, and the rest of his teaching team, thought he had a learning disability.

Silence hung in the air.

Susie, clearly, did not know what to think.

"I appreciate you working with him," I said, "but if you keep using those pattern books you'll be wasting his time, and yours. He won't make any progress. I'm about to teach him the rule for digraphs. If you could find books with digraphs in them, and have him read them, that would really help."

"I'll see what I can do. And I'll do my own research into learning styles."

Cary and I were thrilled. As far as we were concerned, the meeting could not have gone better.

25

"Can we celebrate?" Eric asked as he scampered off the school bus. "Can we go out for hot chocolate?"

The first, and only time, we had ever gone out for hot chocolate had been when Eric had last moved up a reading level. On that day, I had taken Jamie and Eric to City Bakery for its famous, thick, rich chocolate concoction to commemorate the occasion. I assumed today's request meant Eric had once again moved up a reading level, but I wanted to give him the chance to tell me his good news. "What are we celebrating?" I asked.

Eric's school bus stop was at the side entrance of the W Hotel in Union Square. He plopped his backpack on the sidewalk by the hotel's revolving door and pulled out the *Little Bear* book. Brandishing it proudly, he declared: "Purple stick dot!"

"Wow!" I said. "That's amazing!"

That really *was* amazing. Purple was two levels higher than Eric's current level. Purple was the level the school wanted the kids to be at by the end of first grade, and today was only February 1st. Since Susie knew Eric was reading at grade level, the school thinking something was wrong with Eric had to be a thing of the past. That was definitely worth celebrating!

With a spring in our steps, Eric and I retrieved Jamie from the apartment and walked the few blocks to City Bakery.

I must tell you. Hot chocolate never tasted so good.

"Hey, this looks good," Jamie said later that night as he picked up one of the two books Eric had brought home to read for homework.

The book was called *Footprints in the Snow* and the cover featured a picture of a very cute bunny standing on its rear legs in the snow.

As Jamie flipped through the book, his expression turned from interest to disappointment. "What kind of a book is this?" He threw the book down on the couch in disgust. This is what he had seen between the covers:

Words	Illustration
Someone <u>hops</u> home.	A rabbit hopping in the snow.
Someone <u>runs</u> home.	A deer running.
Someone <u>stomps</u> home.	A bear walking.
Someone <u>swims</u> home.	Beavers swimming.
Someone <u>races</u> home.	A fox running.

"Someone _____ home" appeared on the following pages with the words "flies," "hurries," "scampers" and "walks" inserted as the words that were to be guessed from the pictures. That book would have been to great to use for reinforcing the silent /e/ rule since "home" was repeated so many times. But it was not a great book for a child who was reading it in order to learn how to read and had not yet been taught how to read words like races, flies, hurries, scampers and walks.

I picked up the second book, *Bubble Trouble*. It was even more inappropriate for a beginning reader:

> I make bubbles in the air.
>
> I make bubbles in my hair.
>
> I make bubbles big and round and listen for the popping sound.

No beginning reader was able to read words like "bubbles," "are," "hair," "round," "popping" or "sound."

That book was much too hard for Eric to read. Worried that its difficulty would take away the sense of accomplishment he was feeling, I told him to put the book away and ushered him into his evening bath.

At bedtime, Eric and I looked through some of Jamie's old books, searching for a nice story for me to read to him. Eric pulled *Bye-Bye Mom and Dad* off the shelf and leafed through it. That was the story he had brought into the bedroom the other night, asking for help reading the word "slurpy." Back then, he'd looked only at the words in the illustration. Today, he looked at the rest of the words in the book. "Hey!" he exclaimed, "I can read this!"

Notice how this real story, as opposed to an insipid pattern book, is easier for a child to read since so many of the words can be sounded out. Here is how the story opens:

> Today mom and dad went on a trip, and Grandma and Grandpa came to stay with us.
>
> "Bye-bye, Mom and Dad!" I said. "Don't worry. I will take care of everything."

Eric pulled another *Little Critter* book off the shelf. "I can read this too!" He was practically vibrating with excitement.

He looked through a third *Little Critter* book and cried, "I can read all of these, Mommy! Let's make a pile of them! Let's make a pile of all the books I can read!"

Eric carried the *Little Critter* books to the coffee table and stacked them in a neat pile. He was *so* proud.

His joyous proclamation "Hey! I can read these!" kept sounding in my ears long after my little boy was asleep.

The next morning, I sent this email to his principal and cc-d his entire school team on it:

> To: Principal@nyc.schools.gov
>
> From: Me
>
> Subject: Thank you, thank you...
>
> Hi Principal,
>
> I feel like we, as a family, and Eric, as a student, have been given the most important gift any family could get—a school full of teachers and administrators who are open to seeing what works for each individual child. Yesterday, Susie did the most important thing anyone could have done for us—she listened, really listened, when we told her about Eric's experience of learning how to read. She was open to seeing how, and why, the Balanced Literacy curriculum wasn't working for him.
>
> I think she was as stunned as we were to realize Eric had no trouble reading *Little Bear*, a purple stick dot book, when he was stumbling over Level 1 Emergent Reader books in the classroom. That's because, with the Emergent Reader books, he still uses the strategies he used when he didn't know how to read. Whenever he sees a pattern book, he instantly starts guessing from the pictures and assuming a pattern exists, even when it doesn't. So, he, inevitably, gets a lot of words wrong.
>
> I know that if we were in a different school we would not have been listened to. Yesterday Susie listened. She said she had been taught that children learn to read by looking at the pictures, but she was open to hearing how guessing from the pictures hurt Eric. When she worked with Eric yesterday, she saw that he could, indeed, read *Little Bear*.
>
> That astonishing leap happened because we all pulled together as a team.
>
> I am so impressed with how no egos were involved at Hallowed School.

> Everyone was willing to say, "OK. Let's give Eric what he needs" and it worked. I will be forever grateful for that!

I know what you're thinking.

The school and I had not "pulled together as a team." Yes, they had let me assign his spelling words to him but, to me, that was not teamwork. It was allowing me to do their jobs for them. Eric's astonishing leap in reading had happened because of the work I had done with him. But I wasn't going to rub the school's nose in that.

At this point, it didn't matter who had taught him to read.

What mattered was that he was reading.

I wanted the school to see that.

I wanted them to stop thinking there was something wrong with my son.

The next day, Eric came home from school with an announcement: the principal had sat in on his reading time with Susie.

"Really?" I said. "What did she do?"

"She helped me and told me to look at the words."

Did you hear that?

His principal had told him to LOOK AT THE WORDS!!! At the beginning of this school year, I had never imagined that phrase would be a cause for celebration. But now I knew how momentous it was.

"How did you do?"

"Good."

Wanting Eric to realize how proud he should be of himself, I said, "You're going to be the talk of your school."

Instead of looking proud, he looked worried. "Why?" he asked.

"No one at your school realized what a good reader you are because you couldn't read some of the lower-level books in your classroom. And now they know you can read *Little Bear*! I don't think anyone has ever jumped that quickly in reading levels."

"I'm not officially a purple stick dot yet," Eric said. "I'm still yellow." In case you are interested, the order of the stick dots (or reading levels) goes like this: green, blue, red, yellow, orange, purple, pink, white.

"I'm sure you'll be a purple stick dot soon," I said. "Your teacher just needs to sit and read with you and see what you can do."

"I don't know if I can read the other purple stick dot books," Eric said.

"Why not?"

Looking as if he was confessing to a terrible sin, Eric said, "I could read *Little Bear* because I knew the words in the story."

I wish you could have seen the guilty look on his face. Eric thought there was something *wrong* with being able to read a book *because he knew the words.*

I kneeled on the floor and took his hands in mine. "That's the whole idea, honey. That's what reading is. You're *supposed* to know the words in a book before you read it. Or at least most of them. Your school should never have asked you to read books full of words you didn't know. Your school was wrong about that."

That was the first time I had said anything negative about his school to Eric. I had to. There was no way I was going to allow him to feel bad about being able to read a book *because he knew the words.* "You should be very proud of yourself," I said.

And his school should be ashamed.

That night as I tucked him into bed, Eric said, "When I officially become a purple stick dot, I won't need to go to Reading Specialist anymore."

His words surprised me. I hadn't realized that working with Reading Specialist bothered him. He had to keep working with her. She was the only one in the school who would do systematic phonics with him. "Why don't you like working with her?" I asked.

"She works with me during Choice Time or Writing Workshop." Choice Time was the free period during which Eric got to play with his beloved blocks. And Writing Workshop when kids got to write stories. As you can imagine, Eric's spelling was still pretty much a disaster, but he loved to write.

I was sorry he needed to miss those periods, but working with the reading specialist was important. "We'll see what happens in the future," I said.

Eric threw off his blanket and sat up. "You mean I might have to go to her for as long as I'm in that school?" he exclaimed.

"No," I said. "But it may be a good idea to go next year."

"Why?"

"Because she does phonics with you," I said. "Phonics is important."

"You can do phonics with me," he said.

"I hear you," I said. "We'll keep working together and you'll work with her this year and I'm sure you'll get to a point where you'll be able to stop."

That placated him, and he settled down to go to sleep.

His not wanting to work with Reading Specialist introduced a whole new issue—the fact that most kids hate being pulled out of the classroom to work with a specialist. I didn't think Eric saw it as a stigma—not yet anyway. He had absolutely no idea his school thought there was something wrong with him. Cary and I never talked about that when either one of the kids was home, not even when we were behind closed doors. That's how scared we were that one of them would overhear us. We never wanted Eric to know because we were worried about how his school's perception of him would affect Eric's perception of himself.

Eric definitely was not unhappy because his school thought he was learning disabled. He was unhappy simply because he wanted to be in his classroom for his favorite activities and I didn't blame him. Unless there really is something wrong with a child that is causing him to struggle, all kids should be able to learn how to read in their classroom.

His unhappiness over being pulled out to do so was yet another reason for us to make fast progress.

Every year, Hallowed School had a special week during which it invited parents to come in and talk about what they did for a living. On the morning of February 6th, it was my turn.

Standing at the front of Eric's classroom, I told the first graders that I had wanted to be a writer from the time I was a kid. I told them it was the best job in the world because you got to meet all sorts of interesting people if you wrote nonfiction, and you got to make up stories you liked if you wrote fiction. I said that, often, fiction was inspired by a writer's real life and that I had just completed a story called *The Unhappy U* that had been inspired by me teaching Eric how to sound out words. Then I read them the whole story. Here is how the story started:

> In the big, local superstore, in the back of aisle three
> Hang a bag of plastic letters waiting to see what they will be.
>
> What are we meant for? Why are we here?
> At the moment, the poor letters find this very unclear.
> They hang in the toy aisle with cars and with things that can fly
> And the children ignore them. They pass them right by.
>
> "What are we used for?" the letters all say.
> "Why don't children love us? Why do they run away?
> We're not meant for eating. Maybe we stick like glue.
> Are we part of a board game? What in the world do we do?"
>
> More than any other letter, /u/ wanted to know,
> "What am I here for? Tell me and let's get on with the show."
> "U" wanted to be important, he wanted to be great
> To find out his real purpose, he simply couldn't wait.

For the sake of time, I will leave out a section of the story and bring you to...

One day, a boy named Eric and his mom stopped to look at the toys just for fun.

"Look." Eric's mom pointed at letters on a water gun box. "These letters spell g-u-n."

Eric liked to play with water guns, his mother she knew.

But he wasn't interested yet in reading and there was nothing she could do.

Eric ignored her and looked at the water gun.

"Can we buy it please mommy? It looks like such fun."

His mom said, "Today we're just looking but look over here

These letters spell t-r-u-c-k, now isn't that clear?"

Eric took no notice, he took not a look.

But inside the bag of letters, /u/ trembled and shook.

"That's it!" he cried out, "Look! Look! Just look!"

The letters glanced where he pointed, and they saw a book.

The book lay in the mom's shopping cart on top of cookies that cost a buck.

The cover had a picture of a backhoe as well as the word, "Truck."

"I get it," said u. "What we do I now see.

We spell out words. We're as important as can be!"

"We make up books and the things people say

And what's inside a box? Why we give it away!

Look at that cereal! The words on the box make it clear

That when people buy granola they aren't getting beer!"

"Oh, I am so happy!" the /u/ said with glee.

"I wanted to be important! I knew I would be!"

As the story went on, the unhappy /u/ went through all sorts of trials and tribulations until it finally got its wish and became important. It also realized all the other letters were important too and that they all needed to work together to make words.

I was surprised when Eric joined me at the front of the classroom and began acting out the characters' actions: He pretended he was the mother pushing a shopping cart in the supermarket. He put magnetic letters up on his classroom's dry erase board. He turned the /u/ upside down to make it look like an /n/ and took it to the sink in the back of the classroom to wash it, just like the boy in the story did.

After I finished reading, the kids all clapped and a few called out, "That was great!"

I was glad they had liked the story, but I was even happier about how actively Eric had participated in my presentation. His days of sitting in the back of the classroom staring at the rug were over!

Since it was raining, there would be no outdoor recess that day. I asked the children if they would like to stay in the school cafeteria after lunch and draw pictures illustrating scenes from *The Unhappy U*. All of them said yes.

In the cafeteria, Eric passed out drawing paper and markers and gave advice to a few children who needed help deciding which scene they would illustrate. I was thrilled to see him continuing to be a star with his classmates.

I was standing to the side, enjoying watching my son, when a boy named Miles walked over to me. With his collared polo shirt and khaki pants, he looked like a waist-high investment banker. "That was a very good story," he said.

His comment surprised me. Miles was not known for being nice. Last year, he had allegedly thrown a chair at the kindergarten teacher. Recently, he had teased Eric's reading partner, Joshua, about his stick-dot level. To retaliate, Joshua's mother had advised Joshua to ask Miles why he still swam in the baby end of the pool.

Miles did not bring out the best in people.

But Miles had just said something kind.

Maybe he wasn't as bad as everyone said.

I smiled at him and said, "Thank you."

Miles turned and looked at Eric, who was happily assisting his classmates at the long cafeteria table. Miles then looked back at me. Expressionless, he said, "Eric is a very low stick dot."

Okay. I guess he *was* as bad as everyone said.

"He is, huh?" I responded. "Why did you feel it was important to tell me that?"

"I don't know."

I did. Miles was jealous. Eric's mommy had just read the class a story that the kids had loved. Eric was a character in the story and, by acting out various scenes, he had helped bring the story to life. And Eric was still in the limelight as he circulated around the cafeteria table helping his classmates find various colors of magic markers and making suggestions about how they could illustrate the scenes. Miles needed to bump Eric back down to his usual place on the reading totem pole so that Miles could feel better about himself.

A little girl from Eric's class was sitting nearby and had overheard our conversation. "I'm a pink stick dot," she said.

"I'm the highest stick dot," Miles shot back.

Notice that these kids had not said, "I am reading pink stick dot books," or "I am reading the highest stick dot level."

They *were* their stick dot colors.

That's how they defined themselves.

I needed to properly define Eric for them. "Eric is not a very low stick dot anymore. Eric can read *Little Bear*."

"That's a purple stick dot in our classroom," Miles replied. "I'm the highest stick dot. I'm the best reader in the class."

"Does that make you a better person than Eric?"

Miles didn't answer.

"Everyone has their strengths and weaknesses," I continued. "You are a better reader at this point, but Eric swims in the deep end of the pool, and he's the fastest runner I've ever seen."

Miles stood there, digesting this information.

"You know," I continued. "It's not nice to tease other people about their stick dot levels."

"I know."

I would have let things drop, except Eric was walking towards us, and I wanted to nip this conversation in the bud. And, so, I told this six-year-old, "Studies have found that reading very early is not related to later academic success."

"I know," Miles said.

He could not possibly have known that.

"In fact," I continued. "Children who read at low stick dot levels in the early grades are often much better readers in third grade than those who are reading at higher levels in first grade because they read for meaning." (I made that up.)

"I know," Miles replied.

"So, come and see me when you're in third grade and we'll see how you and Eric compare then."

"Okay," said Miles and walked away.

I felt terrible about what I had said to Miles and told another mother in the cafeteria about it.

"Don't worry," she laughed. "He deserved it. He'll be fine."

The time had come for the kids to head back to their classroom. As they packed up their drawings and lunchboxes, the assistant principal walked over to me. "Eric is reading," she said. Her tone implied that there was no denying it. "He is really reading."

I was so relieved. Thank God. If she realized that, it meant the school's wanting to evaluate Eric was a thing of the past. Assuming that was the case, I said, "Great! Can we have a meeting to discuss the best way to move him forward?" What I meant was—can we meet and discuss which phonics rules and sight words he needs to know next? I wanted all of us to, finally, be on the same page in terms of what he needed to learn so that the school could teach him some of it.

"The three of us *(She was referring to herself, First Grade Teacher and to Reading Specialist.)* first need to talk to see what we do with this new information, and then we can all meet. Eric still has his evaluation pending."

My heart sank. "Does he really still need the evaluation? He's made so much progress. It doesn't seem necessary to me."

"He still reverses some of his letters," she replied.

"Is that really unusual at his age?"

"We need to see what the evaluation might turn up."

She left and I walked over to Reading Specialist who was picking up a group of students from the cafeteria. Like the rest of the school team, she had never responded to the thank you email I had sent to the principal.

"Did you see my email?" I asked Reading Specialist.

Her response was not exactly a warm one. Looking very skeptical, she said, "How could he have gone from where he was, to reading purple stick dot books?"

I was stunned! She thought I was lying? Why would anyone lie about something like that?

"Phonics," was all I could bring myself to say in response.

That's how he had gone from "where he was," to reading purple stick dot books.

Phonics.

And learning the most common sight words in their order of frequency of use.

Learning both in a systematic way that made sense.

"I suppose it's possible that he's made a huge leap," she said. "I have to see when I read with him this week. Maybe all the things we've been doing have made a difference. But I've been seeing him only twice a week and Susie has only seen him for a week or so."

Yes, but his mommy has been seeing him every day…

―――――――――

The minute Eric arrived home from school, he threw his backpack on the floor and pulled out a book called *Mouse Soup*. "I read this with Susie today! I want to read it to you right away!"

He was so excited that he didn't even take time to walk to the couch. He sat down on the floor just inside our front door, opened the book, and said, "Susie said I should only read the first story in the book. She said the others were too hard for me."

He read the first story beautifully. It was about a mouse who had been caught by a hungry weasel and tried to keep the weasel from cooking him. When he was done, I praised him and moved to stand up. "Where are you going?" Eric asked.

I was puzzled. "Susie said to stop after the first story, right? Didn't she say you shouldn't read any more stories after this?"

"That's what she said at school, but who says we have to listen to her?" Eric said. "We're not at school anymore. We're home now."

He then went on and read the rest of the book.

26

Two weeks ago, I had asked myself whether I was going to try to help fix things for all children, or whether I was going to focus only on Eric's needs.

Two weeks ago, I had known which type of parent I wanted to be—a crusader, an activist, a fighter for justice and the right to read for all.

On February 6, the opportunity presented itself to be that type of parent. That opportunity was the result of Mayor Bloomberg embarking on another round of seemingly endless school reforms. This time, he was going to change the way teachers got tenure; give principals more autonomy; hold schools accountable for student progress; and change how schools were funded. He was not going to do anything to make sure those funds were spent on curriculums that worked.

At the time, my contribution to trying to change things had been writing my blog. After the New York Times reported the upcoming changes, in my blog I had written…

How can politicians be so woefully out of touch?
Posted by **Helicopter Mom**

Why does Bloomberg continually keep "fixing" things that will not solve the problem? How can he and Klein be so woefully out of touch as to what is really wrong with public schools—curriculums that fail to teach children how to read or do math.

Why, oh why, do politicians continually not look at what parents of the children at "good" schools are doing at home? Why do they not realize fuzzy curriculums like Investigations and Balanced Literacy appear to work because the kids at "good" schools are being taught math and reading by their parents?

It's probably because politicians' kids go to private schools and the politicians are able to afford tutors to help their own children. Somehow, I can't imagine Bloomberg learning the eight comma rules so that he could teach them to his seventh grader who never learned them in elementary school and isn't learning them in his high-performing middle school either because the way his seventh grade English teacher teaches grammar is by having the kids in the class read an impenetrable sheet of rules out loud in class. For example: "Use commas between coordinate adjectives that modify the same noun. Do not separate adjectives of unequal importance." The teacher does very little to make those rules come alive and sends home absolutely no homework in them. That is why I translated those for Older Son, and had printed out worksheets on commas and quotation marks the night before Older Son's English midterm. *(I did not use my family's real names in the blog.)*

No, I don't think Bloomberg ever translated obtuse comma rules for his children. He probably paid someone $125 an hour to do that. We were so desperate for Older Son to learn grammar that we actually paid someone $125 an hour last summer. My husband schlepped Older Son uptown two mornings before work (which is all the way downtown in the financial district) and sat with him while he was tutored by a wonderful English teacher from a private school called Dalton. We stopped after two sessions because we couldn't afford it. Freelance journalists who are completing their Ph.D.s do not make a lot of money. Politicians make more. Especially those who have started information service and media empires before turning to politics. They had the time to start those successful businesses since they weren't at home tutoring their kids, or learning their children's science or social studies curriculums in order to be able to quiz them for their exams.

Many parents at Hallowed School and NEST+m talk openly about helping their kids. Others claim their kids do it all themselves. Don't believe them. After his class finished taking its first social studies exam this year, Older Son's social studies teacher asked the class, "How many of your parents know more about the Mayas and Incas than they did before you started studying about them?" Every single child in the class raised his or her hand.

On February 6, Schools Chancellor Joel Klein explained the upcoming reforms to parents at another DOE Community Education Council meeting. Remember, the purpose of these meetings was to "solicit and encourage public comments on issues important to families."

After Klein had finished describing the reforms, Cary publicly commented. He told Klein that the new reforms did not address the biggest problem of all—the fact that New York City schools had bad curriculums and that those bad curriculums appeared to work in "good" schools because of the work parents or tutors were doing with the kids.

Klein responded that curriculums were not important. Getting good teachers into classrooms was what mattered, he said.

"Of course, good teachers matter," Cary replied. "But good teachers need to use effective curriculums. Otherwise, the kids won't learn."

There was some back and forth between the two of them until, finally, Cary told Klein, "You are so busy defending that you are not listening."

Cary was applauded by the hundred-or-so parents in the room.

Klein continued with his prepackaged speech. Soon, it was obvious that the parents had stopped listening to him. At the beginning of the meeting, I had given every parent printouts of the first two posts in my Helicopter Mom blog. Realizing Klein was not listening to their concerns, many parents began reading the handouts.

From where I was sitting, I heard one of Klein's henchmen ask the other: "What are they all reading?"

They were reading my blog. The politicians I addressed in the first post, below, are long gone, but the changes detailed in the post are still needed, 17 years later...

Dear President Bush, Mayor Bloomberg, and Schools Chancellor Klein,

Posted by **Helicopter Mom**

I know you are doing your best to try and improve the performance of all public school children. I commend you for your efforts. I also know things are not going so well for you. I have some behind-the-scenes information that can help you. What follows in this blog is a first-hand look at the time and effort parents all over the city are expending in order to help their children do well in school, and the toll it is taking on our personal and professional lives.

Many of us feel as if we have re-enrolled in elementary or middle school. My husband, who is an attorney, told a client that he is unable to conduct out-of-town depositions next week because that is when his midterms are being held. (*This was posted the week before Jamie's midterms.*) When his client looked at him uncomprehendingly, my husband explained that it is our seventh grader who would actually be taking the tests, but that my husband would be studying elbow to elbow with him, since studying for tests is a skill his progressive elementary school never taught our son.

There are many, many skills his public elementary school—deemed one of the top 200 in the city, by the way—never taught him. Among them were how to do long division and where to put commas in a sentence. As for semicolons, until recently my son had two words for them: "What's that?"

So how did this elementary school become one of the top 200 in the city? It was thanks to the efforts of parents, who had finally caught on to the fact that they needed to either teach their kids at home, or have them tutored for the state math and English tests. (Those scores are the primary benchmark used to determine if a school is one of the top 200.) When my son was in fourth grade, the school's scores improved so much that the principal was promoted and now teaches other principals how to improve their school's scores. What a joke. The principal, wrongly, gave full credit for those scores to herself and the work of her teachers.

At the time those scores were released, I surveyed parents and found that every single child who did well on his or her 4th grade standardized state math test was either tutored, or taught math at home by his or her parents. Children who did not do well had parents who, innocently, believed that the school was teaching the kids what they needed to know. Their children paid for their innocence since, in New York City, children don't just go to their local zoned middle school. Admission to public middle schools is done on a competitive basis and a child's scores on the 4th grade standardized tests play a large part in determining which middle school they will be accepted to.

Not surprisingly, the kids whose parents taught them the concepts that would be on those tests, or who were lucky enough to be able to afford tutors who did that work for them, were accepted into the highest performing middle schools, while those whose parents left their child's education up to their elementary schools are now enrolled in the lower performing ones.

Mr. Mayor, before you make more changes to our school system, I beg you to really look at what makes a difference in how children perform in school. The difference lies in giving each child the individualized help he or she needs via astute teachers who assess children to see what they know, and don't know, and, either give them supplemental help, or inform parents of what type of supplemental work needs to be done with the child at home. (Even the very best teachers in New York City generally have at least 28 kids in a classroom to attend to and are unable to give each child the individual attention he or she needs.) It will make no difference if you take "good" teachers from "good" schools and put them into the "bad" schools, as you plan to do. You are assuming that the low-performing schools have "bad" teachers. You are wrong. One of the best teachers my older son ever had at his "good" school had been hired away from a "bad" one. At her former low performing school, the students often didn't show up at school because of some problem that was happening at home. The parents didn't show up at parent teacher conferences. There is only so much one single teacher, no matter how outstanding she or he is, can do. To ship this teacher back into a low performing school would not change the real problem, the fact that these kids are not getting the support they need at home. Switching teachers from "good" to "bad" schools will not make a dent in the performance of the "bad" schools.

Last November, *The New York Times* ran a front-page article announcing that U.S. schools were "slow in closing gaps between races." It stated that in spite of the president's attempt to leave no child behind, little progress has been made towards closing the performance gap between minority and white students. (The article did name two schools where minority students had made large gains. The principal of one of those schools attributed the gains to after-school tutoring by volunteers in black churches, while the other principal said progress resulted from "focused instruction, frequent diagnostic testing and (no surprise now) several tutoring programs." In schools where children did not receive individual support from either a parent or a tutor, despite what the article called "concerted efforts by educators," the test-score gaps were so large that, on average, Black and Hispanic students in high school were reading and doing arithmetic at the same level as whites in junior high.

That is not true of the Black and Hispanic students at NEST+m, a rigorous K-12 school in New York City with astonishingly high test scores. There, Black and Hispanic children are on par, or ahead of, their white classmates.

It made the front page of *The New York Times* when the chancellor discovered that NEST+m (one of the highest achieving schools in New York City) was interviewing parents and asking them how much support they were willing to provide their children at home before accepting, or rejecting, the children.

My older son is now a 7th grader at NEST+m. During our admissions interview, we were told that a child's success in that school hinges on parents being ready, willing, and able to academically support the child at home. We were asked if we were willing to commit to providing a large level of support. "Definitely," I replied. "We've been doing that with math since third grade." (That's why his test scores were high enough to earn him an interview at NEST+m, an opportunity very few children were given.) A group of NEST+m parents emailed each other after that *Times* article appeared. One of them bristled at the schools chancellor having a problem with the fact that the school chose students with involved and active parents over non-participatory and non-active parents. "Does he not know that the success of a child does not lie solely (with) the school but with the family and guardians involved?" the email asked about Klein. "How ignorant is he? If it were not for the combination of parent/guardian AND school/teacher efforts NEST+m would not have achieved the kind of academic level that it has now."

That truism applies to children of all races at NEST+m. One of my son's closest friends at that school is a Black boy from Harlem. (*That boy went on to attend Stanford, by the way.*) Academically, he outperforms my son. Not surprisingly, his mom is more adamant about, or perhaps is more effective at, being a helicopter mom.

Want proof?

Last fall this boy came to our country house for the weekend. The kids did hours of homework and studied hard for a social studies exam they were having on Monday. Then, since it was a beautiful, sunny Sunday, we took the kids fishing, something my son's friend had never done before. The boy marveled at the beauty of the bay we were at and collected a few lovely beach rocks to bring home as a memory of this outing, which was clearly very special to him.

My heart filled with joy as I listened to him oooh and ahhh at the beauty of his surroundings. A few minutes later, as my husband was showing the boy how to cast out a fishing line, my husband's cell phone rang. It was the boy's mother calling. "I just wanted to make sure he is studying," she said.

"Um, no," my husband replied sheepishly. "It's such a beautiful day that we took them fishing." Silent disapproval came over the line.

Everything you will read in this blog is true.

Read it and weep.

Then please do something to stop the madness happening within our school system since everyone is losing—both the middle class and the poor. Realize that fuzzy curriculums like Investigations for math and Balanced Literacy for reading appear to be effective because parents at the "good" schools using those curriculums are teaching their kids the crucial fundamentals those curriculums leave out. Once those fundamentals are in place, then those curriculums are able to teach children what they were designed to teach. But without those fundamentals, children's performance sinks like a rock. Savvy parents who are tuned in to the right word-of-mouth parenting network know that. Recent immigrants or members of our city and country's lower socio-economic strata do not. They trust that our city's public schools are going to give their kids the fundamentals of a good education. Many of the schools are not doing that.

Mr. President, there are lots of problems with No Child Left Behind, but at least you are trying to give all children the fundamentals they need, and my hat goes off to you for that. If it was not for mandated state testing, I would not have realized how much was being omitted in my older son's elementary school curriculum and would not have known what to supplement at home.

Mr. Mayor and Mr. Chancellor, I am beginning to think that perhaps you honestly do not realize how important fundamentals are. Mr. Chancellor, you are all for the Whole Language-based Balanced Literacy curriculum because of your own personal experience. *(Klein liked the fact that, in Balanced Literacy classrooms, children choose books that interest them to read.)* As a boy, you loved baseball, and you became a reader when someone gave you a book on baseball. But you were able to read it because someone else had already taught you phonics. If that rudimentary information had not been drilled into your head when you were a schoolboy, you would have been as lost as many of our city's children are because they are not getting a systematic exposure to phonics.

Don't believe me? Take a look at the massive amount of research that says so. Then look at why Balanced Literacy appears to work in "good" (read "wealthy" schools)—because parents at those "good" schools are teaching their kids phonics at home.

Please realize that, until you put in effective curriculums, you need to empower immigrants or parents in our country's lower socio-economic strata with the same knowledge and opportunity that informed middle- and upper-class parents have to devote to supporting their children—or to have tutors work with the low-income kids when necessary. If you don't, you will never be able to close the achievement gap that exists between rich and poor schools.

By pointing out the importance of parents, I am not minimizing the work being done by teachers. My 12-year-old son refers to them as the heroes of America and I agree with him. But teachers have to teach the curriculums they are mandated to teach, and they have to teach them to 28 or more kids each day. In the end, it is parents who make the crucial difference. It's time someone had the courage to stand up and speak that truth. I am that person.

Sincerely,

Helicopter Mom

I never intended to be a Helicopter Mom

Posted by **Helicopter Mom**

I did not set out to be helicopter mom. By that I mean a mom who hovers over every single detail involved with helping her children succeed in school. I always thought of myself as a very well-balanced person who had my priorities straight. As a parent, my goal for my children was simple: I wanted them to be happy. In that I have succeeded. I have two healthy wonderful boys—Older Son, age 12, and Younger Son, age 6—both of whom sparkle with joy and vitality and who are a pleasure to be with.

When they were preschoolers, I never pressured either one of them academically. Instead of drilling them on the sounds that letters make, I took my kids to the playground or let them play with blocks or cars or trains at home. When I hired my younger son's preschool teacher to be his babysitter, she suggested I buy some educational games for her to use with him. I demurred. "He's only four years old," I said. "He should just play." (Younger Son, especially, had a real need to build and create things and I wanted him to have the time to engage in that love and need.)

At the time I was a doctoral student in psychology, and my child-rearing decisions were supported by the academic and psychological experts I was coming in contact with.

A school principal told me that the most important thing parents could do to prepare kids for kindergarten was take them to the park or on playdates so that they could learn to get along with other children.

At Teachers College at Columbia University (where I took several courses for my Ph.D.), I heard fellow doctoral students scoffing at a mother who had called the psychology department and asked for a recommendation of someone who could "cognitively stimulate" her toddler.

"Tell her to let him play with blocks," one of the doctoral students had said. "That's what kids really need."

When I interviewed child development researcher Alison Gopnik, Ph.D., author of *Scientist in the Crib*, for a *Parents* magazine article on how to cognitively stimulate your baby, Gopnik told me that parents had taken cognitive research completely out of context. "Normal, middle-class homes are full of all the cognitive stimulation a young child will ever need," she said. She warned that parents had turned cognitive stimulation into a job and were stressing out themselves and their children.

Not me, I thought. My kids were happy. They were smart without being pressured. They were both curious little people who loved to learn. There were no flash cards in my home. Friends and relatives gave our kids electronic games that beeped the sounds of the letters, but I found them totally annoying. They sat unused in the closet. I believed there was no reason for me to teach my kids how to read when they were in preschool. Early reading had not been found to be a predictor of later academic success. Early reading was not helpful, but pushing, I knew, was detrimental. Kids who were forced to learn to read too early risked growing up to hate reading.

My older son had never been pushed to read. I was forced to become a helicopter mom to him because his elementary school was not teaching him other foundational skills—things like math and grammar. But it did teach him how to read. Today, Older Son loves reading and is in the 97th percentile in reading in the country.

His reading ability earned him an invitation to participate in the Johns Hopkins University talent search, so that he—along with other super-bright kids—could be further groomed academically during the summer.

My smart, skate boarding, hockey-playing son proclaimed the kids on the cover of the Johns Hopkins brochure were "dorks." He loudly stated that he didn't want to go to school in the summer.

He was a sixth grader at the time and had just made the transition from a progressive elementary school to an academically rigorous, traditional middle school. The transition was brutal. His every waking moment was taken up with schoolwork, seven days a week. He couldn't have playdates and couldn't participate in after-school activities. He couldn't even watch TV or read a book for pleasure.

He needed, and deserved, a break. He needed, and deserved, a childhood. We knew that if he continued to be pushed the way his middle school was pushing him, he would lose his love of learning. We threw the Johns Hopkins invitation in the garbage. If there was one thing I knew about myself, it was that I was not a pusher.

That was then. This is now.

Now, I have a 6-year-old who is behind the curve in reading.

When he was in kindergarten, I didn't realize how proactive other parents were being in teaching their kids to read.

In kindergarten, Younger Son said, "I want to learn how to read, Mommy, but my school isn't teaching me how to. They tell us to look at the pictures and guess what the words are, but that's not reading, Mommy. How do you read?" I trusted the school would teach him.

Now I know better.

Now I know Younger Son, like most kids, needs to learn systematic phonics in order to learn how to read. Now I know New York City schools do not teach kids that foundational skill. Now I am teaching my son phonics. I have turned to the other mothers for help and advice. They have given it freely. Now there are flashcards in my home. And phonics workbooks. I create phonics Bingo cards in the little spare time I have between supporting Older Son in his rigorous school, and doing everything else that needs to be done in life, at work, and in grad school.

I have become a woman obsessed. I wake up making lists of words that have the long /i/ vowel sound in them. I walk around phonetically sounding out words on street signs and subway ads and urging Younger Son to do the same. I want to bring Younger Son to the same place the other parents have brought their children.

This morning, I had coffee with another mother. Her son is Younger Son's reading partner. They are the two worst readers in the class.

I asked the mother if she would also ask the teacher to teach phonics in the classroom. "She does teach phonics, but what she teaches is way over our kids' heads," she said. The class is currently working on naming all the possible words that have the long /i/ sound, in them including my, height, freight. The short vowel sounds were never taught in class, nor was the silent /e/ rule.

"Face it, we missed the boat," the mother told me. "We should have taught them at home, and we didn't. The ship sailed without us, and we have to do what we can do to help our kids catch up."

I am helping as fast as I can. I have visions of a huge ship filled with hordes of tiny children with their noses in chapter books while my blonde, adorable son waves to them from the desert island he has been stranded on.

If I could, I would keep Younger Son home from school for a few months and teach him to read. We would work on reading and reading only.

But I can't do that.

I work.

And I worry.

And the ship with all those kids reading way above grade level keeps sailing on.

27

For better or worse, all marriages become predictable. You know how, and when, your husband will reach out to show he loves you. You know how he will comfort you when you are upset, and how his face lights up when he is happy. Over time, every couple comes to share glances, words, and expressions that mean something only to the two of them. As they share new life experiences, new words and expressions are added to that language.

Take snorting for example.

Snorting was new behavior for Cary. The first snort had happened a few weeks ago while he was reading *The New York Times*. Specifically, he had been reading the article that had detailed Bloomberg's new school reforms. That article was what had impelled us to try to talk some sense into Joel Klein.

The second snort happened this morning, February 9th. Again, it happened while Cary was reading *The New York Times*.

"Is Klein reorganizing the school system again?" I joked.

"Read this," Cary said. "You're not going to believe it."

He pointed at a headline that said, "Schools Official Deflects Query About Stocks." The article reported that Klein's newly appointed deputy schools chancellor, Chris Cerf, had just given up stock worth millions of dollars in Edison Schools, a private company that was paid to run some public schools and provided after-school tutoring at some failing ones. Today's article revealed that Edison Schools had been paid more than $9.6 million in the 2005-2006 school year **for its tutoring services alone** and that Cerf's shares of stock in the company were worth as much as $6.7 million.

For this entire school year, I had been struggling to understand why NYC public schools would use a curriculum that caused children to become struggling readers. Now, all of the pieces began to fit together in a very disturbing way.

Could politicians really be so corrupt?

Could it be possible that Bloomberg and Klein had paid millions of dollars for a reading curriculum that did **not** teach kids to read so that they could then pay millions of dollars to tutoring companies that taught kids phonics?

Could it be possible that Bloomberg and Klein, or their employees, or golfing buddies, then made millions of dollars from the profits those tutoring companies made? There was a lot of money to be made by **not** teaching children how to read in school: In 2007, the year Eric was in first grade, tutoring was a 4 billion dollar industry. *(By 2023, that figure had reached 25 billion.)*

"Do you think Bloomberg and Klein are screwing up the school system on purpose so that they can make money trying to fix it?" I asked my husband.

The question seemed farfetched.

Impossible.

But one fact could not be overlooked: By screwing up the public school system, Bloomberg and Klein—intentionally, or unintentionally—had cleared a path for their buddies to come in and make a fortune. (Cerf was a longtime friend of Klein's.) The thought seemed too Byzantine, too John Grisham-ish, to be true but, now that had entered my mind, it would not go away.

Cary said either Klein and Bloomberg and their pals were making money from the tutoring being done as a result of bad curriculums, or they were naïve fools who knew absolutely nothing about education and had put blind faith in employees who were clueless about how kids learned to read.

Which scenario would you vote for?

Cary voted for the first one: politicians were corrupt.

I voted for the second: politicians were clueless.

I had spoken to Joel Klein on several occasions last year when I was part of a group of parents who had successfully fought to keep a charter school from being given valuable space in Jamie's public middle school. I had actually really liked the guy. I thought he had a daunting job that he took very seriously and that he was trying hard to do his best to help all New York City children. But he had chosen to listen to the wrong people.

He certainly hadn't listened to Cary at the meeting three days ago. And he hadn't listened to other parents either.

Later that night, I blogged ...

Be careful who you trust

Posted by **Helicopter Mom**

My advice to you, Joel Klein and Mayor Bloomberg? Be careful who you trust. It seems that some of your highly paid employees and consultants may be taking total advantage of you. They are making you look like fools, and they are hurting our children's ability to learn reading, writing, and arithmetic.

Like medical doctors, your credo when it comes to selecting curriculums should be "first do no harm." By putting in ineffective curriculums like Balanced Literacy, you are doing great harm. I worry about all the New York City children you continue to damage day, after day, while you or your buddies or employees continue to make a profit from the children's lack of progress in New York City public school classrooms.

Shame on you.

Here are two more blog posts from that time. They show how our needing to teach our kids so much of what they should have learned in school was affecting me and Cary. Our experience is a window to what many other families all across the country are experiencing...

Valentine's Day

Posted by **Helicopter Mom**

(February 14) If your life is anything like mine—and it probably is if you are reading this blog—then your Valentine's Day will not resemble a scene from a Hallmark movie in spite of your best efforts to be romantic. But if you take a minute to look beneath the frantic busyness of the life that you and your husband share, you might find the love your husband has for you is even stronger than you could have imagined.

However, you have to look—really look—at the ways your husband is saying he loves you. And that may not involve taking you out to a romantic restaurant.

Husband did his best to try and make this Valentine's Day romantic. Two weeks ago, he had asked me if I could meet him for lunch or dinner on that day.

His question showed that he not only remembered Valentine's Day, but that he wanted to take me out to celebrate it. It also put my preference before his. It also acknowledged that, since I work from home and pick up Younger Son at his the school bus stop every day, my workday is very short. Because of that, lunch would not work for me. (I usually eat it standing up in the kitchen.)

If we had a normal life (read: no child enrolled in an academically rigorous middle school and another in a school that was failing to teach him how to read) I would have said, "Dinner."

Instead, I said, "Let's wait and see how much homework Older Son has, or if he has a test the day after Valentine's Day, before we make reservations anywhere. That way we won't be disappointed if we have to cancel."

Turns out Husband is driving Older Son to Brooklyn this afternoon, and picking him up at night, so that Older Son can complete a science project with two of his classmates. Older Son also has a big social studies test tomorrow. (I'll bet his teacher is going out to dinner with her husband tonight. She doesn't have any kids enrolled at NEST+m.)

I told Husband that I don't need to go out to eat on Valentine's Day to know how much he loves me. Husband has already shown me how much he loved me when:

1. After I said I was totally burnt out from helping the kids so much with their schoolwork, he took over helping Older Son prepare for his midterms.

2. This morning, when we both heard Younger Son start throwing up at 5 a.m., Husband leaped out of bed and was the first one to reach him. While I tended to Eric, Husband cleaned up the vomit that was all over the floor.

3. He surprised me with a beautiful arrangement of flowers this morning, right after I got back from putting Younger Son's sheets into the washing machine in the laundry room down the hall from our apartment. The flowers were exactly the kind I like—a small arrangement of wildflowers and miniature roses. For the first ten years of our 17-year marriage, Husband would buy me big, impressive arrangements that really didn't do anything for me. After I told him the truth about what kind of flowers really make me happy, he's made sure to buy what I like, rather than what he thought was more romantic.

4. He went to a lot of trouble to surprise me with those flowers. He'd made a special trip to the florist on his way home from work last night. He left the flowers with the doorman last night and then snuck them into his closet after I had left for the 6 pm stats class I was taking in grad school.

5. Even though he went to the florist, he was home in time for me to go to my class and then he fed the kids and checked Older Son's math homework.

6. He designed and set up a website for me so that I would be able to post this blog.

7. Even though he is swamped with a big case at work, he is leaving the office early today to pick up Older Son and his friends after school and drive them to Brooklyn. Their science project is due the day after tomorrow and tonight is the only time this week that the dad overseeing that project was available. (I guess those parents aren't going out for Valentine's Day either.)

8. He makes me laugh. Just this morning he snorted while reading *The New York Times*. This is new behavior for him that means he is reading an article about Bloomberg and Klein making some other ineffective change to New York City public schools. Yesterday he snorted because (true story) they are opening a public school that will teach half of its classes in Arabic. (When Husband told this to someone at Younger Son's school, they refused to believe him.)

This morning, when he snorted again, I steeled myself for another crazy plan from our mayor or schools chancellor. Husband held up the newspaper and appeared to be reading the lead article: "Bloomberg has done away with teaching math and reading in public schools. He says the kids learn it better at home anyway."

I realized he was kidding. Husband and I laughed and laughed. I hope that you and your husband find time to laugh together today. The ability to laugh is what is helping me and my husband survive the brutal work load helping our kids do well in school has placed on us.

Being able to laugh helps us remain close, even though we don't do the traditional things that are supposed to bring you close as a couple, like go to the movies or out to dinner. We don't even have time to watch a TV show together.

But we do love each other, and we both know it.

In memory of Celia Rose
Posted by **Helicopter Mom**

(February 16) Two years ago, over February break, 7-year-old Celia Rose FitzGerald—a second grader at a downtown public school and a student at the Lee Strasberg Theater and Film Institute—went on a ski vacation with her parents and 4-year-old sister.

At her Saturday acting class, Cece told her instructor that she wouldn't be there the following Saturday, gave her a hug, and said, "Save me a lollipop."

A week later, Cece (as everyone called the joy-filled little girl), died in a skiing accident. She left a huge hole in her school community, and in her family's heart.

Imagine. Her family went on a happily anticipated ski vacation with their exuberant 7-year-old child and came home with her dead body.

The sheer horror of that has never left me. It probably never will. I will probably remember Celia Rose, and her family's grief, every winter break for as long as my kids are in school.

This coming week, New York City public schools are closed for winter break.

This coming week marks the two-year anniversary of little Cece's death.

This coming week, as we vacation with our kids, let's allow Cece's tragic death to help us remember what is most important—our kids are alive and well. They are with us. We can reach out and hug them. That is what matters most. Not the color of their stick dots. Not their ability to count by doubles, or to recite The Bill of Rights (as Older Son is being required to do in his social studies class), or put commas in the right place in a sentence.

This winter break, consider putting away all schoolwork.

I just stood up and pulled *Green Eggs and Ham* out of the suitcase I have packed for our ski vacation in Vermont.

Younger Son can make progress in reading next week.

This week, I will read to him only at bedtime and only for the sheer joy of it. This week, I'm going to ski with him and play with him in the snow. I'm going to buy him a lollipop and look strangely sad as he eats it, since I will have bought him that lollipop in honor of Celia Rose.

Bloomberg tells parents: You are responsible for the education of your children

Posted by **Helicopter Mom**

(March 5) Husband snorts as he reads *The New York Times*. Loyal readers, by now you know what that means. Bloomberg and Klein are at it again.

Turns out, the *Times* has compiled an article from remarks Bloomberg made on his weekly radio show and during visits to two churches. The paper noted that "while his overarching goal seemed to be to mend fences with parents, Mr. Bloomberg also offered some tough talk about the need for parents to take responsibility for the education of their children."

Please excuse me while I choke.

I couldn't be any more responsible for the education of my kids without being their actual classroom teacher.

"If your child is going to do well, parents have to be involved," he said.

No kidding.

If I had left the teaching of reading up to Eric's school, he would still not know how to read.

Bloomberg also stated that, "It's the teachers who are the professional educators, but it's the parents who have the children most of the day, most of the year."

And that's when we are supposed to teach them how to read, and do column addition, and write their way out of a paper bag since most NYC public schools are failing to do so.

Remember when we thought that being an involved parent meant baking cupcakes for school bake sales, volunteering at fund raisers, and attending parent teacher conferences?

Those days are over.

We've thought so for a long time.

Now the mayor has publicly said so.

Now an involved parent is his or her child's teacher.

As my cousin, a child psychologist, recently said: The world of education has irrevocably shifted.

It has placed the entire weight of properly educating children squarely on parents' shoulders.

28

I had spent weeks getting ready for this moment.

I had scoured the internet and the shelves in various bookstores throughout Manhattan looking for workbooks with at least a few good pages on digraphs. I had created digraph Bingo games consisting of words beginning with /ch/, /sh/, /th/ and /wh/. Because I had not been able to find any early readers focusing on digraphs, I had pored through Dr. Seuss books, line-by-line, looking for words that began with them. I had found enough to give us something to work with. I was ready and raring to go.

Eric was not.

He was exhausted.

As I had feared, Extended Day had extended his day much too much. Eric's bus stop was almost the very last one on his route, and his bus always got stuck in Manhattan's rush hour. That meant the bus didn't drop him off until 5:15 at the earliest. He then needed to unwind, play, and have dinner. He didn't start his schoolwork until 7:00 p.m. At that point, he needed to do his homework and then do a reading lesson with me. He drooped like a parched plant in need of water by the time he got to my lessons. It seemed useless to try to teach him something new when he was so tired. But he needed to learn digraphs.

Imagine my surprise when I realized he already knew them! His knowledge wasn't 100 percent solid, but it was pretty good.

"Did you learn these in school?" I asked.

"With Reading Specialist," he replied.

Hallelujah! I was so happy she had taught him something! But why hadn't she told me she was working on digraphs with him? Why hadn't she told me she was moving him ahead in his lessons and that his homework with short vowels in Explode the Code Book 1 ½ was just to reinforce what he already knew? I asked Eric more questions and realized something that was even more surprising.

When Eric had initially been labeled "at risk," his teacher had told me that the reading specialist would be doing a "push in" with him in the classroom. All along, I had thought she was working with him one-on-one and targeting what he needed to learn most. Only now did I learn that Eric had been placed into a group of kids who had been working with the reading specialist since the beginning of the year. Some of them had been working with her since kindergarten. The group was working on digraphs, and that meant Eric was working on digraphs too. The fact that he had been put into a group of kids who were more advanced explained the much-too-hard sight words Reading Specialist had sent home earlier in the year. Instead of giving Eric the words he needed, she had sent home the words the group was memorizing. I wish she had explained all of that and that she had told me she was teaching him digraphs. I would have been thrilled to know that, and it would have saved me a lot of work.

Because Eric wasn't totally solid with digraphs yet, I spent our next few lessons trying to get him to complete some digraph worksheets. But he was usually too tired. Often, he would ask if he could "just read." Seeing how exhausted he was, that is what we did.

Eric began reading out loud from the Dr. Seuss books I had found at the East Hampton Library. He read the digraphs in *One Fish Two Fish*. Then he started *Fox in Socks*. When he got to page 15, he moaned, "Oh God. Was this book written to torture children?" He absolutely hated it and I didn't blame him. Not only was the book very difficult, but there was no story line. It went like this:

> Chicks with bricks come
> Chicks with blocks come
> Chicks with bricks and
> Blocks and clocks come.

And...

> Clocks on fox tick
> Clocks on Knox tock.
> Six sick bricks tick
> Six sick chicks tock

"The book did come with a warning from the author," I said. I showed him the opening page where it said, "Take it slowly. This book is dangerous."

"It's not dangerous," Eric said. "It's terrible."

I decided not to torture him with it anymore and we began working our way through *Bartholomew and the Oobleck*. I read him the hard words and he read the words he could sound out or knew by heart, as well as the sight words he was working on. That book was great for reinforcing "do," "down," and "out" because those words appeared repeatedly in the story.

When we were done with that book, he began *Green Eggs and Ham* which was great practice for the words do" and "could" and "would."

"This is easy!" Eric exclaimed. He was relaxed and happy as he read:

> Do you like green eggs and ham?
> I do not like them, Sam-I-am.
> I do not like green eggs and ham.
> Would you like them here or there?
> I would not like them here or there.
> I would not like them anywhere
> I do not like green eggs and ham.
> I do not like them, Sam-I-am.

I wanted to put flowers on Dr. Seuss's grave. Except for *Fox in Socks*, his books were absolutely amazing for practicing early sight words and phonics rules.

Turns out, that was no accident. Dr. Seuss had written his books expressly for that purpose. Believe it or not, the whole Dr. Seuss phenomenon happened because of a 1954 article in Life magazine examining why so many children were having trouble learning to read. That article was written 70 years ago and it could have been written today.

The story described parents crying in "dismay" because their children could not read or spell. It said, "Many a college has blamed high schools for passing on students with average or better I.Q.s who cannot read adequately to study college subjects; high schools have had to give remedial reading instruction to boys and girls who did not learn to read properly in elementary school; the sixth grade teacher has blamed the fourth grade teacher; the fourth, the first; and all the teachers have now and then blamed parents."

The article found fault with the whole word/look-say method of teaching reading. It also said that part of the problem was that kids were not motivated to learn to read because the Dick and Jane books were so boring. It suggested that a whimsical author like Dr. Seuss (who had already published some books) would be better suited for writing a children's primer. The director of Houghton Mifflin's educational division thought that was a great idea and he asked Dr. Seuss to do it. He gave Dr. Seuss a list of the 348 words the average six-year-old should know and told him to choose 225 of them for a story.

Seuss thought the assignment would be easy, but it took him a year-and-a-half to find a way to rhyme all of those words and write an entertaining story to boot. Another reason it took him so long was because his heart wasn't in it. That's because he was a strong opponent of the look-say method of teaching reading. He thought the lack of a focus on phonics was why so many kids were illiterate. That is why his books also included so many words kids could easily sound out in his books.

His first commissioned sight word book was The Cat in the Hat. It was a runaway bestseller. Dr. Seuss's career took off, and the rest is history. To this day, his books are among the few that give kids a chance to both sound out words and to practice frequently used sight words.

I soon saw that silent /e/ words were making very frequent appearances both in the stories Eric was bringing home from school, and in Dr. Seuss books. Even though Eric had memorized some words that followed the silent e rule—words like "Jane," "like" and "home"—any time he came across a new silent /e/ word in a story, he would be stumped. I had done a lot of research on how to teach him that rule and was almost done preparing the materials I was going to use to do so. The timing was perfect for me to start teaching him.

Turns out, the timing was more perfect than I realized. The next day, I was volunteering for lunch duty at his school. After I was done supervising the kids in the cafeteria, Eric took me to his classroom to show me the building he had constructed out of blocks during choice time. I oohed and aahhed over his building but was more excited to see a list of silent /e/ words hanging on the wall.

Did you hear what I just said?

There was a list of silent /e/ words hanging on the wall!

YIPPEE!!!!

That meant THE CLASS WAS WORKING ON SILENT E WORDS! And not in the helter-skelter way they had done in the beginning of the year when silent /e/ words like Pete had been lumped together with works like me, flea, and glee. The list hanging on the wall now was clearly intended to teach only the silent /e/ rule. It consisted of word pairs like this:

can/cane
pin/pine
pet/Pete

Excited to see what he had learned in the classroom, I pointed at the word Pete, and asked, "What's that word?"

"Pet," said Eric.

Oy.

That was worrisome. His teacher had, clearly, taught silent /e/ to the class. Why had Eric not learned it? *(Next month, his teacher would tell me that Eric had not been in class when that lesson was taught. He had been pulled out to work with Reading Specialist. The teacher had done only one lesson on the silent e rule and Eric had missed it. But I did not know that at the time and, so, thought the problem lay with my son.)*

It was clear that I needed to teach Eric the silent /e/ rule. He needed be awake and alert for those lessons. Alert and awake was not going to happen if I couldn't start teaching him until 7 p.m.

On February 27th, I emailed Eric's teacher and told her I was pulling Eric out of Extended Day. Within a few hours, Susie called to ask me to keep him in it. I also received an email from the school social worker saying she wanted to meet with me. That email meant the school was setting the evaluation in motion. (Before a school does an evaluation, a social worker needs to get something called a "social history." The social worker will ask parents about a child's mental, physical, and emotional development, as well as about any factors at home might be impeding the child's progress in school.)

Three weeks ago, on the day I had read *The Unhappy U* to Eric's class, I had asked both Susie and Reading Specialist for a meeting so that we could discuss which phonics rules and sight words Eric needed to learn next and who would be teaching them to him.

That meeting had never happened. I did not respond to the email from the social worker. Instead, I emailed the school team asking if we could meet to discuss how we could work together to move him forward.

―――

That meeting happened on March 12th. I thought we were meeting to come up with constructive ways we could all work together as a team to ensure Eric's continued progress. But that was not the reason the school team called the meeting. What Eric needed to learn next was not even mentioned.

Instead, the meeting we had was a required part of the evaluation process. In it, each member of the school team recounted what she had worked on with Eric and why she thought an evaluation was necessary. There were two main reasons:

<u>Reason #1</u>: "He still has those funny reversals," Susie said. "Sometimes he reads 'was' as 'saw.'"

But reversals were normal at his age.

<u>Reason #2</u>: "He may have an issue with phonemic awareness," said Speech Therapist.

Because Eric sometimes misheard sounds in spoken words, he had been working with the school's speech therapist on phonemic awareness. Phonemic awareness is the ability to recognize the sounds in spoken words. Eric did not have a big problem with that, but he did mishear some words. For example, when he first began working with Reading Specialist, he had heard the /dr/ sound as /gr/. He had pronounced drawer as "grawer" and drool as "grool." That specific problem had been rectified, but he continued to, sometimes, mishear other sounds. For example, he had recently thought the word elephant was elethant.

"Poor phonic awareness may be why he mispronounces some words," Speech Therapist said, referring to his previous, incorrect pronunciation of drawer.

"But he mispronounces just a few words," I said. "Don't all little kids mispronounce some words? Isn't that normal?" *I knew phonemic awareness was important: the National Reading Panel had identified as one of the five essential components of reading instruction. But, at the time, I did not know that phonemic awareness was something that should be explicitly taught in kindergarten and first grade. It was not a disorder Eric should be evaluated for.*

"It may be normal, or it may be an issue for Eric," she replied. "Lack of phonemic awareness is a large cause of reading difficulties."

So was a reading curriculum that taught kids to read by looking at pictures, instead of at words.

Cary put his hand on my knee. He could tell I was upset and might say something I would regret.

"Thank you," he said to the assembled educators. "We will think about it and get back to you."

"We have to do it," Cary said as we headed for the subway. "If we don't let them evaluate him, they will always think something is wrong with Eric. An evaluation is the only way we can prove the problem is with the school and not with him."

I stopped dead in my tracks. I could not believe what my husband was saying. "You want Eric to be evaluated so that we can prove to the school that *there is nothing wrong with him*?"

Cary nodded. "I know it sounds crazy. I know most families have evaluations to prove something is wrong with their kid. We need to do it to prove that there is something wrong with the *school*. It's the only way they will believe us. It's the only way things will change."

Almost everyone I talked to about the evaluation agreed with Cary. Almost everyone said I should let the school evaluate Eric.

"I've been fighting for years to have my kid evaluated for dyslexia and they won't do it," said the mom who had backed me up at the CEC meeting with Daria Rigney. "If they are willing to evaluate your kid, you should definitely take advantage of it. It will get your son services at the school. Most parents have to really fight to get services for their children."

"There is nothing negative about an evaluation," said my cousin, the child psychologist. "Most people are doing everything possible to get their kid evaluated. You get to take the SATs untimed!" She said this in the same tone of voice you would use to say, "You get the Holy Grail!"

Do you remember Learning Disabled Mom? Back in November, she had wondered if her son had been labeled learning disabled because Hallowed School had not taught him how to sound out words. She had wondered if, maybe, there was nothing wrong with her son.

That thought had been too horrible for me to contemplate at the time, and it must have been too horrible for her to contemplate as well. Even though she now knew the school did not teach explicit, systematic phonics, she still fully supported the school. "Think of it as the school trying to help," she said when I asked for her opinion about the evaluation. "I'm surprised at the lengths they are going to. Everyone else I know had to fight for an evaluation. Why are they pushing one on you?"

"It has to be my blog," I said. "I am publicly posting about what is happening. I think they want to do the evaluation so they can say something is wrong with Eric, and not with them. I'm afraid they'll unearth every stone, looking for something that could be a problem when it really may not be."

"Be careful with the blog," she replied. "You are right about the school not teaching the kids. Every mother I've talked to is teaching her kid to read at home. I know you are trying to make things better for all kids with that blog, but other people's kids are not your problem. I hate myself for giving this advice but, when my kids needed help, I went in very quietly and made sure to never rock the boat. I've always been very polite. I've never questioned anything about the school, and I've always gotten my kids what they needed. You need to play the game. Stop being a muckraker. Don't be too concerned about the system because that could hurt your child."

Wow.

She had "always gotten her kids what they needed?"

Did she not remember that there was a huge probability that her son had been labeled learning disabled simply because the school had not taught him how to read?

The system had not helped her child.

It had hurt him.

And it had hurt mine too.

The system had failed to teach him how to read.

If that wasn't hurting a child, I didn't know what was.

Out of all the moms that I talked to, only one said we should be very careful about having Eric evaluated. Her son was in a higher grade at Hallowed School, and she had allowed the school to evaluate him when he was younger. He had been having trouble learning how to read. The evaluation had found a very slight issue with language processing that may, or may not, have been causing his reading difficulty. She and her husband had allowed the school to label their child learning disabled, and he had been working with Reading Specialist for a few years now.

The mother told me that being labeled learning disabled had made her son feel less than. "It really affected his self-esteem. It was the worst thing we could have done," she said. Her gut told her that there was really nothing wrong with her son, and that the school had made him feel not capable for no reason. "Evaluations are subjective," she said, "and I feel like the school was looking to find a problem."

That last comment echoed my biggest fear about the evaluation. I was afraid the school team would keep looking and looking for the slightest issue so that they could say something was wrong with Eric and not with their teaching methods. And so, I continued to put off the evaluation.

The permission form for the evaluation had arrived in the mail weeks ago. I had stuck it on the very top shelf of my closet to ensure the kids would never see it and had continued doing everything in my power to help Eric make progress.

But the school's strong conviction that something might be wrong caused me to keep a laser-sharp eye out for any sign of trouble. I remembered that Eric had not learned the silent /e/ rule when his teacher taught it in class. *(That's what I thought at the time. I did not yet know he had not been in the classroom when his teacher taught the class the rule.)* I worried every time Eric read a word backwards. He still frequently read "on" as "no." And he began doing something new —"reading" words that were different than the words on the page. In one story, instead of reading the word "children" he said "kids." In another one, instead of "pretty," he said "beautiful" and, instead of "dark," he said "black."

That was so worrisome, that I emailed Reading Specialist about it.

"What do those substitutions mean?" I asked. "What is that a sign of?"

She never replied. *(Those substitutions meant Eric was still guessing what words could be, using context or the pictures to help him. If you remember from Chapter 5, Whole Language and Balanced Literacy do not care if a child reads a word correctly, as long as the word the child "reads" has the same meaning as the actual word on the page. In Balanced Literacy, if the child reads "horse" instead of "pony," the teacher will accept "horse" as correct. To me, however, his using synonyms for the words on the page was weird and I couldn't understand why he was suddenly doing it.)*

Then, one afternoon, Eric drew two stick figures on his painting easel. They were supposed to be me and him. The stick figure of the little boy had a talking circle coming out of its mouth, the way cartoons do. In the talking circle, Eric had written, "I love you Mommy."

But this is what those words looked like:

> M ʊoy ǝvol I
> ommy.

The top line was written completely backwards. The y and e were also flipped in the wrong direction. The second line—"ommy"—was written correctly.

I thought he had written backwards on purpose. "Wow," I said. "How did you do that?"

"What do you mean?"

My blood ran cold. Eric had no idea he had written "I love you M" backwards.

That was a problem.

A BIG problem.

"You wrote the first line totally backwards," I said in a lighthearted tone, as if he had done something fun and interesting.

"I did?" Eric squinted at the letters but didn't seem to realize there was anything wrong.

He picked up the eraser, but I stopped him. "Leave it," I said, keeping my voice as natural as possible. "What you did is really cool. I want Daddy to see it."

Eric put down the eraser and picked up a piece of chalk. On the other side of the easel, he wrote, "I love you Mommy," correctly.

I nodded. "Those letters are going in the right direction."

I didn't say anything more.

I didn't want Eric to sense my concern.

Writing backwards was not normal.

Not realizing you had done so was even worse.

Feeling stunned, the way you do after you witness a terrible accident, I walked into the bedroom and retrieved the evaluation permission form from the depths of my closet.

It was time to learn whether there was something wrong with my son.

It was time to see if the school had been right all along.

29

It took a month for the school to complete Eric's evaluation. Cary and I never used the word "evaluation" with Eric. We told him that we wanted him to continue getting speech services in school and that the Department of Education required all kids who got speech services to have the equivalent of a check-up. "They just want to make sure that there isn't something else that maybe they should be working on with kids," I said. That made sense to him, and he didn't ask any questions about it. I was glad that Cary and I had made sure to never talk about the evaluation while the kids were anywhere near us. Even while he was being evaluated, Eric had no idea the school thought there was something wrong with him.

But I knew. During that long, long, long month of waiting, not a day passed that I did not wonder what direction our life was going to take.

Were we going to Holland or were we going to Italy?

If something was wrong with Eric, I would embrace life in Holland. I would become fully informed about his learning disability and I would help him in every way I could.

But, in my heart, even with his backwards writing, I still believed we belonged in Italy. The main sign that a child had a learning disability was an inability to make progress. Eric had made—and continued to make—great progress.

We were now working on silent /e/. I had introduced the rule with flashcards alternating short and long /a/ words: the flashcard for the word "can" was followed by a flashcard for "cane"; cap was followed by cape; mad was followed by made, and so on. After Eric had read all the flashcards, we played a short and long /a/ Bingo game that I had created for him. He learned long /a/ easily, so I didn't have him do any worksheets.

The next day, we reviewed the long /a/ flashcards. He read them all correctly, so I moved on to teaching him long /i/ using flashcards that alternated short and long /i/ words. The flashcard for "Tim" was followed by a flashcard for "time"; "kit" was followed by "kite"; "pin" was followed by "pine," etc. After that, we played short and long /i/ Bingo.

The following day, we moved on to the next vowel. By the end of the week, he had mastered all five of the long vowel sounds and began reading Dr. Seuss's *Cat in the Hat*:

The Cat in the Hat, by Dr. Seuss

"The sun did not shine.

"It was too wet to play.

"So we sat in the house

"All that cold, cold, wet day.

"I sat there with Sally.

"We sat there, we two.

"And I said, "How I wish

"We had something to do!"

The book was 61 pages long. Over the next few days, Eric easily read all the short vowels and blends in the book, as well as the digraphs (fish, dish, wish) and words with y at the end of a word (sunny, funny). Sight words like "down" and "little" were also no problem. The sight word "should" was hard for him, so I added "should" to his list of sight words.

The book was great for reinforcing his silent /e/ lessons because it contained lots of silent /e/ words: cake, rake, shine, like, made, games, bite, tame. A few of those words were a little tricky for him, but any time he came to a word he didn't know, he would put his hand over my mouth to make sure I didn't tell him what it was. He wanted to figure out the words on his own.

I tried having him read some of the books he brought home from school, but they continued to be harmful since their leveling (level of difficulty) continued to be driven by the number of words on a page and the size of the font. It had nothing to do with which phonics rules or sight words the kids had learned.

One day, Eric began reading a book called *Guard the House, Sam*. That book was a yellow stick dot, which was several levels *lower* than *Little Bear*, which Eric had read beautifully. Since it was a lower level, *Guard the House, Sam* should have been significantly easier. It was very hard for a child at Eric's stage of reading. Yet, Eric read the following...

> Rosie's dog Sam loved staying home alone.
>
> Guard the house, Sam!" Rosie always said.
>
> Guarding the house was what Sam did best.

So what's the problem if he read the words?

As he read, **he was looking at his feet** and not at the page.

That meant his teacher had read this book with him in class and he had memorized it. He had no idea how to actually read the words on the page. Once again, instead of "reading" the words, he was reciting them from memory. From then on, we permanently ditched the school's leveled books and stuck with Dr. Seuss and other books I found for him in the library.

By the end of March, Eric had mastered silent /e/ and I used *The Cat in the Hat* to decide what his next phonics rule should be. That book had lots of words with /ea/ in them, like "near" and "fear." Those are called vowel digraphs—the first vowel makes its long (or "alphabet") sound and the second vowel remains silent.

I began teaching Eric the /ea/ sound. He worked this way through the /ee/ and /ea/ pages in *Explode the Code Book 3* and read a Little Critter book called *Just Me and My Puppy* that was full of "ea" and "ee" words. For a few nights in a row, we played an /ee/ and /ea/ Bingo game that I made him using the lists of /ee/ and /ea/ words in the Phyllis Schlafly book I had ordered last summer when I first realized there was a problem with the way Eric's school was teaching reading. (That book had ended up just being full of word lists.)

With each passing day, we were one step closer to Italy.

At the beginning of April, however, Eric's school gave us what appeared to be an itinerary for Holland. It sent home a flier about an all-day symposium for parents of children with learning disabilities. That worried me. I figured his school would not have sent home that flier unless the evaluation had already found something wrong.

I registered for the conference. If my son was learning disabled, I would go to any, and every, conference I heard about. I would do everything I could to help him.

A week after registering for the conference, I received word that Eric's evaluation was finished. We would be meeting with the school on Friday, April 20th, to get the results.

The conference for parents of children with learning disabilities was the day after that—Saturday April 21st.

On Friday, I would know the direction our life was taking. On Saturday, I would either be at Eric's hockey game or at a symposium for parents of children with learning disabilities.

If there was something wrong, I would humbly apologize to the school for not believing them sooner.

If nothing was wrong, I would have proof that the school was guilty of educational malpractice.

By the way...

The name of the conference for parents of children with learning disabilities was...

"Parents: The Essential Piece for Student Success in School."

"What Eric knew how to do, he did very well and took into the highly superior range," the school psychologist said. "The things he couldn't do, were simply because he hadn't been taught how to do them."

I sagged into my chair with relief.

Eric had aced his evaluation. There was nothing wrong with him. His subscores in all categories of his evaluation were "above average" or "superior," including phonemic awareness.

The school had thought poor phonemic awareness was Eric's biggest problem, meaning the biggest issue getting in the way of him being able to read at grade level in school. (Remember, he was reading much better at home.) When the high phonemic awareness score was read out loud, Cary gave the principal a pointed look.

She shrugged her shoulders, as if to say, "I don't get it."

The only "issue" found was that his reading performance was not as high as it should have been, given his high IQ.

No surprise there.

It was also no surprise that not having been taught certain things had affected his performance on the IQ test. For example, his score on a math subtest was lower than it would have been if he had known what a subtraction sign was. When the psychologist expressed surprise at his not knowing the subtraction sign, Eric's teacher said, "We don't use the minus sign in the classroom. We use the words 'take away,' so he's never seen a subtraction sign."

I was happy about her honesty and glad that my paranoia that the school would go out of its way to find something wrong with him had been unjustified. These people were operating with the best intentions.

I had not told the school I had agreed to the evaluation because Eric had written "I love you mommy" backwards. I wanted to see if, on its own, the school would find some reason for him to have done this. In the meantime, I had researched backwards writing and learned that it was perfectly normal for children this age. It is called "mirror writing" because the letters are reversed but are correct when looked at in a mirror. Some people, most famously Leonardo Da Vinci, remain comfortable with it into old age.

(Da Vinci used mirror writing when he was writing notes to himself. Some people think this might have been because he was making it harder for people to steal his ideas. When he was writing something he wanted other people to read, he wrote normally.)

"Well, that was great news," I said. "Thank you." I moved to stand up.

"Because his reading performance does not match his IQ, we are classifying him as learning disabled," the principal said.

My knees literally gave way and I fell back into my chair. "What do you mean you're classifying him as learning disabled? School Psychologist just said there were no issues. So, why would you classify him as learning disabled?"

"Because his reading performance does not match his IQ," the principal said again. "That is the definition of a learning disability—a child's performance in school does not match his level of intelligence."

But his "reading performance" at home was great. It appeared to be much worse in school because the school assessed him based on whether he could read one of those ridiculous leveled books. Those books assessed how well kids could guess, not which foundational phonics rules they had mastered. That's why Eric was still stuck at two reading levels below purple, even though he had been able to read purple stick dot books like *Little Bear* and *Mouse Soup*.

"No way," I said. "I am not going to let you label my kid learning disabled. He is not learning disabled."

"There's nothing wrong with the words 'learning disabled,'" First Grade Teacher said in a reassuring tone. "When I hear those words, I just think that a child has potential but isn't reaching it in the classroom and needs extra help."

"But the reason Eric is not reaching his potential is **not** because he is **learning disabled**. You just told us there is nothing wrong with him."

"If you want him to continue getting services at school, he needs to be classified as learning disabled," the principal said.

If this was a movie, and I was the hero of that movie, I would have stood up and given these people a piece of my mind. I would have told them how wrong their teaching methods were and how those teaching methods had harmed my child.

I would have stormed out of the room as the theme from *Rocky* swelled in the background. I would have swooped into the classrooms and rescued all the other children who were being evaluated because the school thought there was something wrong with them. I would have started my own school. My school would have taught systematic phonics and the joy of literacy would have shone like a beacon throughout Manhattan.

But this was not a movie, and I was not a hero.

I was just a very upset and very tired mom.

Tired to the bones tired.

I sighed.

I have not yet told you this part of the story: Cary's law firm was on the verge of disbanding. He was looking for another job, and not having any luck. (Maritime lawyers were not in great demand.) Soon, we might be living solely on my freelance income, which would barely cover rent and food. It would not cover the mortgage payments on our house. We had two college tuitions looming in our future, and my school loans to pay off. We needed help. I needed help teaching Eric so that I would have the time to write more articles to make more money.

As if she had read my mind, the principal said, "He would have SETSS three times a week next year to work on his writing."

At that time, I still thought the initial "S" in SETTS stood for "supplemental," as opposed to "special" as in "special ed." Eric could certainly use supplemental support. He needed to work on his spelling and on writing neat and clear sentences and paragraphs. Imagine if this team taught him what he needed to learn. It had happened with digraphs. It could happen again.

The school now had definitive proof that the problem, all along, had been with the Lucy Calkins/Teachers College curriculum, and not with my son. Because of that, the school might do a better job next year. By turning down their help, I would be saying that they did not know how to help my son. I would be saying they did not know how to teach effectively. That was true, but communicating it so blatantly was bound to cause hurt feelings and friction going forward.

Everyone was silent. The sound of the wall clock's tick-tock, tick-tock was audible as the principal, assistant principal, first-grade teacher, speech therapist, reading specialist, school psychologist, and the social worker waited for my decision. My husband waited as well. He knew the burden of teaching Eric would fall on me if we turned down the SETSS services, so he was letting me decide what to do.

I thought of the advice I had been given: be grateful for any services the school provides, other moms had told me. Parents fight hard to get their kids those services.

Eric's school was offering me those services on a silver platter.

I longed for those services to be effective. I longed to have time to enjoy my child's childhood and not spend almost every moment I had with him teaching him subjects he should have learned in school. If there was a chance the school could help him next year with spelling and writing and, therefore, free up time I could spend enjoying my son, I would let them do it.

And so, I allowed the school to label my son learning disabled.

Typing those words years later brings tears to my eyes.
I am still ashamed of what I allowed them to do.

Cary and I walked out of the principal's office accompanied by the school psychologist and the social worker.

In the hallway, I turned to the psychologist and asked, "Did I do the right thing?"

"Yes," she said. "The more support he gets, the better. He, clearly, isn't getting what he needs in the classroom. He should have been taught what a minus sign is."

"I could work with him at home."

"You shouldn't have to."

"It's terrible how much parents in the city have to do to support their kids in school," the social worker said. "Unbelievable. I live in Chappaqua and have four kids. (Chappaqua is the upscale Westchester town where Bill and Hillary Clinton reside.) One of my kids is at Duke, one is at the University of Michigan, and I have twins at Greeley High School. We're lucky to live in a good school district. I didn't do anything with any of my kids when they were in school. Nothing."

"We need to move," I said.

"You should," she replied, quite seriously. "You need to get into a good school system."

At a conference I would soon attend, this is what a teacher in the excellent Scarsdale, New York school system had to say about good schools: "If you want to find a good school system, look for the system that has the most mothers with Ph.Ds. in it."

Those moms were either teaching their kids at home, or they knew how to get quality curriculums into their kids' schools so that all kids could learn.

There must be a lot of moms with Ph.Ds. in Chappaqua and Scarsdale.

There must NOT be a lot of moms with Ph.Ds. in New York City.

I say that because, on April 28th, nine days after Eric was labeled learning disabled, *The New York Times* reported that many of the most dedicated, crusading parents in New York were giving up the fight to help make New York City public schools better.

Almost no parents were running for election to Community Education Councils, the only place where parents allegedly had a voice in what was happening in the schools. (The CEC meetings were where Daria Rigney and Joel Klein had so blatantly ignored what parents were telling them.)

Parents were "fuming that the councils have no real authority, no power to institute policy and no influence with the Department of Education," the *Times* said. They feel, "participation is pointless ... because the Department of Education did not listen to their complaints."

The fact that even the most active and involved parents are giving up the fight is "an indication of how bad things are," said Tim Johnson, the chairman of the Chancellor's Parent Advisory Council. "I think, over all, the Department of Education really doesn't want parents at the table advising them on much of anything. Nothing (the parents) do seems to get any attention."

You would think the message that aware parents were educating their children at home would have gotten through to *someone* at the DOE by now.

At a recent CEC meeting, it had been announced that our principal had gotten a $5,000 bonus because of the school's high state math test scores and the assistant principal had gotten $2,500. The mom who had supported me in trying to convince Daria Rigney that Hallowed School did not teach systematic phonics had stood up after the bonuses were announced and said, "Hey, the parents at Hallowed School are all tutoring their kids at home. Do you think we could get a piece of that bonus?"

I had laughed when the mom told me what she had done, but the fact that so many parents were teaching their kids at home was not funny. Imagine how different our lives would be—how much more time we parents would have to enjoy our children—if schools actually taught kids how to read, write, spell, and do math.

The mayor and schools chancellor were probably thrilled that involved parents were giving up. In time, they wouldn't be mayor and chancellor anymore and another mayor would revamp the school system yet again in some unnecessary, bureaucratic way. The new mayor and chancellor would continue to allow the ineffective curriculums to remain in place and would continue wondering why the disparity between wealthy and poor school districts continued to exist.

That disparity continued because politicians did not listen to the well-educated, middle-class parents who told them the curriculums were terrible.

Those parents then did what any reasonable people who needed to earn a living and couldn't spend all their valuable time talking to deaf ears would do—they stopped wasting their time telling the Department of Education what was wrong.

They spent their valuable time making things right for their own kids.

Sadly, and frighteningly, they left everyone else's kids to City Hall.

30

At the end of first grade, Eric was officially a purple stick dot. ☺

On his final report card, he was at grade level in every reading skill except for "reads with expression and attends to punctuation." Once his reading had improved, so had other aspects of school—he was at, or above, grade level in all subcategories of math and in behavior.

This was his teacher's written appraisal of him on his report card: "Eric has shown a lot of growth this year both socially and academically. His desire to read, combined with all of the support he has gotten at school (*Barf*) and at home (*Yes!*) have helped him to become a more confident and successful reader... Eric is confident in his mathematical solutions and likes to share his ideas with the class. **I hope that Eric continues to work hard throughout the summer.** *(Emphasis mine.)* I am so glad that we have gotten Eric the services and support that he needs. (*He doesn't need services and support. He, and all kids, need good teaching to happen in the classroom.*) Have a great summer!"

Summer

You better believe that Eric continued to work hard over the summer.

Eric and I worked on his reading every single day. We finished up our work on vowel digraphs—/ee/, /ea/, /ai/, /oa/, /oe/—and that was the last phonics rule I taught him using any supporting tools like worksheets or Bingo games. Now that he knew how to sound out words, he picked up the rest of the rules on his own or after just a brief explanation by me. Those included a group of vowels I referred to as "oy-oy-oy" vowels: /oy/, /oi/, /ow/, /aw/, /oo/, as well as words with /ght/ in them like night, knight, fight. (Maybe my lesson on how to spell "right" had stayed with him. ☺)

Most of Eric's summer work consisted of simply reading out loud to me. He made his way through every book in the *Henry and Mudge* series and then moved on to *Poppleton* books. The more Eric read, the more confident he became, and that confidence trickled down to consistently engaging with words in his environment.

One day in late July, he walked around Amagansett reading out loud every sign he saw. He did this spontaneously, with no prompting from me. On a police car, he read "Town Police." While sitting in the car outside the local gym he read, "Body Tech" and then wanted to know why the /ch/ was pronounced like a /k/ instead of /ch/ as in "chicken." In the beach parking lot, Eric read "Parking by Permit Only." An advertising blimp flew over the ocean, and he read the name of the product being advertised: "Hood milk." He also announced that his name was spelled wrong: "It should be Erick."

A few days later, in the car on the way home from his birthday party, he, totally unselfconsciously, read out loud a long birthday note It-Was-Nothing-Mom had enclosed with his birthday present. He read it out loud even though he was sandwiched between several of his school friends in the back seat. Last year, those kids had all been much better readers than Eric. Last year, he would have been ashamed to read in front of them. He would not have known how to read any words besides "and" and "the." Cary and I held our breaths until Eric finished reading his birthday card, worried that he would stumble, and his friends might say something hurtful.

He did not stumble. He paused when he came to three unfamiliar words, sounded them out, and kept reading to the end of the note.

I silently cheered for my son. His friends did not comment. They couldn't have cared less. They took reading for granted and took Eric's ability to read for granted too.

I, on the other hand, would never, ever, take any child's ability to read for granted again.

Second grade

There are many precious firsts in a child's life. First steps. First words. Of course, those are momentous moments, but the most monumental moment of all—the one I remember to this day as a flashbulb memory—was the day Eric first picked up a book to read for pleasure. With no prompting from me. Here is how that came to happen…

In September of second grade, as Eric moved into harder books, I saw that words with "ed" and "ing" suffixes were tricky for him, and I set about making him lessons on those. Over the weekend, I retrieved a bunch of books from Jamie's bedroom at our house and left them on the coffee table, planning to look through them later to search for words with suffixes.

I went into the kitchen to make lunch and, from there, saw Eric walk over to the books. He picked up a book about a boy named Brady who was obsessed with hockey, leafed through the first few pages, and then sat down on the coffee table and began reading it.

I froze.

He had just picked up a book and was reading it on his own!

I didn't know what to do.

Should I praise him for reading?

No. That might make him self-conscious and ruin his enjoyment. I wanted it to seem as if what he was doing was the most natural thing in the world, but it did not feel natural to me. It was new and it was awkward, and I didn't know what to do. I was scared that if I said the wrong thing, he would stop reading.

My heart began beating faster. I didn't want Eric to notice me noticing him, so I avoided looking at him and got busy in the kitchen. I pulled a tray of chicken nuggets out of the oven, flipped them, put them back in the oven, set the timer for another 10 minutes, and turned on the flame beneath a pot of broccoli I had set up for steaming. Then I reached for four plates. As a frequent writer of parenting articles and a soon-to-be developmental psychologist, I knew how important it was to give kids chores. It helped them develop a sense of responsibility, cut down on feelings of entitlement, and made them remember they were part of a family unit. Setting the table was usually Eric's job.

I put the plates on the kitchen counter and snuck a look at Eric. He was still sitting on the white, wooden coffee table, completely engrossed in the book. I was torn. Should I let him keep reading, or should I have him set the table? Having him set the table risked ending a moment that might not happen again for a very long time, if ever. But then I decided I was being overly cautious. Now that he knew how to do it, reading *should* be a perfectly natural part of his life and our family life should go on as usual. And, so, I said, "Eric, set the table please."

No response.

"Eric?"

He looked up. "What?" He had been so focused on reading, that he hadn't heard my request.

"Please set the table."

"I will, as soon as I finish reading this book."

Oh God. How I had longed to have him say those words one day.

The time had come.

Now, life needed to go on and absorb the immensity of this new normal into it.

"You can finish reading the book as soon as you set the table. The book isn't going anywhere but I need your help now."

He set the table. Below, by the way, are the opening lines of the book Eric had been reading, *Brady Brady and the Great Rink*. Pretty impressive for a kid who, only a year ago, could read only two words: "the" and "and."

> Brady loved winter. He loved winter because he loved to skate.
>
> He loved to skate because he loved hockey.
>
> Hockey was all Brady thought about.
>
> It drove his family crrrazy!
>
> They had to call him twice to get his attention.

Eric did not pick up the book again. At first, I worried that I had handled the situation improperly but, as the weeks passed, Eric continued to read spontaneously on his own. He read ads on the subway and on street signs. He read memos that came home from school in his backpack. One day, after he read a memo the school sent home requesting that children's artwork be submitted for a school calendar, Eric said, "I really like reading now. I don't understand why I like it. I used to hate it."

I hugged him. "You like it because now you know how to do it. Now you can read and enjoy the stories."

Eric became a voracious reader. Over and over again, I found myself saying things like, "Eric, stop reading. Help me set the table." Or "Eric, stop reading. It's time for bed." At first, I couldn't believe I was saying those words but, in time, they came to feel natural. Soon, Eric was reading above grade level, zipping through books like *Magic Tree House*, *Geronimo Stilton*, and even the *Childhood of Famous Americans* series, which was meant for middle schoolers.

Eric's second-grade teacher played a role in his love of reading. Early in the year, he had seen that Eric liked to read books about pirates and he kept him supplied with a steady stream of them. His teacher also stoked Eric's love of math. Eric had always enjoyed math, and, thanks to the work he was doing in his classroom, in second grade it became an obsession. He constantly begged us to give him math problems. We made up math problems, and he solved them until we reached the point where we had to say, "Stop. That's enough for today." At Eric's request, he and Cary did math for the entire length of their train commute to school every morning.

Earlier in the book, I had promised I would tell you how the math at Hallowed School turned out for us. The school taught the constructivist way of doing math—breaking numbers apart and then adding or subtracting from left to right. That method was not an issue for Eric because I explicitly taught him about place value (which his school did not) as well as the traditional way of doing column addition, subtraction, multiplication, and division. Eric did constructivist math in school (and enjoyed it very much) but, on his homework and on tests, he used the traditional way I had taught him.

Everything about second grade would have been perfect had I not allowed the school to label him learning disabled. Because I had done that, he was mandated to work with the school's learning specialist.

The reading specialist he had worked with last year was pregnant and had resigned to prepare for the birth of her baby. Her replacement was terrible. She, literally, taught Eric nothing. The only structured lessons she did with him involved teaching him the sounds that letters made, which he had already mastered in kindergarten. (I am not kidding. Instead of doing an assessment and seeing what he knew, and what he needed to learn, she started him at the beginning of a structured phonics program called Wilson. Every time she met with him in her office, she had him recite "A/apple/ah" etc. This shows you that, even when a solid structured phonics program is used, it may not be being used efficiently.) Other than reviewing letter sounds with him, she simply showed up in his classroom and corrected any mistakes he made in his math or writing. Because no learning goals were set, he began to feel like the learning specialist was just constantly looking over his shoulder as he worked, ready to pounce on any, and every, mistake. She never used those mistakes as a springboard to lessons that would prevent those mistakes in the future.

Eric adored math, and he loved to write. Cary and I worried that having such an inept learning specialist involved with his work in math and writing would turn him off to those subjects.

On November 1st, Cary emailed the principal and said the learning specialist was not to work with Eric anymore.

"You can't just stop," the principal replied. "He's mandated for SETSS."

After listening to our concerns, and investigating whether they had any merit, the principal agreed that Eric could stop working with the learning specialist and tried to find someone else in the school to work with him. That never came to pass, but it did not matter. I worked with him on writing and spelling, and he continued to get better at both. By the time February came around, his spelling had taken off astonishingly. He mastered his class spelling words, literally, overnight.

Every night, I still read out loud to Eric at bedtime. One night, I closed the book and Eric said, "Can I keep reading please, please, please?"

"Why?" I thought maybe he wanted to know what happened next and, if so, I would read him a few more pages.

"I like to read," he replied. He took the book into bed with him and read until I insisted he turn out the light.

In March, he was "decertified," which meant the "learning disabled" label was removed. Happily, he no longer "qualified" for Special Ed Services, services he never, *ever*, should have been mandated to receive.

I DIDN'T BELIEVE HIM

In kindergarten, when I had observed Eric's class during Open School Week, he was sitting in the back of the room, ashamed of the fact that he could not read. During Open School Week in second grade, he sat in the front of the room, eagerly raising his hand every single time the teacher asked a question. My happiest moment came when the teacher posted a paragraph at the front of the room and asked, "Who wants to read this out loud?" My son's hand shot up into the air.

I watched with joy as he raised his hand over and over and over again. I listened as he inserted proper punctuation into a sentence, identified a word that should have been capitalized, and described how he got from 27 to 79 on a number line using addition and subtraction strategies. A parent who attended Open School Week on a different day told me he had enjoyed a lecture my son gave the class on the safety merits of 747s. Cary told Eric that other parents had said he was an excellent student. His response? "I'm only like that when there are visitors in the classroom. When no one is there, I have my hands behind my neck and my feet up on the table."

Of course, he was joking, and his joke made me happiest of all. He was back to being the Eric he had been before going through the trauma of not being taught how to read in school. His wonderful, dry sense of humor was, once again, in full bloom. And so was his confidence.

One morning towards the middle of second grade, Eric washed his hands in the kitchen and then turned around to get the dishtowel to dry his hands. As usual, the white towel was draped over the top of our kitchen door. In the past, I had always retrieved it for him whenever he needed it but, today, he said he didn't want me to get it for him. "I want to jump and get it myself."

He jumped once and missed.

He jumped again. His jump was higher this time, but he still missed.

He jumped a third time. This time, he grabbed the towel, pulled it down, and dried his hands.

"I always succeed!" he said.

And so he did.

Epilogue

Eric did, indeed, succeed.

He became an academic superstar. He got excellent grades for the rest of elementary school, won numerous academic awards there before he graduated, and was proficient in both reading and math on his state tests. While still in elementary school, he was accepted to the Johns Hopkins University Center for Talented Youth. In middle school, he took a coding class there and that class helped him discover his professional calling. He was salutatorian of his very rigorous high school and went on to major in computer science at one of the top computer science programs in the country, graduating early with a GPA of 3.9.

At the end of his freshman year in college—when he was just 17 years old—Apple came to his campus to recruit interns. Even though Eric was just a freshman, and the event was geared towards upperclassmen, Eric took a chance and, without an interview appointment, pitched an idea to one of Apple's recruiters. His idea was that the camera on iPhones and iPads could be used through the device's keyboard to take a photo and of, say, a recipe or business card and the words in the photo would be typed out for you. (He had already created, and was selling, a recipe app with similar functionality.)

Apple loved his idea. That summer, the company flew him to its headquarters in Cupertino, paid him, housed him, and gave him the support and resources he needed to begin making his idea a reality. After Eric went back to school, Apple continued developing his project. It came to be known as Live Text in the keyboard and was put into use beginning with iOS 15. When you use that feature on your iPhone or iPad, think of Eric! He always did like to create things, as you know from our story.

Although Eric loved working at Apple, and interned there again the following summer, he decided he wanted to work in artificial intelligence. In his junior year, he landed an AI internship at another tech giant and, after graduating, began working there full-time. At age 23, he is already seeing great success in his field. I am sure his life path would have been very different had he not—at age six—found a way to get me to understand his school was not teaching him to read.

Jamie also ended up in a wonderful place. He is now a surgical resident at one of the top 10 surgical residency programs in the country. That would not have been possible had I not taught him math, and other foundational skills, in his younger years.

My story also has a happy ending. As you know, I was earning a Ph.D. in psychology at the time Eric was not taught how to read in school. Living through that experience caused me to dedicate my professional life as a psychologist to helping kids reach their full academic potential. Instead of trying to fix reading problems after they happened, I chose to help kids avoid those problems in the first place. I am now the owner and director of a thriving K-12 tutoring company where we help students succeed in all academic subjects. It is rewarding work that I love doing.

Through the grapevine—actually from Eric's former kindergarten teacher—I heard other happy news. Thanks to my lobbying the school for phonics, to my blog posts, and—most of all—to the lessons the school learned because of Eric, his school had begun using a systematic phonics program called Fundations in its kindergarten classrooms. That had happened the year Eric was in second grade.

Things were still not perfect. The school was still using the Lucy Calkins curriculum to teach reading. Reading experts would call the addition of Fundations a "phonics patch," meaning that adding a separate phonics program was just trying to patch up a curriculum that was badly broken, as opposed to actually getting rid of the problem. Although the kids would now be learning phonics rules in a systematic fashion, those rules would be taught in a vacuum, separate from their reading "lessons." In their "reading lessons," the kids would still be told to guess what the words were from pictures or context, and they would still be given pattern books to read instead of decodable readers. They would still be guessing at many words instead of sounding them out. Their path to becoming good readers would not be as smooth as it could be if their work was being supported by decodable readers, but at least they would have a rudimentary knowledge of how to sound out a word. (Unfortunately, the same cannot be said for kids attending many other schools.)

And how did things end for Joel Klein, the schools chancellor who proclaimed that curriculums don't matter? He made a complete 180-degree turn. Klein is now on the board of the Foundation for Excellence in Education, a nonprofit that, according to its website, "supports state leaders in transforming education." One of the foundation's main missions is trying to get all states to use research-based, effective reading curriculums. Those curriculums all teach explicit, systematic phonics.

How does Klein explain the tragic mistake he and Mayor Bloomberg made when they mandated Columbia University's Teachers College curriculum into all New York City classrooms?

In his book *Lessons of Hope: How to Fix Our Schools*, he says he was "let down by my teaching and learning team. They were the people who were supposed to have my back when it came to…curriculum issues, but … they had not adequately prepared me." The educational news site *Chalkbeat* quoted Klein as saying he was sorry he had forced schools to "adopt a uniform curriculum that embraced philosophies of progressive education over more traditional instruction."

At least he said he was sorry.

Lucy Calkins has not.

Even though the internet and her published writings are full of statements she made denouncing the teaching of phonics rules to beginning readers, Calkins is now telling the media that she has been a big proponent of phonics all along.

She is trying to salvage what is left of her reputation and stature, but there is no pulling the wool over the eyes of the many school districts whose students were damaged by her curriculum. Someone who had always supported the explicit teaching of phonics would not have needed to do a sea change in her approach to teaching reading and issue a revised curriculum, which is what Calkins did in 2022. Her revised curriculum still uses a workshop model, but now includes daily systematic phonics lessons and has dropped three-cueing (guessing what words could be from pictures, context, and just the first letter of a word). But her curriculum is expensive, and her publisher is offering a discount on it only to schools that have purchased the old version in the past three years. That means the old version will remain entrenched in many classrooms.

Even districts that can afford the new version are not buying it. A Palo Alto school board member told APM's Emily Hanford that the Palo Alto school district would not consider the revised curriculum. "There's a trust issue there," he said. "You'd have to decide you could trust her again. Um, that's hard."

New York City is not trusting her anymore either. NYC is the nation's largest school district and the place where, according to Calkins, her curriculum has been used "with the greatest intensity and for the longest period of time." How did that turn out? It caused "hundreds of public schools (to) ... teach reading the wrong way for the last two decades, leaving an untold number of children struggling to acquire a crucial life skill," *The New York Times* reported in 2023.

New York City is, finally, giving her curriculum the boot. In September 2023, half of the city's 32 school districts began using a new research-based curriculum, and the other half will start in September 2024. (Principals will have the autonomy to choose one of three curriculums identified as being evidence-based and effective.) According to *The New York Times*, the only schools allowed to apply for a waiver to opt out of the curriculum change are those where more than 85 percent of students are proficient in reading.

New York City has about 700 elementary schools.

Do you know how many schools meet the criteria for opting out?

Twenty.

Let me put that another way: in only 20 out of 700 New York City schools are kids reading proficiently enough to allow those schools to possibly keep Calkins' curriculum. And you have seen how the kids at those schools most likely learned how to read—via parents or tutors.

Columbia University has, finally, come to see the error of its ways. In September 2023, the university responsible for giving Ivy League credence to Calkins' curriculum, announced that it was going to be dissolving the Teachers College Reading and Writing Project (TCRWP), that Calkins had stepped down as its director, and that she was going to be on sabbatical for the 2023-2024 academic year.

In its written announcement, the university stated, "Dr. Calkins shares her expertise as a consultant through her own LLC. Teachers College is not involved in the operations or provision of services provided by Dr. Calkins in her LLC." Even though Columbia is clearly putting as much distance as it can between itself and Calkins, its written announcement said the university was "grateful to Dr. Calkins for her service." Nowhere in its statement did the university apologize for incubating the curriculum in the first place.

Even though David Banks has been schools chancellor in New York City for only a year and a half, and had nothing to do with the Teachers College curriculum being placed in New York's schools decades ago, he graciously took the fall for it. *The New York Times* quoted him as saying, "It's not your fault. It's not your child's fault. It was our fault."

Clearly, the fact that New York City's reading curriculum is a disaster is not Banks' fault. It is the fault of the schools chancellors who came before him and of Balanced Literacy curriculum developers like Lucy Calkins and the Teachers College Reading and Writing Project. How they could have spent decades turning their noses down at reading research that was definitively settled in 2000 (THE YEAR ERIC WAS BORN!!!) is beyond comprehension. But, as *The New York Times* reported, Calkins "does not believe she has anything to apologize for."

Teachers would beg to differ. Because Calkins refuses to take the blame for training teachers incorrectly, teachers have been left feeling responsible for the damage their ineffective teaching has done to so many children.

"I feel horrible guilt," a Pennsylvania teacher told Emily Hanford in her APM podcast *Hard Words: Why Aren't Kids Being Taught to Read*.

"I thought, 'All these years, all these students,'" said another teacher, referring to the kids she had failed to teach how to read for 26 years.

A teacher named Margaret Goldberg, who is now a literacy advocate and co-founder of The Right to Read Project, told Hanford, "One of the things that I still struggle with is a lot of guilt. I did lasting damage to these kids."

Goldberg blames herself, yet she was simply doing what she had been trained to do by people with seemingly impeccable credentials. In an open letter to Calkins, Goldberg wrote: "It may be impossible to retract from classrooms all the materials grounded in (three-cueing) instruction that carry your name, or the logo of (Columbia University's) TCRWP, but here is my wish—I hope ... that you will speak out openly, honestly, and directly to teachers to say something like this...

> "I got a lot right about reading, (the importance of great books, print-rich classrooms, read-alouds, and more), but I misunderstood something really important: the role of foundational skills in reading ... The chasm between reading research and the classroom was so wide that even I, an expert at an Ivy League university, didn't know the information about reading necessary to write evidence-based lessons.
>
> "This means that you, classroom teachers, should not carry the blame for the number of students we did not teach to read. You did the best you knew how to do with the guidance and materials you were given. And now it's time for all of us to embrace changes in practice."

Did Calkins bravely and honestly fall down on her sword and admit she had trained teachers incorrectly for decades? Did she help ease some of the pain teachers are feeling? Did she lead her teacher acolytes into a new dawn of effective reading instruction?

Nope.

Instead, she wrote an open letter back to Goldberg in which she said, "Had TCRWP not supported foundational skills all along, our kids would not be outperforming other students in ... New York City." Any teacher ever trained by Calkins knows it is absurd for her to say she has supported foundational skills all along.

And the kids taught to read with her curriculum in New York City were not outperforming anybody. Schools Chancellor Banks made that point very clear. In his very first policy speech, he had one thing to say about

Calkins' curriculum: "Across the city, it has not worked. There's a very different approach that we're going to be looking to take."

He was a man of his word. As I mentioned earlier, he is in the process of throwing the Teachers College curriculum out of New York City classrooms. "This is the beginning of a massive turnaround," he has said.

Let's hope so. Already, there is pushback from New York City schools. As *The New York Times* reported, "The new plan ... has attracted immediate skepticism from some teachers, who often say major changes come with insufficient training. It has also drawn ire from the city's principals' union, which has called a uniform curricular approach 'pedagogically unsound' in such a large system."

To date, four states—Indiana, Arkansas, Louisiana, and Ohio—have made it illegal for teachers to use the three-cueing methods that are at the heart of Balanced Literacy. It is literally *against the law* for teachers to tell kids to guess what words could be by using picture clues, context, and just the first letter in a word. (See the Appendix for a copy of Louisiana's bill.) But there is pushback in those states too. Principals and teachers say there is no such thing as a one-size fits all curriculum and that states should not be telling local school boards what to do.

And, so, the reading wars continue.

The good news is that there is more interest in moving to evidence-based reading practices than ever before. Almost every state has passed at least one bill to get schools to use effective curriculums, or improve teacher training, or have better screening to identify kids who are struggling. But legislation has been implemented in the past with little, or no results. When phonics curriculums were mandated into some classrooms, most teachers did not use them. The curriculums arrived, but the boxes remained unopened. (Remember how Whole Language co-founder Ken Goodman gave "a shout out for all those teachers who...have quietly nodded their heads as they were told what to do and how to do it—and then closed their classroom doors"?)

One place where legislation was soundly ignored was California. In 1995, in a move to ban Whole Language from its classrooms, California passed—without a single dissenting vote in either house—a bill mandating phonics be used to teach reading. That never happened. Despite ongoing efforts of literacy advocates and educated parents in places like San

Francisco and Silicon Valley, California remained a hotbed of Whole Language and Balanced Literacy.

In 2001, George Bush denied federal funding to any school district that did not use phonics, but Bush's effort to get schools to use systematic phonics also failed for political reasons.

Let's hope this time is different. Change is beginning to happen and let's hope that this time the change is real and deep and that science triumphs. I think that it will because what makes today's move towards evidence-based reading instruction different from any prior effort is that many teachers have gotten on board with it, and they are spreading the news about it to other teachers via social media. Several teacher-leaders like Margaret Goldberg and Anna Geiger in the United States and Kim Lockhart in Canada have emerged on various online platforms. They are mobilizing their fellow teachers to accept the science of reading and telling them which books to get, and which articles to read, in order to become more informed about it. Many teachers across the United States spent their summer vacations this year reading and learning about evidence-based reading instruction on their own personal time. Others saved, and used, their own hard-earned money to pay to attend literacy conferences. They stated that they did so because they were tired of seeing kids fail.

For the first time, change is happening at the grass-roots level, but, to date, change has happened in only a small percentage of classrooms. Not every teacher can afford—or is dedicated enough to—use his or her own money to attend literacy conferences. In places that have passed laws mandating evidence-based practices, retraining tens of thousands of teachers will take years. As Lockhart tweeted this summer: "In (Ontario) we have a new science-based language arts curriculum (being implemented this fall) yet few of us were trained in the science of reading in our teacher training programs. Mentoring programs will be extremely important this fall, throughout the year, and for years to come to help support teachers who are new to the science of reading."

At the moment, many teachers are not only new to the science of reading, but oblivious to it. They are still teaching phonics in a superficial, sporadic manner. Even in schools that have implemented systematic phonics curriculums, teachers teach those lessons separately from reading lessons. In their reading lessons, children are still told to guess what words could be by looking at the pictures.

As a reading professional, this is what I currently see happening in schools that think they are doing everything right by teaching systematic phonics alongside a Balanced Literacy curriculum: Kids tend to know their phonics rules. I've witnessed little first graders rattle off the phonics rules they have learned and use terms like "r-controlled vowels." But those kids still often struggle with reading because they have not had enough practice in applying those rules via worksheets or decodable readers. Kids continue to be given pattern books with lots of big words in them that they do not yet know how to sound out. So, even though kids *know* the phonics rules, they are not able to apply them to reading big words and are forced to guess what the word could be. Guessing becomes their default method of reading, and they continue to read poorly. (See my website, www.StepstoReading.com, for some real-life video examples of that.)

And we must not forget the millions of children who have already passed through kindergarten and first grade without learning how to sound out words. Those children are now struggling with reading, and they may continue to do so for the rest of their lives.

So, what's a parent to do?

Your best defense is to teach your child to read. I firmly believe that every parent should know how to do so. Initially, I resented having to teach Eric how to read. I wanted to be playing with, and enjoying, my son instead of spending all my free time figuring out how to teach him. Eventually, I realized that needing to figure out how to teach him was what had been hard. Actually teaching him how to read was one of the most wonderful things I could have done with, and for, him. It caused us to forge a special bond.

I found that I missed working with Eric once he was a fluent reader. I missed it so much—and ended up finding the process so rewarding—that, as you know, I decided to spend my workdays teaching other people's kids how to read. I also give presentations and have made videos in which I teach parents how to teach reading.

I'm going to tell you something many people find surprising: If you have the right materials to use, and if you use correct methods from the very beginning, teaching a child to read is very easy. Anyone who speaks

English, and knows how to read, can do it. No higher education or special training is needed.

By saying that, I am not minimizing the important role of teachers. Their job is extraordinarily valuable and extraordinarily difficult. As Dr. Michael Pressley, former director of the Literacy Achievement Research Center at Michigan State University, said, "We have analyzed teaching up, down, and around and I cannot imagine how anything could be more demanding than teaching first grade well ... It is much harder than flying a 747."

I agree. I am in awe of how teachers manage to keep a classroom full of 6-year-olds engaged, motivated, behaving, and learning. Not all of them do and that affects how—and if—kids learn. That's when parents will need to step up to the plate.

To enable all parents (and teachers) to teach kids to read, I have written a series of easy-to-follow workbooks called *Steps to Reading*. Those books contain the exact same curriculum I use with my students. They give you step-by-step instructions on how to systematically teach both phonics and the most frequently used sight words. They are chock-full of fun and engaging worksheets, Bingo games, board games, online activities, and recommendations of decodable readers kids can read at each step of the way. You can find information on the workbooks at www.StepstoReading.com as well as free videos on how to teach a child to read and free worksheets for you to download.

Why reveal the secrets of my success?

Because my goal never was to start a successful tutoring company.

My goal always was—and continues to be—to help children succeed in school and to give their parents the tools they need to help them.

Of course, phonics is only the first step to becoming a proficient reader. Kids also need to have a good vocabulary and be able to read fluently. Both of those skills, along with an understanding of the subject matter they are reading about, will enable them to understand what they are reading. But without phonics, reading never gets off the ground. It would be like trying to teach someone how to drive without ever telling them how to start the engine. I hope this book, and my workbooks, serve as a key to getting your children on the road to reading.

Every child deserves the right to read. Help yours do so, and then spread the word to other parents so they can do so too.

Appendix I

The following page is Louisiana's bill outlawing three-cueing.
The relevant paragraph is underlined in the bill.

ENROLLED

2022 Regular Session

ACT No. 517

HOUSE BILL NO. 865

BY REPRESENTATIVE NELSON

AN ACT

To amend and reenact R.S. 17:24.10(A)(4), relative to literacy; to require public schools to ensure that certain textbooks and instructional materials are not used in reading instruction; and to provide for related matters.

Be it enacted by the Legislature of Louisiana:

Section 1. R.S. 17:24.10(A)(4) is hereby amended and reenacted to read as follows:

§24.10. Early literacy instruction and assessment; parental notification; reporting

A. Each public school shall:

* * *

(4)(a) Ensure, pursuant to R.S. 17:351.1, that all textbooks and instructional materials used to teach students to read are high-quality, fully aligned to state content standards, and based on literacy strategies that are scientifically researched with proven results in teaching phonological awareness, letter formation, phonics, decoding, fluency, vocabulary, and comprehension.

(b) Ensure that no textbooks or instructional materials that employ the three-cueing system model of reading, visual memory as the primary basis for teaching word recognition, or the three-cueing system model of reading based on meaning, structure and syntax, and visual, which is also known as "MSV", are used in reading instruction.

* * *

_____
SPEAKER OF THE HOUSE OF REPRESENTATIVES

_____
PRESIDENT OF THE SENATE

_____
GOVERNOR OF THE STATE OF LOUISIANA

APPROVED: _____

CODING: Words in struck through type are deletions from existing law; words underscored are additions.

Appendix II

The following is an excellent guide from the Louisiana Department of Education explaining what three-cueing is and how to recognize it.

Act 517 of the 2022 Louisiana Legislative Session **prohibits** the use of the three-cueing system, or the MSV technique, in curriculum and instructional materials. This approach has been **proven ineffective** by empirical research in teaching students to read. This guidance document provides an explanation of what the three-cueing system is, what to look for when identifying these strategies in curricular materials, why it is **not** best for students learning to read, and what instructional strategies are proven effective for teaching students to read and comprehend.

What is the "Three-Cueing System?"

The three cueing system is an approach to *foundational skills instruction* that involves the use of three different types of instructional cues: semantic (gaining meaning from context and sentence-level cues), syntactic or grammatical features, and grapho-phonic (spelling patterns). When students encounter words that they cannot read automatically, they are prompted to question themselves using the following three questions: *Does it look right? Does it sound right? Does it make sense?*

At the earliest stages of learning to read, students are prompted to default to semantic or syntactic cues before attempting to use grapho-phonic cues. Students are encouraged to use illustrations to "guess" the meaning of words in predictably-written texts.

As part of the three-cueing system, teachers analyze student reading errors using the "MSV" technique and seek to determine if reading errors are related to "meaning, structure, or visual" issues. If students' errors are meaning-related, the teacher will focus instructional efforts on supporting a student in using semantic cues to read passages. If the issues are related to structure, the teacher will focus on supporting students' use of syntactic cues, and if the errors are visual, the teacher will prompt students to use grapho-phonic strategies.

As evidence mounts against the three-cueing system, many programs no longer refer to this instructional approach using this terminology, so identifying three-cueing in curricular resources requires careful observation of the strategies used to guide students as they learn to read.

When Might I See "Three-Cueing?"

The three-cueing approach is most-often found during foundational skills instruction in grades K-2. Some of the common prompts associated with this approach - "Does this make sense?" or "Look at the picture" - can be appropriate in other instructional contexts, such as when a student is encouraged to use illustrations to support deeper comprehension of stories, or when students are monitoring their own reading, but they are not effective strategies or prompts for teaching students to read words on a page. Instead of relying on multiple, varied cues, students should instead be consistently prompted to decode words using learned spelling and syllabication patterns.

As the three-cueing approach typically involves teachers prompting students to use different cues, this type of instruction is often found in small-group or individual settings. It is a hallmark of "Balanced Literacy."

Common Features of Programs that Use the "Three-Cueing System"

Leveled Readers - Unlike decodable texts, which include only words that contain spelling patterns for which students have been explicitly taught, leveled readers are books that are designed to encourage students to rely upon three-cueing strategies to be able to successfully read them. At the earliest levels, these books contain predictable patterns (*I see a red ball, I see a blue ball, I see a green ball*) and heavy picture support. As students progress through grade levels, the texts become increasingly complex. While there may be descriptions of what characterizes books of different levels, they are rarely tied to learned spelling and syllabication patterns and are instead leveled according to sentence and/or vocabulary complexity. When reading from leveled readers, students may read books that are "on their level" that contain spelling patterns for which they have not been explicitly taught.

Reading Strategies - In many classrooms using the "three-cueing system," you may see posters encouraging students to use strategies such as "Lips the Fish," "Eagle Eye," or "Chunky Monkey." Some of these strategies encourage students to engage in reading behaviors that are not aligned to best practices in reading instruction. More effective prompts will encourage students to decode words using learned spelling and/or syllabication patterns.

The following table shares some of the clear differences between instruction grounded in science of reading research and balanced literacy instructional approaches.

Foundational Skills Instruction	
Science of Reading	Balanced Literacy
decodable texts	leveled texts
systematic, explicit phonics instruction	phonics instruction provided "as needed;" not systematic
students prompted to "decode" words	students prompted to ask "does it look right, does it sound right, does it make sense?"
	students prompted to look at pictures for support in figuring out the meaning of unknown words (most often in grades K-1)
	guided reading

Access the Literacy Library for additional guidance and resources that support best practices in literacy instruction. Contact louisianaliteracy@la.gov with any questions.

www.ingramcontent.com/pod-product-compliance
Lightning Source LLC
Chambersburg PA
CBHW032027290426
44110CB00012B/705